D1431831

Marianne Moore

Marianne Moore
Imaginary Possessions

Bonnie Costello

Harvard University Press
Cambridge, Massachusetts
and London, England
1981

Publication of this book was aided by a grant from the Andrew W.
    Mellon Foundation

Library of Congress Cataloging in Publication Data
Costello, Bonnie.
    Marianne Moore, imaginary possessions.

    Includes bibliographical references and index.
    1. Moore, Marianne, 1887–1972—Criticism and interpreta-
tion.   I. Title.
PS3525.05616Z6   811'.52   81-1133
ISBN 0-674-54848-5   AACR2

Excerpt from the unpublished writings of William Carlos Williams,
    copyright © 1981 by the Estate of Florence H. Williams.

To Christopher Costello and Marjorie Costello

Acknowledgments

I am grateful to Helen Vendler for her inspiration, advice, and encouragement through many drafts of the manuscript, and to Neil Hertz for his ideas and his guidance in earlier versions. I should also like to thank Sandra Siegel, David Novarr, and Cecelia Tichi for reading various versions and for their criticism and support. Patricia Willis, at the Rosenbach Foundation, provided many clues and directives from her intimate knowledge of the Moore archive. Jonathan Loesberg helped me to identify Victorian sources. The teaching and conversation of Richard Tristman have influenced my ideas in ways I could not begin to document. Frank Cespedes offered unfailing enthusiasm and support throughout this project.

My work on this book was supported in part by a summer stipend from the National Endowment for the Humanities and by a faculty fellowship at Harvard from the Andrew W. Mellon Foundation.

Contents

Marianne Moore

Citations to the following books by Marianne Moore are given in the text:

Poems (London: Egoist, 1921).

Observations (New York: The Dial Press, 1924).

Selected Poems (New York: Macmillan, 1935). Abbreviated SP.

Collected Poems (New York: Macmillan, 1951).

Predilections (New York: Viking, 1955).

The Marianne Moore Reader (New York: Viking, 1961). Abbreviated MMR.

Complete Poems (New York: Viking, 1967). Abbreviated CP. This volume is about to be reissued with minor alterations. Page numbers here may vary from those in the second edition.

Introduction
Sincerity and Gusto

W E RELINQUISH many satisfactions—consistency, symmetry, logic—when we are caught in the choreography of a Marianne Moore poem. While her subjects are often marked by their particularity, her imagining of them seems to follow no predetermined course. Moore does not seem to speak immediately to urgent personal and communal needs, but she does speak to our need for strong enchantment. And through these dithering poems we can feel a gaining steadiness, can see a hummingbird's iridescent poise revealed in the flurry of words.

When she collected her criticism, Marianne Moore began with a foreword of characteristic humility. "One feels that what holds one's attention might hold the attention of others."[1] My first task in drawing Moore's poems yet again to the attention of contemporary readers is to analyze their hold on us. What mode of attention keeps our interest through these unballasted poems, which seem to break every expectation of structure, perspective, voice, argument? What current carries us over long sentences we can scarcely at first sort out, and leads us on to epigrammatic statements we seem not to arrive at but to run up against? What motive, as Kenneth Burke would call it, what inscape, as Hopkins would name it, has brought together these words, images, idioms from different dictionaries and atlases of the mind?

Moore's foreword to *Predilections* asserts the existence of a "language of sensibility of which words can be the portrait." Here, where moral and aesthetic categories converge, I found my clue in approaching these poems. Moore never expresses her "sensibility" in a personal manner, but she reveals her predilection for the irregular, the densely varied, the elusive, the fluid, by imitating these qualities in her style.

R. P. Blackmur has called criticism "a fiction to school the urgency of reading."[2] Our reading of Moore requires such schooling, and the poet herself often provides the lessons. Moore gives many names to her predilections, but always double ones, pairings of moral and aesthetic or intentional and expressive categories: feeling and precision, idiosyncrasy and technique. Sincerity and gusto emerge, as I hope to show, as the most inclusive terms to identify Moore's poetic character. They denote a way of thinking and responding in any occasion or context, not just in the field of major human actions.

"Sincerity" as Moore uses the term (and its analogues: integrity, genuineness, authenticity), is "a magnetism, an ardor, a refusal to be false," (*Predilections*, vii) which "precipitates a poem" (*Predilections*, 18). Moore is not alone, of course, in demanding sincerity in art. Sincerity was a major criterion of Romantic art, particularly in Rousseau and Wordsworth. Both Henri Peyre and Lionel Trilling have traced the concept of sincerity in philosophy and literature through recent centuries.[3] But in the modernist period sincerity is no longer connected with the private or social self, or with the egotistical sublime, but is directed outward, toward an accurate rendering of objective reality, away from both discursive abstraction (rationality) and emotional abstraction (personality). In its insistence on the concrete image, modern sincerity is almost a turnabout to classical sincerity, which was attributed to objects that were free of impurities. Epicures still speak of "sincere" wines. For T. E. Hulme sincerity was the abhorrence of approximation; it was the desire to get the "exact curve" of a thing, "to hand the thing over bodily." For Ezra Pound, too, it was antirhetorical, seeking to go "beyond formulated language." Louis Zukofsky found sincerity unsatisfactory as a principle of reality in art, deciding that it was only "a portrait of the author's character intent upon the object." But his preferred "objectification," the ideal fusion of imagination and reality into the "rested totality" of medium, bears an unmistakable resemblance to Hulme's "sincerity."[4] The term, not the ideal, had changed.

While Moore passionately embraces the ideal, she also recognizes that "precision is a thing of the imagination" (*Predilections*, vii); it cannot, we infer, be a thing of language, since language always approximates, always puts itself between the observer and his world. Moore's poems are restless because they place "the refusal to be false" in constant tension with rhetoric. Sincerity, for Moore, is not poised objectification or the transcendence of rhetoric, but what Herbert Read (whom Moore had read) called "a state of openness."[5] Recognizing the contradiction buried in the impulse of modern art to abuse the very thing it uses, to make language (a medium) unmediated, Moore made this contradiction a source of energy and reflection.

In Moore, sincerity is a blend of eagerness and restraint, of ambition and humility. She leaps, precipitously, into speech, and then checks herself, paradoxically producing more speech by recording her revisions. " 'The deepest feeling always shows itself in silence; / not in silence, but restraint.' " Her "conscientious inconsistency" struggles to match what it knows, at the outset, it cannot match, "life's faulty excellence," its "regal and excellent awkwardness." Failing to "objectify" her medium, she makes it resemble the density, irregularity, and motion of life.

For Moore, integrity is the opposite of tedium, and sincerity and gusto are two sides of the same coin. As sincerity is connected with the urge for truth and accuracy, gusto is, as Hazlitt says, "power or passion defining any object."[6] Moore's "gusto" is also like the classical *enargeia*, which modernists appropriated. It is the emotional byproduct of the flux and tension of form. This flux and tension are set in motion by sincerity, which accepts no single-minded description of reality. But Moore's gusto is not, as is the energy in Pound's vortex, the eye of the storm, a perfect center created from the collision of perspectives. It is the feeling of pleasure accompanying bafflement, the energy released in the poem by the resistance of an object to each onslaught of form. Her acts of description and definition repeatedly give way to exclamation of delighted defeat. The desire for possession is displaced by passion and admiration. Gusto is an emotion connected with failure, not with mastery, with relinquishing, not attaining, "what one would keep." Few writers deal with failure so enthusiastically. Moore celebrates the world's elusiveness, its superiority to our acts of appropriation, seeing the world's freedom as intrinsic to our own. And "gusto thrives on freedom," on the repeated discovery of difference. Thus her poems do not seek a still center in the turning world; they are distinctly temporal, and turn with it in constant astonishment.

While Moore denies poetry its ideal satisfaction of realizing the genuine in form, of overcoming its temporality and limit, she allows for many consolations. She entertains orders and meanings, while keeping them highly constricted and qualified; she allows herself an "imaginary possession" of experience through acts of association, allegorical paradigms, epigrammatic statements, formal structures, which make no claim to resemble the actual order of the world. In this sense the poet is a maker as well as a seer or sayer. Although ideas are illusory and things elusive, poems nevertheless have validity as individual, creative realities. And lacking a grasp of the world, Moore contents herself with the fleeting assurances of self-reflection.

Moore's words portray her sensibility, not just by saying what she feels or thinks, but by enacting over and over again an essential imaginative structure. I assume therefore that Moore's poetry is consistent in its inconsistencies. While her art is daringly asymmetrical, its parts are nonetheless cooperative and mutually reinforcing; one aspect of her work can be understood in terms of another. Her moral vision is the counterpart of her aesthetic practice, her images repeat the structure of her themes, her themes are enacted (not "dressed") in her forms, and so on. But I assume as well that no one aspect controls the whole. They turn, together, as the "machinery of satisfaction." Moore presents her poetry as process as well as product. It records, and engages the reader in, the act of ordering the raw materials of sensation, thought, and language.

This book is primarily designed as a critical analysis of the structures, images, and modes of representation in Moore's poetry. But no reading of Moore can be precise, let alone complete, without careful attention to the exhaustive, detailed record of a creative process that she left behind. Until recently critics had been satisfied, for the most part, to make general statements about Moore's style and subject based on the evidence of *Complete Poems*, which is far from complete and represents only one phase of her long and varied career. Many impressions of Moore's practice prove inaccurate in light of the larger record of her work. Revision and composition were one to Moore's restless imagination. With every new publication (and even in printed copies she sent to friends) she would set to work adding, deleting, reworking lines, to the dismay of critics like myself who have tried to trace the record. Many fine early poems never found their way into collections, others underwent such drastic stylistic or thematic changes as to become new works. I have tried wherever possible to draw attention to the variants, suggesting a line of thinking from one version to the next.

More important, perhaps, than the published record of Moore's work is the unpublished one, collected at the Rosenbach Foundation. This collection probably constitutes the single most complete record we have of any literary career. Moore's literary correspondence with T. S. Eliot, Ezra Pound, William Carlos Williams, Wallace Stevens, Hilda Doolittle, e. e. cummings (to name only the most familiar figures) provides a fascinating view of her contemporary scene. Her notebook of conversations—among other writers, colleagues from *The Dial*, artists, and critics—offers not only an eyewitness view of the times but also many clues to poems. The most regular exchanges took place among members of her family. The letters and remarks to and from her mother and brother, containing numerous sources of and references to poems, suggest an intimacy about Moore's creative practice which critics ignorant of the correspondence have repeatedly missed.

Anyone familiar with Moore's poetry knows she was a kleptomaniac of the mind. She kept several file drawers of clippings, photographs, postcards, in which are hidden away the sources of many poems. She was once impressed by the remark "a good stealor is *ipso facto* a good inventor," and made a note of it in her reading diary. Her career proved the statement's wisdom. Moore was a compulsive reader and note-taker, copying out verbatim in her tiny scrawl page after page of others' observations—more than a dozen volumes during her career. Many writers keep commonplace books, but few have demonstrated such absorption not only in literary materials, but in fashion columns, zoological features, travel chronicles, an astonishing variety of written or spoken observations. It is difficult to determine Moore's attitude toward these passages, but they do mark out areas of fascination. The critic can trace here not only Moore's selectivity as a reader, but her further selectivity as a writer. From long passages, and often from many different time periods and contexts, she culled and molded the lines that served her poetic purpose. At the back of every diary, Moore kept a personal index— these volumes were compendiums of the represented world, resources she could draw on in creating an individual reality. The working out of that individual reality is traceable from its inception to its final expression. A comment in a family letter, a remark in a news column, review, or journal, a photograph or postcard (often not documented in her notes) would send Moore off on a rapid chain of abstract associations—to an epigram read two years earlier, a remark made by a friend in her childhood, a vase described in an auction column. Moore often discovered these associations in workbooks in which we can see her not only transforming the observations of others into her own unique arrangement but converting prose to poetry, free verse to syllabics, highlighting possible rhythms and rhymes as they occur to her. We also discover from these notebooks that Moore worked on several poems at once, that they would often only late emerge as individual works, and that many passages would be transferred from one poem to another.

With only Moore's quotation marks, notes, and public remarks to go on, a reader might dismiss Moore as a sort of curator of the choice observations of others. But with all her attention to accuracy and documentation, she was often rather free with her borrowings, revising the statements of others to fit her needs or predilections, or transforming and undermining their remarks by quoting them in a contrastive contest. Though some of Moore's poems are almost entirely made up of quotations, they remain remarkably original and individual. If we examine her quotations in their original settings (as we can by exploring the notes, clippings, pamphlets, and books collected at the Rosenbach), we can develop a much more complete sense of Moore's poetic independence and ingenuity.

The Rosenbach collection provides insight not only into the poems themselves but into the mind that made them. We find that most poems have a private as well as a public layer—that they contain allusions and references that only her family and friends would recognize—references that are unessential to an appreciation of most poems, but which endow them with a personal dimension missed by the uninitiated reader. Moore's imagination, we learn, was private rather than impersonal. Similarly, we learn that many of the images and observations in the poems are overdetermined—that they frequently have several sources (from a considerable range of contexts) where only one is noted. This multiplicity of sources is quite different from the multiplicity of references; it has nothing to do with an understanding of the poems, but it has a great deal to do with their creation.

The Moore archive also makes clear the extent to which this poet wrote from a world already represented. Direct experience of nature was seldom the seed of her poetry. Rather, she visited museums and exhibitions, bringing home reminders of what she had seen, and worked from books, pamphlets, reproductions. One could never master the real world, but one could draw emblems and descriptions of the world into a private setting where the world might be brought under imaginary control. There is no fraud in this activity—it is words and pictures she is selecting and arranging, not life—but from this practice she seems to have derived, and transmitted to her reader, a humble satisfaction.

This indirection, this imaginary possession, accounts too for Moore's apparent subject matter. She has often been criticized for a triviality of subject, but her exotic bestiary, her collections of antiques and curios, need to be interpreted on several levels. At one level, certainly, we can say that Moore's motive is an aesthetic one—subject is a secondary matter to a lover of style. But a deeper motive is the working out of experience in a realm where precision is possible. We cannot render clearly the things that affect our humanity most directly. But we can begin to find a symbolic satisfaction and understanding in an impersonal, imaginary realm of animals and objects. Moore's insistence on accuracy, her compulsion to lay out facts, forces this imaginary activity back into the real world without threatening or disturbing it with personal prejudice or anxiety. The private world we can begin to uncover in the Rosenbach collection suggests that this symbolic action is a primary motive of the poems.

One can speculate as to the biographical causes of this symbolic action—the failure and eventual madness of Moore's father, her mother's efforts to create orderliness and strong cohesion between herself and her two children against the financial and social precariousness of their condition. Clive Driver, Moore's literary executor, is writing a biography which will provide us with an invaluable picture of the life behind these unusual poems. I have not attempted biographical criticism here. But I have tried in my discussion of Moore's poetry to begin integrating critical analysis and scholarly research. This is an enormous project which will engage many future critics of Moore. While fine critics and fine scholars have both attended to these works in the past, there has been little cooperation between them. A passive reiteration of the facts surrounding Moore's compositions cannot recreate the enthusiasm and originality of this creative imagination. And the poems themselves can seem impersonal, obscure, and alien until we are more intimate with the practice of their maker, as it is recorded at the Rosenbach.

We feel relieved when we find, among a difficult poet's works, a poem about poetry. It is, we tend to think, like finding a hospitable friend in a room of strangers. Not surprisingly, critics gravitate toward those poems of Moore's which offer reflections on art. But while these sometimes simulate prose argument, they in fact move as obliquely, as illogically, and as enigmatically as the rest of her work. They are abstract emblems of her more particular mosaics of consistent inconsistency. Moore's famous mottoes must be read in the contexts in which they occur. But thus enriched, they offer valuable clues to the poetic character of other "portraits." They reveal an ambivalence about the authority of form, an ambiguity as to the nature of the genuine, and a constant difference between the genuine and the forms we contrive to express it. These poems describe efforts to embody "truth" that repeatedly turn up images of subjective intensity.

Genre classification, too, often schools the urgency of reading; and so I take up, in these pages, Moore's chief and favorite genres. The title of Moore's second volume, *Observations*, incorporates two genres—description, and social or moral reflection—which merge in interesting ways. In the poems that deal more directly with human subjects—the poems of social and intellectual criticism and praise and of moral reflection—sincerity causes her to refute absolutes and simple oppositions, and turns criticism in on itself in perpetual revision and ironic reversal. She freely emblematizes objects, but she works against the grain of conventional symbolism to promote active thought within revitalized images. Moore will allow us to deal no more complacently with ourselves than we do with nature. In the descriptive poems sincerity turns up differences while at the same time it leaps to identifications. Particulars exceed the grasp of generalities, observations resist assertions. Moore indulges freely in these poems (which ostensibly describe nonhuman subjects) in the play of association and the pull between eye and mind, word and thing, fiction and fact, human meaning and nature's indifference. But in the process of casting out and reeling in associations, she catches glimpses of the self at the poem's surface, consoling her when objects swim away from the lure of meaning.

Like other commentators on Moore, I see her original and revealing images as central to her genius. Image clusters usually suggest to Moore wider areas of fascination. "It is human nature to stand in a middle of a thing" (CP, 49), to assign meanings to all the qualities and configurations we see around us. If such a practice is natural to human beings, it is even more native to poets, and Moore is relentless, however self-conscious, in correlating value and fact. She is an allegorical poet, in that she does not pretend a natural continuity between physical qualities and the meanings she assigns to them. Moore's obsession with combat and armor, which many critics have noted, penetrates beyond the moral and social sphere to become an intellectual and aesthetic principle, at work everywhere in her poetry, in "the angle at variance with angle" and the "collision of knowledge and knowledge." Animals armored against aggressors figure the self galvanized against inertia and complacency. While an aggressive mind constricts experience and meaning, the sincere mind that internalizes combat enlarges the world, and paradoxically frees itself by restraint. Moore stabilizes and sweetens the war within and the "warfare between imagination and medium" by creating images of dynamic poise, converting explosion to "implosion," combat to reciprocity, "adversity" to "conversity." Perhaps less conspicuous, but no less dominant, in Moore, are images of luminosity, suggesting the power of the invisible beneath the surface of things. Indeed, in modern literature generally luminosity is an image of essential reality, of the thing itself in its true unity. But usually in Moore, who sees real presence as the absolute that exceeds art, this center of light and spiritual identity only shows itself as iridescence, or as its temporal counterpart, metamorphosis. Both imply an infinite multiplicity beneath apparent finitudes. Moore is drawn like a moth to any form of inherent light, and though she tends to discover light in the minutiae of nature, she represents it as a modest form of sublimity. Again, these qualities of light and iridescence, admired by Moore, at the level of subject and imagery, have their stylistic counterparts.

When I pass on to consider Moore's forms, it is in the belief that form is never a transparent vehicle of meaning in poetry. In Moore, it is sometimes almost opaque. Moore's art is impeccable, but not cooperative. The "novices" who are "deaf to satire" and understand only single-minded assertions are lost in her chiasmic square dance of wit. The oddity and difficulty in the form of Moore's poems, whether short, swift epigrams or effusive lists, draw our attention away from reference and toward the fact of composition, as that alembic in which our relation to experience is transformed. The asymmetries of utterance are played against the symmetries of artifice. Dense quotation, open, associative structures, and competing levels of organization are, in Moore, marks of sincerity and agents of gusto. "Plain speaking" is Moore's ideal, but a rigorous, dynamic "plain speaking," not rhetorical simplicity. Since forms of expression grow habitual, the poet's task is to renew our engagement in the process of ordering experience through words. The pull of the sentence against the pull of the eye generates the sparks that come from her kindled lines. Grammar is stretched and twisted (though never broken) to accommodate the variety, irregularity, and motion of life. An independent, persuasive but uninsistent rhythm, along with other formal structures, sustains us through the poem's unharnessed density and plurality. A discussion of Moore's form naturally includes her method of quotation. Here again, her aim is to revitalize language in the crucible of the poem.

While Moore's poems look peculiar next to other poems, it seemed to me that they might be clarified in some other context. The many poems about art objects and the many references to paintings and sculpture suggest possible influence by and analogy with the visual arts. In visual sources Moore found not only examples of the tension between the flux of life and the stasis of art but also ways of expressing and mediating that tension. In her search for the genuine she found her closest kinships among those who actually *looked* for it.

A book about Moore would not be complete without some reflection on her critical practice. A poet's critical remarks are often the best resource in understanding her poetry. But we err, I think, in approaching an artist's criticism principally as a tool for our use. Moore's critical brilliance is equal to her poetic brilliance, in style as well as substance, and it ought to be approached with similar interpretive effort. Kenneth Burke has said that Moore's critical *Predilections* are the perfect analogue of her poetic *Observations,* and with this in mind, I look closely here at three essays, describing their rhetorical movement and enactment of meaning. In each Moore mediates between "the burning desire to be explicit," which moves forward into speech but threatens to consume its subject, and "natural reticence," which restrains speech but also threatens to snuff out the energy of the line. Sincerity accounts in these essays for Moore's delight in disorder, her fascination with minor flaws and deviations as the marks of authorship. For Moore, style exists in the gap between "the genuine" and "the raw material of poetry," a gap marked by hesitations and imperfections of form that I have called "rhetorical reticence."

Whether we approach Moore's themes, methods, images, forms, theories, or influences, we find the same artist, absorbing the contradictions of her enchanting art and enchanted imagination into the aesthetic of sincerity, and turning them to the effect of gusto, making art an enactment, rather than the fulfillment, of desire for a genuine and inclusive portrait of reality. And in the meantime, in the course of that enactment, she achieves what Wallace Stevens called "an individual reality," as a reciprocation, not a reflection, of the world.

Moore was not a poet neglected in her time. Though recent criticism has undervalued her work, her contemporaries and those who immediately followed recognized an important talent. But early commentaries on her poems were less notable for their critical insights than for their passion. After Moore's *Poems* was brought out by H. D. and

Winifred Bryher in 1921, Harriet Monroe published an essay called "Symposium on Marianne Moore," in which Moore is condemned, by some, for her "gymnastics" and eulogized by others ("young radicals" Monroe called them) for her ingenuity and courage. Either way, she had created an impression. Moore's first defenders, mostly fellow poets, tended to present her in terms of their own current obsessions. To Aldington she was an imagist, to Zukofsky an objectivist. Pound linked her with Laforgue and the art of "logopoeia"; Eliot with ritual and classicism. She became the heroine of Williams's *Spring and All*, where he praised her for precisely the qualities he was trying to achieve. Stevens read Moore as a new romantic, like himself. As Williams observed in his *Autobiography*, "She was our saint . . . in whom we instinctually felt our purpose come together to from a stream . . . She was like a rafter holding up the superstructure of our uncompleted building . . . What were we seeking? No one knew consistently enough to formulate a 'movement.' To my mind the thing that gave us most a semblance of a cause was the poetic line and our hopes for its recovery from stodginess." Moore's response, many years later, typified her strong sense of independence: "I never was a rafter holding up anyone!"[7]

Moore published *Observations* (*Poems* with a few subtractions—some regrettable—many revisions, some dazzling additions) on her own initiative in 1924 and again, with a few changes, in 1925. In 1925 she also became editor of *The Dial*, to some extent interrupting her writing career, but poems were clearly in gestation, for in 1935 she published *Selected Poems*, which placed her at the center of contemporary American letters and remains her most significant volume. As Eliot wrote in his introduction to the selection, "Miss Moore is, I believe, one of those few who have done the language some service in my lifetime" (SP, viii). In 1948, after the publication of *The Pangolin and Other Verse* (1936), *What Are Years* (1941), and *Nevertheless* (1941), and after many grants and awards, *The Quarterly Review of Literature* brought out a special issue on Moore, showing her as a poet who had won the reverence not only of her peers but of the generation of poets following after her. During the Fifties, books on modernist poetry began to include chapters on Moore, and the Sixties saw several book-length studies that offered preliminary descriptions of her themes and style. Moore criticism is now entering a new phase of critical and scholarly depth. Laurence Stapleton makes substantial use of Moore's letters and reading diaries in order to trace the evolution of her unusual works. Marie Borroff has begun the essential work of stylistic analysis, suggesting analogies with feature articles and promotional prose.[8] My own work, benefiting from these previous studies, undertakes a detailed description of the imaginative structures determining Moore's poems, through a full-length theoretical reading. I have preferred to trace the path of Moore's imagination through whole poems rather than fragments, showing her motives, her modes of proceeding, her contradictions and inspirations. Because these poems are integrated imaginative acts, I have tried as well to show the interrelation among their various elements.

We lack a truly complete edition of Moore's poems. The 1967 *Complete Poems* (recently reissued with emendations and addenda) is by no means complete, and though "omissions are not accidents" there is a great deal we miss in this last collection. Since Moore was a relentless reviser (most often deleting descriptive digressions, but sometimes changing the sense significantly), we need a variorum edition, and one that includes not only the many versions of the poems published in book form, but the many poems that appeared only in magazines and the many that remained unpublished. A recent bibliography has been of some use in drawing this material together, but it is incomplete and often incorrect.[9] I have used *Complete Poems* unless otherwise noted, but I frequently draw on earlier drafts and publications.

Moore was an exceptional essayist as well as a poet. In addition to *Predilections* and the few pieces in *The Marianne Moore Reader*, there are many uncollected essays, including her regular, anonymous "comments" in the *Dial*. The collection and study of these writings will place Moore among the major theorists and prose stylists of her generation. She was also an imaginative and skillful translator, and while several critics, notably Laurence Stapleton, have touched on her translation of La Fontaine, there is still a great deal to be said about the place of translation in her career. Moore scholarship is, then, in its infancy. I have dealt very little with the sources of and influences on Moore's poetry (a slightly different subject from the sources of her quotations), though the topic is an important and neglected one. As T. S. Eliot observed, Moore's art is the product of "many soils." She is a modernist in her use of juxtapositions, of particularity, and of unconventional materials. But she is also a classicist, in her high civility, her Latinate diction, her fondness for epigram, her obsession with neatness. Her extended metaphors sometimes recall the Metaphysicals; her long descriptions resemble the work of Cowper. In her fascination with the invisible beneath the visible and her love of the Hebrew sublime, she is a modern romantic. The influence of the Victorians, well documented in her notes, needs to be explored. The sciences are almost as important as the visual arts to Moore's development as an observationist. Her study as a biology major at Bryn Mawr was the beginning of a long fascination with natural fact. I touch on each of these strains, but a great deal more documentation and analysis are needed. I have dealt with Moore's "feminine" qualities elsewhere.[10] But sincerity and gusto are peculiarly American traits, and for all her idiosyncrasy there is no poet more American than Moore, albeit a "superlative American," as she called Henry James.

In discussing Moore's poems I have tried to define a canon. Unlike Laurence Stapleton, I do not see an "advance" so much as a decline in Moore's writing after *Selected Poems*. As she became more of a public poet she became less of a poet's poet. In the latter part of her career, in my view, she surrendered the warfare between imagination and medium to sentimentality and simplicity at times, and at other times to a manner became mannered. Much of her late work lacks sincerity and gusto. This falling-off is, I think, directly responsible for her relatively minor position in the history of modernism. One of my aims in emphasizing the many brilliant early poems is to restore her to her proper importance in that tradition. Anthologies have tended to distort her real achievement, preferring the most accessible, most conventional poems to the more engaging and characteristic ones. Thus "An Octopus," one of Moore's greatest poems, has been anthologized only once, by Jerome Rothenberg in his deliberately revisionary selection, *The Revolution of the Word*.[11]

Moore's greatest poetry does not deal directly with the major myths of our culture, with tragic or comic themes. Her truths, excerpted from her poems, may seem proverbial. But if we consider her subjects and themes as occasions for significant imaginative acts we can have no doubt about the value of her art. Like "impassioned Handel" in "The Frigate Pelican" who was "meant for a lawyer and a masculine German domestic / career—" but who "clandestinely studied the harpsichord / and never was known to have fallen in love," Moore is "unconfiding" and "hides / in the height and in the majestic / display of her art." Like the frigate pelican and his fellows, without cosmic purpose ignoring the more obvious lures of the romantic sensibility, she "wastes the moon."

But he, and others, soon

rise from the bough and though flying, are able to foil the tired
  moment of danger that lays on the heart and lungs the
  weight of the python that crushes to powder.

[CP, 26]

Moore's poetry is opposed, above all, to complacency, inertia, dejection. Her objective in the aesthetic of sincerity and gusto is to keep the
mind alert and free, the world large and abundant.

1. Defining the Genuine
Poems about Poetry

MARIANNE MOORE'S comment on a photograph of herself is typically poetic and personal. As Alfred Kreymborg observed in his autobiography, her conversation was as strategic as her poetry; the sincerity here has a double edge:

> I'm all bone . . . just solid pure bone. I'm good natured but hideous as an old hop toad. I look like a scarecrow. I'm just like a lizard, like Lazarus awakening. I look permanently alarmed, like a frog. I *aspire* to be neat, I try to do my hair with a lot of thought to avoid those explosive sunbursts, but when one hairpin goes in, another seems to come out. Look at those hands: they look as if I'd died of an adder bite. A crocodile couldn't look worse. My physiognomy isn't classic at all, it's like a banana-nosed monkey. (She stops for a second thought.) Well, I do seem at least to be awake, don't I?[1]

These self-deprecating remarks are presented with a certain exhilaration. We need only recall how much Moore admires toads, lizards, monkeys, and the like. They make up the menagerie of her subject matter, as proud emblems of all that cannot be circumscribed in any neat form. In fact, we learn as we go through the poetry that Moore sees most things this way. The particular is always peculiar because precision in coming to terms with it remains a thing of the imagination. Nothing does fit the curve of our expectation, if we are awake. We "aspire to be neat," but put aside the classical confidence in generalized decorum for the sake of the genuine. In consoling herself as "awake at least" Moore implies that her appearance is a consequence of being awake to a world that is permanently alarming.

Curiously, some of the likenesses Moore observes are alarming images, others images of alarm—the two glide together, the alarmed figure is itself alarming. "I look like a scarecrow . . . I look permanently alarmed, like a frog." But by implication, to be awake is to be alarmed, to be alarmed is to be alarming.

The ideal of poetry, a perfect reciprocity between the world and its representation, is, as she says of marriage, "an interesting impossibility." The poet is bound to fail, like the child in "Critics and Connoisseurs" who attempts "to make an imperfectly ballasted animal stand up." Awake to nuance, to deviation, to distinction, the poem will never be "neat." Moore believes in decorum, but an ultimate decorum that does not exclude or falsify. This wakefulness is not just an austere agent of sincerity, however. Clearly deviation is delight as those "sunbursts" resist their pins. Sincerity always turns up something beyond one's control. Moore's best poems express a conflict between her desire to form and delimit thought and experience and her alertness to the unassimilable detail. Sometimes she expresses this as the imagination's power to reach beyond reason. But ultimately she traces the recalcitrance of objects to their separate reality, which poetic form can conjure but never capture. The motion of these poems is toward the repeated discovery of this area of conflict, centered in the notion of the genuine, and the resulting friction in the language has an affective power of "gusto."

This is not to suggest that Moore's poems are fundamentally unruly. She orders her poetic materials even as she declares the recalcitrance of her subjects. Thus her poems have a presence and a wholeness quite apart from their references. Not only through verse form but through repetitions, juxtapositions, extended metaphors, and implied analogies, Moore takes quiet possession of language without denying the density of life. She satisfies a natural impulse for identification and order, but claims no authority for such gestures. Moore's realism and her "poetry" are thus simultaneous, but not synonymous. Her tentative, imaginary harmonies hold out for more ultimate harmonies. Her discreet, incidental self-portraits give the mind's eye a place of rest while it tries to take in the larger portrait of the world. Moore's world is both its opaque, substantial, unrepeatable self and a natural resource for allegories of poetry. Characteristically, her poems are at the same time descriptions of reality and representations of imaginative activity. They inevitably fail at exact description, though they are redeemed by integrity and enthusiasm. But they succeed in imaginative representation, which becomes an imaginary possession in consolation for the reality that poetry can never possess.

In one way or another almost every Moore poem alludes to aesthetics. Contemporary critical theory is fond of finding self-reference in literature, but in Moore the argument can be made without special pleading. Many of her poems deal directly with the subject of art. And while a work of art can never directly trace its own activity, these poems confront in a general way the same problems they illustrate in the particular.

Because Moore's poems about art contain more direct statement than her other poems, we tend to treat them as prose. Indeed, they invite us to approach them familiarly, since they make straightforward, personal assertions; then they shrink on contact, or dissolve into a coruscation of luminous details and tantalizing circumlocutions. If one approaches poems familiarly, she tells us, "what one says of [them] is worthless"; on the other hand, "if one is afraid of [them], the situation is irremediable." Embracing the epigrams, aphorisms, and maxims in these poems, critics have evaded their idiosyncrasies and obscurities. Moore herself sets the standard for this critical behavior, approving plain speech and scorning interpretation, but her own poetic activity suggests a rule of discretion rather than prohibition. If we experience these poems as wholes they reveal a more complex understanding of the "phase of life" called "literature." Though perhaps with less revolutionary fervor, Moore was, like her contemporaries, defining a new poetic. But she is less willing than others of her generation to overthrow the past, or to claim victory for the present. She is not only making a rhetorical appeal to the reader but echoing her fellow poets, in asserting "I, too, dislike it." But she is willing to find a place for the genuine in the flawed.

In Moore's many approaches to the subject of art, we can discern a consistent pattern of concerns. Each of these poems seeks "the genuine" and condemns "humbug"; but underlying this relative contrast is an absolute one, in which all art is "humbug," though it can "make a place for the genuine." All art involves an opposition between "original" truth and "derivative" form (Moore's own terms), paradoxically and ideally resolved in uncompromised fusions of reality and imagination into medium. Each poem approves simplicity, humility, and naturalness in art, and deprecates ostentation, narcissism and contrivance. But beneath this simple opposition Moore develops a more complex picture, in which things and meanings are superimposed, in which things seem to be valued for their own sake, but are finally valued as figures. The poems enact and figure a play (sometimes of reversal, sometimes of reciprocity, sometimes of equivocation) between the world observed and the observing of it, the voice of things and a voice for things. This play ultimately arises from the relation of poet to subject and reader to poem. The genuine, which ideally denotes the achievement of a sense of reality in art, becomes instead a sign of imaginative intensity. While at one level Moore attacks narcissism in art, at another she finds it inevitable, useful, and delightful. While other modernists made the major claim of achieving the genuine in form, closing the gap between human constructions and the order of nature, Moore admits the elusiveness of truth, connecting the genuine with the acknowledgment of limits. The poem does not reveal the thing in all its realness, but puts us on the scent with lively images of pursuit.

In the poem entitled "Poetry" Moore's relative contrast between "half poets" and genuine poets runs parallel to a more fundamental opposition between the raw materials of poetry and the genuine. Moore pursues an explosive resolution ("imaginary gardens with real toads in them") which she knows to be ideal, offering "in the meantime" a list of ordinary objects in a formal setting which are also images of pursuit. The genuine thus takes on a double meaning, as stimulus and as response. "In the Days of Prismatic Color," Moore's modern paradise lost, and a poem rich with allusion, contrasts a haughty, advancing obscurity to a golden age of simplicity and clarity. But underlying this complaint against excesses of form is a more inclusive picture of our fall from original immanence into absence and illusion. At the end of the poem truth speaks defiantly against ephemeral form, but the voice of truth can only be presented, in the poem, as an echo of the poet. "The Monkeys" creates a similar ambiguity of voice which complicates a simple contrast between object and audience, and between genuine and fraudulent art. The play of perceiver and perceived, buyer and seller, occurs on many levels of "When I Buy Pictures"—its lists, its epigrammatic phrases, and its status in relation to its theme. The poem associates the genuine with humility, so that, paradoxically, to be genuine is to disclose one's sources. Once again Moore's sense of the immediacy and primacy of the genuine is complicated by her sense of the separate and secondary nature of art.

"Poetry" (CP, 266–267), the most famous and the most direct poem addressing the question of the genuine in art, provides the best starting point for defining Moore's usage. Though critics have long taken this poem as a statement of Moore's poetic, few have really confronted its peculiar procedures and examples. Moore's brilliant solution, "imaginary gardens with real toads in them," is often quoted, but the prestidigitation that produced it is rarely traced. In fact Moore never really does define poetry or the genuine, but through the labyrinths of ambivalence and ambiguity, skeptical restraints and imaginative leaps, she presents her conception of their relationship. She posits an ideal in which the genuine is absorbed into form, reference into poem, the real into the imaginary. In the meantime poetry turns out to be a magic trick that does not quite succeed, but which absorbs us in its dazzling sleight-of-hand, in which we think we glimpse the genuine before it turns into the poet once again.

Our initial question in reading "Poetry" is one of reference: what is the "it" of "I, too, dislike it. There are things that are important beyond all this fiddle"? Clearly "it" is poetry—but why does Moore avoid the noun? Is the poem a prescription for or a definition of poetry, or do these converge in Moore's mind? While she "dislikes" it at the beginning of the poem, by the end she has made it a distant ideal. Syntactically "this fiddle" could stand either in apposition to "poetry" (in the generic sense) or as a reference to the immediate poetic activity. Naturally both the general and the particular are complicated in this poem in which the speaker refuses to stand in one place, moving from "I, too" to the impersonal "one" in a defensive defense of poetry.[2] We discover that there are three poetries referred to here: one that won't do at all, the pretentious and narcissistic products of "half poets"; one that is transcendent, ideal, and purely imaginary, that fuses the genuine with artifice; and finally, the poem at hand. The problem is to separate them.

Before we have even begun to consider this ambiguity others have arisen. The ambiguity of reference is related to the ambivalence of the poem, which declares, at the outset, a dislike of "it" but immediately begins to retract. "Reading it, however, with a perfect contempt for it, one discovers in / it after all, a place for the genuine." Is the contempt part and parcel of the discovery? Or is it erased by the discovery? One finds in "it" a "place for the genuine"—does one find the genuine itself or is it extraneous to the poem, imported in or substituted? "Place" could imply either an occasion or a space. Which does Moore intend? If the "it" so far is "fiddle," is the genuine part of the fiddle or a transcendence of it? Is Moore discovering the magnitude of uselessness or overcoming it? The early problem of defining poetry has slipped into the problem of defining the genuine, as imaginative intensity or the achieved presence of reality in form.

What immediately follows "the genuine" could stand in apposition to it, though this is not entirely clear: "Hands that can grasp, eyes / that can dilate, hair that can rise / if it must, . . ." Typically Moore speaks through concrete particulars. But what, precisely, do they say? That we should stick to sensory detail when writing, to "finite objects"? It is worth noticing that these images all belong to a specific *realm* of particulars: they are all physical manifestations (body language) of internal reactions. Is the genuine, then, the stimulus or the response? Is it "objectification" or "a portrait of the author's character intent upon the object, which is sincerity"? Moore shifts persepctive. Given the details of grasping hands, dilating eyes, rising hair, we would tend to say "the genuine" was a matter of response, except for what follows: "these things are important not because a / high-sounding interpretation can be put upon them but because they are / useful." They are here seen as objects eliciting our response, "useful things," not responses. What is useful about them? A defense of poetry, even a definition, ought to answer the question. Instead Moore gives us more information about what is *not* appropriate:

> When they become so derivative as to become
> unintelligible,
> the same thing may be said for all of us, that we
> do not admire what
> we cannot understand:

The word "derivative" linked with "unintelligible" implies a definition of the ideal poetry as original and lucid. Originally, in *Others* 5 (July 1919) and *Poems* (1921), this section ended in a period. Moore returns to the thread of the previous assertion, but the colon suspends our expectation, suggesting that the examples could illustrate the antecedent negative or the following positive observation.

> the bat
> holding on upside down or in quest of something to
> eat, elephants pushing, a wild horse taking a roll, a tireless wolf
> under
> a tree, the immovable critic twitching his skin like a horse that
> feels a flea, the base-
> ball fan, the statistician—
> nor is it valid
> to discriminate against "business documents and
> school-books"; all these phenomena are important.

Moore has evaded all questions. Reduced, the argument runs: these things are useful because they are important; these things are important because they are useful—a mere tautology, but in poetry, if not in logic, something is accomplished. We do have the peculiar illusion of an answer, by virtue of the very struggle of getting to this point. An engagement is recorded. Here, it seemed, we have the genuine: real physical objects—elephants, horses, wolves, fleas, full of smell and feeling, not "discriminated" for their symbolic value but "objectively" interesting. And yet the list is far from a random sampling of the world's objects. Once again these "important" phenomena are all of one type: animate beings investigating other objects, "in quest" or pursuing things, though admittedly also objects of our own inquiry. They play both sides of an equation between subject and object, derivative and original. What is interesting about them is how they reflect our own acts of investigation—our curiosity depends on theirs. Is this the genuine, then: the act of finding? Moore's method of argument through the first two-thirds of the poem, as we have seen, is not to answer a question, or to resolve a duality, but to get at the question from ever-new vantages. We have on the one hand exploration, on the other hand discovery, joined by ambiguity.

Moore's next strategy in the poem is to condense distinctions into paradoxes, or abstract oxymorons. We shall "have it" she says, when we become "literalists of the imagination." Moore tells us in the notes that she condensed this phrase from an essay Yeats wrote on Blake:

> The limitation of his view was from the very intensity of his vision; he was a too literal realist of imagination, as others are of nature; and because he believed that the figures seen by the mind's eye, when exalted by inspiration, were "external existences," symbols of divine essences, he hated every grace of style that might obscure their lineaments. *Ideas of Good and Evil* (A. H. Bullen, 1903), p. 182 [CP, 267–268]

From what Yeats poses as undesirable opposites, realists of the literal (or natural) and literal realists of the imaginative, Moore derives a new ideal posture. The extremes of nature and imagination come together. Grace and the literal are one. But is the distinction "resolved" in her phrase? She holds out its fulfillment as a prospect, but the phrase is still, to us, paradoxical. "Precision is a thing of the imagination" (not, one infers, of reality), she writes in "Feeling and Precision" (*Predilections*, 8).

> One must make a distinction
> however: when dragged into prominence by half poets, the result
> is not poetry,
> nor till the poets among us can be
>   "literalists of
>   the imagination"—above
>   insolence and triviality and can present
>
> for inspection, "imaginary gardens with real toads in them," shall
> we have
>   it.

The "literalist of the imagination," we infer, not only is "sincere" in his vision ("untempted by any grace of style that might obscure its lineaments"), but also is successful in rendering that vision supremely graceful. In him, the formal and the natural are copresent, even cooperative; he produces "imaginary gardens with real toads in them." What follows is a contradictory demand for "the raw material of poetry," language and its various ordering devices (surprisingly aligned with the garden), and the genuine, things as they are (aligned with real toads). We lack the means to bring them into the same ontological status.

> In the meantime, if you demand on the one hand,
> the raw material of poetry in
>   all its rawness and
>   that which is on the other hand
>   genuine, you are interested in poetry.

Clear enough. But why toads? Why not "real roses" or "real princes"? Why must the oxymoron be double? A practical answer is that Moore feels an affinity for odd creatures. Indeed, her poems are full of them: her octopus, pangolin, jerboa, lizard, all "supreme in their abnormality," work against the curve of the general, the average. They are original and individual. The peculiar is linked in her mind with the particular. By their peculiarity they demonstrate the inclusiveness of the genuine, which will not discriminate against toads any more than against "business documents and school-books." The "poetic" ideally is a totally inclusive class. Moore "dislikes" poetry that statically congratulates itself on remaining within a class of what is "properly poetic." The wakeful mind is challenged to extend the class it can embrace. The genuine pressures decorum. Still, though the ideal objective viewer has no predilection for beauty but responds genuinely, we in fact do find toads "and the like" disconcerting, or if we do not, we know we are unusual in this. The norm of response to toads is, in life, not garden ease but hands that grasp, eyes that dilate, hair that rises, responses that also accompany the sublime.

Toads belong to a lexicon of symbols and have their own literary history, as rich as the history of the imaginary garden, even part of the same tradition. Together with other amphibians and reptiles (snakes, basilisks, chameleons) they often represent the power of the irrational in the midst of controlled elements. Their shocking, irregular appearance, their way of leaping out of camouflage, produces an effect of the uncanny, or gothic horror, in some versions of the sublime. Though "natural symbols," they are often cousins to the demonic or supernatural—the incubus, the satyr—as creatures outside the realm of human understanding. They are present in literature not as "things in themselves" but as challenges to the boundaries of beauty, decorum, human order.

We have not learned the method of Moore's "literalists of the imagination" who are at ease with toads. We have only their raw materials and their intentions. Indeed, their accomplishment seems to us miraculous, a matter of enchantment or alchemy—such as would turn princes into toads, and vice versa. It is hard to resist the conjecture that such suggestions of magical transformation were present in Moore's mind in a poem about poetry, about image-making. To the "literalists of the imagination" the toad is a prince again, welcome back into the decorum of the garden. Similarly, things and words, nature and spirit are for them all of the same order of being. But such an ideal belongs to an imaginary, Edenic garden. We, on earth, can create "conjuries that endure" (*Predilections*, 32), but they remain fictions. Our toads are conspicuous and vulgar, challenging the perimeters of formal beauty. It is the incongruity that stimulates us, not the perspective it ideally provides. In this realm of pseudomagic, of conjuring, what has happened to the genuine, which had been implying the mundane world, "things in themselves," "dry, hard, finite objects"? Freud suggests that the effect of the uncanny (*heimlich*) involved the strangeness of the familiar, as its etymology (both homely and strange) implies. Perhaps this same doubleness obtains in Moore's use of the genuine. As ordinary as toads are, we cannot find forms that can domesticate them. Indeed it is the very effort to frame them that makes them seem extraordinary.

Until the toad is a prince, the ideal "garden" is only imaginary.

The toad is, in a sense, the emblem of failure, the rough edge of our attempt to bring the real world and the world of formal beauty together. It is also, becuase it confounds, an object of admiration (making our eyes "dilate"). That which is beyond language produces the effect of gusto, cousin to the sublime. But the toad is not an emblem of defeat. The point is not that we want to capture the toad in all his naturalness, the physical object itself as toad. Why should we? We have it aplenty in the world as it is. But "lit with piercing glances" (whether of reflected or radiated light Moore doesn't specify) the poeticized toad has the occasional look of a prince. It is "hair-raising" when you think about it, how we catch these transformations in transit but cannot complete the charm. We make mutations, gargoyles. We do read poetry, do become for moments "literalists of the imagination," but we cannot sustain our transformation. Sincerity, which started out as honest vision, becomes an expression of desire (not attainment), and the energy that accompanies that desire is "gusto." Moore's poems are "conjuries" that can make "real toads" appear in fictive gardens. But she always reveals what's up her sleeve, brings her images round to reveal the conjurer. She quotes, with approval, a saying of Kenneth Burke's: "The hypnotist has a way out *and* a way in" (*Predilections*, 8). Working against the beliefs of the literalist of the imagination, for whom poetry is presence, is the skeptic, for whom it is mere illusory "fiddle."

It is not surprising, given her view of poetry as a process of competing dualities, that Moore should have gone through many revisions, never fully settling on one. We have been looking at the form of the poem published in *Collected Poems*—the one most often anthologized. But it went through several forms.[3]

An intermediate phase in the second edition of *Observations* displays a frustration with ambiguities and an attempt to silence them. Not only is the poem shortened, but the famous "imaginary gardens with real toads in them" is removed and in its place is the phrase "enigmas are not poetry" prefacing a reminder that poems should not be "fashioned into that which is unknowable." Moore's vacillation about whether the "mysteries" she celebrates are natural or rhetorical, important or self-indulgent, will be the subject of another chapter, but it is clear enough here that she is subjecting her art to some hard criticism. Still, as if to say that these abrupt moral dispensations were too easy a resolution of complexity, she returned with minor changes and deletions to the original version when she published *Selected Poems*. And as though to acknowledge that art and the genuine are not yet resolved into one, she returned to syllabic patterns after an excursion into free verse, attempts to simulate natural speech. But in 1967 she lashed out against herself again, printing only part of the first three lines of the poem in *Complete Poems.*

Moore seems to have struggled with the Horatian precept *dulce et utile* in revising "Poetry." What had at first been "important" was now only "pleasing." But a draft of this version in the Rosenbach archive suggests that her ambivalence carried over into the act of composition. After "enigmas are not poetry," which abruptly concludes the version printed in the 1925 edition of *Observations,* she wrote:

> and not until the misled literalists of the imagination
> present for inspection
> imaginary gardens with real toads in them
> shall we encounter its misrule.

Here Moore changed the positive meaning that her phrase "literalists of the imagination" had borne in *Others,* but she was clearly turning against the pragmatic line this new poem was taking. She delightfully inverted values by neatly opposing "misled" and "misrule," celebrating poetry's recalcitrance, its rebellion against those whom she had called in the *Others* version "autocrats." Perhaps she was resisting the autocrat in herself.

The final, 1967 version of "Poetry" (CP, 36) reduces it from its original thirty-eight-line movement of rhetorically persuasive point, example, counterpoint, to a bare expression of ambivalence:

> I, too, dislike it.
> Reading it, however, with a perfect contempt for it, one discovers
> in
> it, after all, a place for the genuine.

The two versions stand not as original and revision but as two alternative statements. In an interview after the publication of the *Complete Poems* Moore said her change arose from dislike of unnecessary verbal display in the early poem. And yet she did publish the original in the notes to *Complete Poems,* and in her work "notes" are an integral part of the whole. It was not her usual practice to include her variorum. If, as she says, "omissions are not accidents," the corollary may be "inclusions are intentional." The ambivalence in the two versions of "Poetry" is basic to Moore's aesthetic: poetry embodies a continual tension between the desrie to concentrate all thought into a unity, into epigram, into implied vision (and silence), and the desire to make distinctions, to be explicit, to find the right words (and perhaps simply to assert one's existence by saying more). A line in the original published version of "Poetry" in *Others* reveals this temptation: "Case after case / could be cited did one wish it." Later Moore sees this wish as self-indulgent, claiming that the 1967 version contains all that the earlier version spells out. But could we divine the earlier version from its vestige? Language is not an instrument of precision, as Moore is the first to admit. Reducing the poem to three lines may be Moore's attempt to uncover the genuine, but a short poem is no more genuine than an expansive one.

Revision, whether within the text or between texts, is an essential part of Moore's aesthetic. It is motivated by an essential ambivalence about poetry's capacity to assert and form an elusive, multifaceted world. The imagination must continually catch itself in its complacencies and wipe away the smudge of accumulated thought. And the poem must have the same effect on the reader; it must elude his settled understanding. A passage in her reading diary (among many Moore copied from H. Festing Jones's *Diversions in Sicily*) expresses this need for constant renewal: "During the voyage through time the words of one's own language become barnacled over with associations so that we cannot see them in their naked purity as we see the words of a foreign tongue."[4] Too rigid an ideal of sincerity will reduce the poet to silence, because literature is by its very nature insincere. "If one is afraid of it [literature], / the situation is irremediable." On the other hand, "if one approaches it familiarly, / what one says of it is worthless" (CP, 45). The effect of Moore's poems is always to make her subject (and her poem) unfamiliar, without allowing it to become alien.

It should be said that Moore is not an austere moralist in upholding the value of sincerity. The "difficulties" she encounters (and produces) are in fact the proper pleasure of art. While resolution may be held out as the ideal, paradox clearly has a delight of its own. Her alert discovery of nuance, her fastidious resistance to blunt closure, suggest not only a sincerity of attitude but a dislike of ending. Moore's sincerity, then, is the agent of gusto. Failure in terms of precision becomes success in terms of energy generated, by the genuine discovery of a world bigger than our words for it.

In "In the Days of Prismatic Color" Moore's "literalist of the imagination" lives in the past rather than in the future, a luminous

Edenic past, obscured by a history of half-poets and their high-sounding interpretations. Though truth was once immanent in prismatic form, "it is no longer that"; we have fallen into representation, into form as a mask rather than as an extension of truth.[5] The continuity of pure and fractured light has been replaced by the discontinuity of light and darkness.

The imagery of light and darkness pervades Moore's poetry from her first to her final work. We think of the "black glass through which no light can filter" in "Black Earth," the "black jade" water in "The Fish," the "sea-serpented regions 'unlit by the half-lights of more conscious art' " in "Novices," the refracted light of "The Egyptian Pulled Glass Bottle in the Shape of a Fish," the "ray of whimsicality on a mask of profundity" in " 'He Wrote the History Book.' " Repeatedly Moore protests willful obscurity and the elaborate masks of elegance and praises the simple light of sincerity, the deep inner radiance unmatched by the brassy light of superficial wit. Light, of course, is identified with truth, darkness with obscurity. But Moore acknowledges that little in life or art is black and white. Life and art are translucent at best. The world itself is a kind of "screen" (as in her poem "He Made This Screen"), and filtered or reflected light is often better than no light at all. Art may not be able to present the genuine in its natural radiance, but it can sometimes seem to be penetrated by it, and it can sometimes represent it with a secondary, but still illuminating luster. Just as "Poetry" begins in denial and ends in aspiration, "In the Days of Prismatic Color" (CP, 41–42) attempts to admit a ray of light through its shadowed forms.

In this poem Moore criticizes excessive artifice as an uncreating word, as diabolic as any in Pope's *Dunciad.* And like the younger Pope in "Essay on Criticism" (a possible allusion and source of the imagery), she yearns for the days when art and nature were the same. But she does not pretend to offer a pristine alternative for the modern age. We fall into art, which is by its very character distant from nature and truth, from the genuine. Like Andrew Marvell in "The Garden," Moore describes an ideal that precedes all duality, a time not "of Adam and Eve but when Adam was alone." Moore is privately revising a comment someone, perhaps her mother, made about an exhibition of paintings by her friends Marguerite and William Zorach: "the fineness of early civilization art—I have never seen such primeval color. It is color of the sort that existed when Adam was alone and there was no smoke, when there was nothing to modify it but the mist that went up."[6] The speaker assumes that art had a golden age of innocence to which certain artists return. Moore admired the Zorachs' work (Marguerite painted her portrait a few years after the show), but even the work of superior artists is necessarily a representation of truth, not its revelation. For Moore all art is the result of duality; she presses back before art, which is derivative by definition, to a time of originality. While poetry cannot contain that originality, it can "make a place" for it, can introduce it in quotation. Thus the insistent monstrosity of baroque art, with its "classic multitude of feet" is not practically opposed to a genuine art such as "literalists of the imagination" might create, but to a discreet art written in syllabics, which acknowledges its own limits by breaking form in the last stanza.

In the days when Adam was alone, there was no difference between reality and imagination, between truth and form.[7] Objects and meanings were apprehended in an immediate unity. But "obliqueness" in the fallen world of art has lost its root meaning, and is no longer "a variation of the perpendicular." Form is uprooted from nature. Art is no longer innocent. Moore acknowledges her own fallen state, her own impulse to mystify and complicate simple truths, when she remarks of the subject at hand "it also is one of / those things into which much that is peculiar can be / read." But there is a sense in which the fall is a happy one for Moore, though the immediate mood of the poem is nostalgic. What artist more enjoys reading peculiarities into things? Just as Adam through his fall is brought to recognize the grace and omnipotence of God, so Moore, through the constant encounter with the limits of form, is able to make a place for the intervention of the genuine. The poem moves through a series of assertions and denials to arrive at its negative capabilities. The "wave" of art is not stilled in the poem, only humbled, as the expansive, pauseless sigh gives way to tirade, tirade to simple wisdom, and wisdom to "truth." But this "truth" is, after all, only an echo of the poet's own enthusiasm. "The wave may go over it if it likes. / Know that it will be there when it says, / 'I shall be there when the wave has gone by.'" The quotation marks a difference, but the words mark an identity. We have at once the illusion of truth's presence and the awareness of a proxy.

The notes to each edition of Moore's poems alert us to borrowings. But there are almost always other sources which Moore leaves undocumented perhaps because they are not only borrowings but gestures and allusions. Where the sources are personal Moore may have intended private gestures enclosed within public statements. Where they are general, as in the echoes of Pope, Moore's reticence frees the poem from the strict confines of tradition while allowing allusions to it. The editors of the *Marianne Moore Newsletter* have recently traced the quoted lines at the end of this poem to a letter from Moore's brother shortly after he entered the Navy: "I feel sometimes as if the wave can go over me if it likes and I'll be there when it's gone by."[8] This does not mean that the poem is primarily addressed to or about her brother, any more than it is addressed to or about the Zorachs, Pope, or Nestor (whom she notes for the first quotation). But it does suggest, as so many such sources do, that Moore's aesthetic reflections have a personal dimension, that she brought the separate events and observations of her personal relations into the more general and independent sphere of art. The source also suggests that her brother represented for Moore an ideal of fortitude and faith that she hoped to emulate in her poem.

Moore's lines are usually overdetermined. Keats may have provided the literary source of these final lines as Moore's public predecessor. But Keats had more confidence in the union of art and eternity, even if these leave the poet and his reader wounded in their mortal state. It is art, as the vehicle of truth, that survives to speak its message as the waves of generations go by.

> When old age shall this generation waste,
>   Thou shalt remain, in midst of other woe
> Than ours, a friend to man, to whom thou say'st,
>   "Beauty is truth, truth beauty,"—that is all
>   Ye know on earth, and all ye need to know.

For Moore, not only man but art is ephemeral; there is no urn to speak the words of truth. But her own poem is implicitly that urn, the quotation its caption, with all the Keatsian ambiguity as to where the poet's voice merges with, or separates from, a transcendent voice.

"In the Days of Prismatic Color" exemplifies Moore's ambivalence about the mask of art, an ambivalence that returns throughout her work. For every poem condemning obscurantism there is another poem approving disguises and protective coverings. Moore's satiric impulse is to tear the veil, to expose motives and break through pretensions, to penetrate a mist of confusion to simplicities and primitive truths. But her allegorical impulse is to veil and mask those truths, as the only way of bringing them forward into art. The genuine must be figured to be known, though the figure at once reveals and conceals it.

"The Monkeys" (CP, 40) also concludes with the voice of truth enclosed in quotation marks, and this time much less reticent. But the source and substance of the remarks become ambiguous through the many layers of figuration, pronoun reference, quotation, and indirect statement.[9]

"The Monkeys" deals chiefly with a taste for art that sacrifices the "magnificence" of nature for the narcissistic satisfactions of baroque complexities, high-sounding interpretations, and intellectual emphasis. Ironically, a "flattery" of our intellectual power can make us vulnerable. But within this simple dichotomy Moore suggests several others which deepen and complicate it.

The subject of art is not raised until the final third of the poem; the first part consists of a casual recollection of a trip to the zoo. Characteristically, Moore lures us in with a "feigned inconsequence of manner." But ultimately the zoo becomes a metaphor—comically suggesting artists in cages and spectators gawking at them. Moore does not reveal the analogy until the image has registered in a literal way. Such a method allows her, in keeping with her theme, to respect the particularity of objects, but also to open their range of significance. This is undoubtedly why she changed the title from the earlier "My Apish Cousins," which announced the notion of artist as ape of nature. The zoo is an ideal metaphor in which to engage this play of identification and difference, for it is precisely to see ourselves in the alien and the alien in ourselves that we visit the zoo. What we find is not always flattering, but it is, to some degree, familiar. In the first stanza, Moore seems to be discriminating among these creatures, the zebras "supreme," the parakeets "humdrum"; and yet from a distance, seen as representatives of the variety of nature, they are collectively "magnificent." As characters from the world of art, too, they are both satirized and praised. We find the same tolerant irony in "Poetry," in which "all these phenomena are pleasing" though some are lightly mocked.

Most critics dismiss the first half of "The Monkeys" as a digression and move on to the "meanings" in the second half. But the two parts depend on each other, in several ways. In the first half the images are presented primarily as literal ones, though a complete reading of the poem brings out their figurative value. The figure in the second half is obviously allegorical, bearing only a secondary relation to the creaturely setting from which it is drawn. Thus the poem maintains a tension between the particular and the figurative, between the animals as examples of nature and as figures of artists. While the tension is resolved, by implication, in the notion of the artist as a natural genius, the tension is sustained throughout the poem in an equivocation about that "Gilgamesh" of the carnivores, and what he represents. The artist remains on both sides of the cage, as a "natural" but also as an artificer who converts nature to flattery.

The digression on memory serves as a fading device. Moore throws a veil over nature to create an allegory. When she focuses again after the dimming she is a purely imaginative sphere in which animals speak. The allegory allows a representation of nature, which is otherwise silent to us. But the question remains whether this is the voice of nature or only an echo of ourselves.

Is this cat, personified as the epic hero, speaking on behalf of nature or on behalf of the artist? Ideally, these are on the same side; the artist's orders attempt to tap the vitality of nature. Gilgamesh, in this sense, might well be Ezra Pound, spokesman for artists, who condemned the interpretive activity of critics, who criticized "culture" for its inflationary values, in which NATURA is bartered off to hollow usury, and who developed the dynamic art of the vortex. (Wyndham Lewis, while painting a portrait of Pound, observed that he had the head of a lion.) The relative complaint of the artist-hero against critics who view art in strictly formal terms gives way to an absolute: nature is set against the impositions of form. In the days of Gilgamesh, perhaps, we saw prismatic color; nature and artist were allied. (Although the legendary Gilgamesh was known for his strength to defy the force of nature in a great deluge.) But for the modern artist form is always attained by a bartering with the raw materials of nature. In a sense the poem *does* barter nature for flattery, using its industry to convert things to human use, making nature represent humanity.

The voice in quotation represents many constituencies at once. As the voice of nature it speaks against impositions of human forms. As the voice of the isolated artist it speaks against a public, including critics, who put art in a special category. As the voice of the public it speaks against critics and their high-sounding interpretations. So we have several possible allegiances in the ambiguities of "us" and "them"—nature against man; artist and nature against public; artist, nature, and public against critics.

But after the dash the language is more sympathetic, seeming to speak of what is rather than of the false impositions on what is. The superior voice of Gilgamesh gives way to the more generous voice of the narrator who invoked him, and who spoke from outside the cage. Art indeed has a power over us even greater than the power of nature, for it is a sign of our ability to order nature, to put it to our use. The sea (always, in Moore, an image of the sublime, inhuman power of nature) may draw our imaginations to its profundities, but the lure of art, which proffers flattery, which demonstrates our power to surpass nature in its creative force, is even greater. Pound's vortex, for instance, would capture in its dead center all the vitality of nature. But Moore resists the lure of art, at the end of her poem, and surrenders her industrious orders, including the fiction of Gilgamesh, to the deluge of simple raw materials that support human culture, "hemp, rye, flax, horses, platinum, timber and fur." Art is created out of nature; nature is prior to art, and art returns to nature. The poem begins and ends with the things, the particulars, from which it was constructed; and the fiction of Gilgamesh, of truth speaking through art, remains only as a memory.

The comparable ambiguities of buyer and seller in "When I Buy Pictures" create an infinity of pictures within pictures which works against the grain of the poem's rhetorical simplicity. The speaker approaches the reader with the same apparent openness as in "Poetry," moving Donald Hall to write: " 'When I Buy Pictures' says what it has to say in prose-like sentences that would be hard to misinterpret . . . Miss Moore is writing criticism."[10] But this is "prose with a heightened consciousness" in which there is nothing wasted or random. Its choice of words, its images, its structures, are an integral part of its meaning. The familiar, direct manner dissolves on contact, giving way to the idiosyncratic and indirect.

Like many others, the poem begins in revision and skepticism, drawing a direct connection between restraint, humility, and the genuine as it goes on.

Moore often uses the metaphor of buying and selling in representing relations between artists and audiences, as in "Novices" for instance:

> the little assumptions of the sacred ego confusing the issue
> so that they do not know "whether it is the buyer or the seller who
> gives the money"—
> an abstruse idea plain to none but the artist,
> the only seller who buys, and holds on to the money. [CP, 60][11]

Buying is a transfer of ownership, an act of appropriation in which an object becomes identified with someone. But "imaginary possession" allows the mind to identify with the object while permitting the autonomy of both. Enclosed in acts of imaginary possession are acts of self-reflection and self-possession which confer the sense of ownership that is objectively denied. "When I look at that of which I may regard myself as the imaginary possessor"—pursued objects become oblique mirrors of the pursuer in Moore but retain their position as objects. Such gestures of selfportraiture are everywhere in her poetry, at the level of individual lines and at the level of whole analogies, but they are never obtrusive; we are drawn into the imaginary sense long before we spot the mirror in it. Moore's self-reflexiveness is not aggressive or arrogant, as is that of "novices." But she, too, is both a buyer and a seller. For while she gathers these images in she is also projecting them outward in her own picture, not only in this poem but in all her galleries of quotation and description.

Moore's humility prohibits her from placing "too stern an intellectual emphasis upon this quality or that" and critics have tended to take the "average moments" as random and indiscriminate. But while Moore's antihierarchical attitude keeps her from conspicuously ordering her list, she takes possession of it through repetition and association. What is perhaps first striking about the list is its range and inclusiveness. Because of Moore's manner of presentation, our inclination is to skip over this list and return to the more "significant" language at the end of the poem. But the argument the poem makes prohibits us from preferring the "intellectual emphasis" to the "life of things." And indeed, if we return to the list, it seems to ask for consideration by its very peculiarity. These are not objects that would please everyone in his "average moments." We might explain it to some extent as a simple, meaningless chain of associations: sounds suggest other sounds (parquetry . . . parchment . . . parts), silver suggests blue, age suggests images of age (hatboxes that bear images of old fashioned hounds that are shaped like hourglasses).

But more suggestive orders are also accumulating, though they do not account for every element. As in "Poetry" and "The Monkeys" observer and object are reversed. In the first two images, the "intensity of the mood" is paired with a picture (on a hatbox) that might provoke such a mood. The pair create a regress in which we see a picture of someone looking at a picture—a mirror of Moore's situation, and, at a further remove, of our own.

Moore sets objects of associative value off against objects that have none, in order both to attract and to repel our curiosity. Thus the square of parquetry is juxtaposed to the biography, and the biography is attended to not for the story it tells but for its formal appearance (making the biography literal in the most extreme sense). Typically, Moore distracts us from our impulse to interpret by presenting objects of symbolic value but drawing attention to their nonsymbolic elements. So the hieroglyph is admired for its "snipe-legged" form rather than for its hidden meaning, making it equal in value to "an artichoke in six varieties of blue," a purely formal image. But while an element of significance may be ignored in the immediate introduction of an image, it is drawn out by other elements. While there is no "intellectual emphasis" on the subject of time, the "old thing," the "hourglass," the "parchment-like expanse" of the biography, and the hieroglyph work together to introduce it. Moore asks us to look at "the silver fence," but we know we are looking at "Adam's grave" and thinking of the fall which Constantine's pompous silver fence tries to deny.[12] We know that Michael showed Adam human history, including his own grave (in *Poems* the vision of Adam's grave is "prefigured by himself"), and the vision is indeed like a biography, a parchment-like expanse. And Adam looking over human history is indeed like the "satire on curiosity" and like its opposite, the vision of diminishing things. Moore's sincerity requires restraint, but not utter silence. She plants associations, if she does not underline them. As she wrote in the *Poems* version, Adam's grave means "just as much or just as little as it is understood to mean by the observer." But in the subject of Adam's fall, she tells us in "In the Days of Prismatic Color," "much that is peculiar can be read." In Moore's poetry we do not know who is the buyer and who the seller, not because there is so much intellectual emphasis but because there is so little. But the sense of humility Adam feels from the fall, his acknowledgment of the spiritual forces that have made him, prefigures Moore's writing. Again writing is cast as a postlapsarian art, removed from the genuine but struggling to make an imaginary place for it. From earliler versions it is clear that the poem is concerned with making as well as buying pictures. Moore seems to be talking to herself about her method of borrowing, when she writes, in *Poems*, not that a picture must, like Adam, "acknowledge the spiritual forces that have made it" but that it must "acknowledge the forces that have made it" and "must admit that it is the work of X, if X produced it; of Y, if made / by Y. It must be a voluntary gift with the name written on it." Art is derivative in a literal as well as a figurative sense. The pictures she buys are already bought, and indeed all her examples are already once removed from "the life of things" though they may be "lit with piercing glances" into it. On the other hand, to buy a picture is inevitably to make it, to infuse it with personal significance. The energy in the phrase "lit with piercing glances into the life of things" flows two ways, drawing light from inside and outside at once. That Moore has borrowed the phrase from A. R. Gordon's *The Poets of the Old Testament* only extends this doubleness.

In the version of the poem that appeared in *The Dial* (July, 1921) Moore takes up pictures "as a savage would take a looking-glass." The savage sees himself in the glass, but what he sees is strange and new. This simultaneous identification and distance sustains the energy of the glance, as Moore explains directly in a draft of the poem, which states that a good picture "compels analysis and does not disappear under admiration."[13] The relation between picture and purchaser is one of steady magnetism and skepticism, identification and distance. Moore wrote in a version of "Humility, Concentration and Gusto," (in the Rosenbach archive) "I have always regarded readings of poetry—even talks about poetry—with the scepticism and curiosity of a savage."

The "place for the genuine," then, which is ideally filled by the presence of "truth," is in the meantime filled with images of the artist's intensity. "Picking and Choosing," with its plea for accuracy and sincerity, ends with an image of desire and gusto, " 'a right good salvo of barks,' a few strong wrinkles puckering / the skin between the ears." The small dog, like the poet, does not yet "have it," does not possess the meat of transcendent truth, though perhaps he has "put us on the scent." But lingering in all Moore's poems is the possibility that this truth is itself an illusion created out of the artist's superfluous desire. Moore acknowledges Xenophon, himself a model of accuracy, for the lines "a right good salvo of barks." But this is another of Moore's overdetermined images; lurking in the line is another passage from Conrad, which she copied into her reading diary shortly before she composed the poem. "An artist's touches are sometimes no more articulate than the barking of a dog who would call attention to something without exactly knowing what. This is as it should be and he is a great artist who can be depended on to bark at nothing."[14]

"Determination with resistance" is the theme and action of all Moore's poems, and it sums up the situation of art since the days of prismatic color. Artists are not incarnate gods, not "literalists of the imagination." Art is genuine not because it captures "truth" in "form" but because it has sincerity and gusto. Quarrelsome and subjective in their judgments and forms, artists harmonize in the intensity of their genius.

In a "Comment" hidden at the back of an issue of *The Dial*, Moore addressed the problem of rivalry and disagreement in the arts, finding a more abiding harmony within it. While it has Moore's usual offhand manner, the essay is a remarkable and inclusive statement of her poetics. It gathers up under one rubric many of Moore's major insights and structural preoccupations. Speaking directly of differences among artists, she evolves a theory of the composing process and the negative capability of art. After a brief introduction on international tensions, she writes:

> The unquiet nature of the artist is proverbial, genius being in some sense always in revolt. But . . . the aesthetic malcontent is out of court, for wherever there is art there is equilibrium . . . It is determination with resistance, not determination with resentment, which results in poise . . . Agitated in the disposing of his own turbulent business as were "the Egyptian sculptors who set themselves problems a little beyond their comfort," the artist is in a state of profound activity, emerging from darkness into light like the grain which he eats, unable often to recognize in himself that "summer in December" of which enduring art consists. The ruffled genius might in his acuteness realize that sometimes he fights with that with which he is agreeing, and is like the hour, marked by a shadow which seeming to cut the sun, defines it. Although "the judgment of experts on one another is at variance," their genius is not; perception is always as Traherne would say, "innocent": insurrection being contrary to that sensitiveness and receptiveness which
>
> ". . . like the fairest glass,
>   Or spotless polished brass,
> Themselves soon in their object's image clothe."
>
> In making works of art, the only legitimate warfare is the inevitable warfare between imagination and medium and one finds it impossible to convince oneself that the part of the artist's nature which is "rash and combustible" has not been tamed by the imagination, in those instances in which the result achieved is especially harmonious.[15]

Repeatedly in Moore we find that perception and imagination are innocent and genuine while form is combative and artificial. The consequence is that art is a constant struggle, a "martyrdom," as she wrote in a letter to William Carlos Williams (January 26, 1934), one is willing to make for the "cat nip," the "ignis fatuus" of art. The sunbursts of imagination and reality will always resist the pins of artistic order. But art can define the genuine by its very failure. While form is always dark, its darkness can define a light, "like the hour, marked by the shadow which seeming to cut the sun, defines it." Moore's is an art of reciprocity and conversity. In every conflict or opposition there is a potential equilibrium, a lively poise. In the struggle between form and form, or between imagination and medium, a balance is achieved from which emerges a "summer in December" which can never be contained, but which is yielded as a consequence of struggle. The ultimate conversity, for Moore, is that between the imagination and its object, for by becoming absorbed in the object the artist discovers an image of herself.

2. The Spontaneous Symbol
Emblems and Meditations

MODERNISM was a kind of deprogramming, a breaking down of automatic associations to restore "contact," as Williams put it, with experience. Like other modernists, Moore advocated rigor and spontaneity in thought and representation, but she found ways of working within the symbolizing process, allowing natural phenomena to be yoked to abstractions that interpret experience, while preventing these images and ideas from hardening into catchwords and dogmas. Unlike the imagists, for whom the natural object was the adequate symbol, Moore drew objects into a realm of fancy where they could stand conspicuously for ideas. And yet they retain the specificity and tangibility of the original world from which they are cast. She is always observing while she is making observations. Moore may challenge conventional associations, but just as often she brings a symbol back to life, treating it as though it were just discovered at the primary juncture of fact and concept. She engages the reader's attention with the thrill of unexpected resemblance. Spontaneity and symbolism would seem to be opposed, but for Moore they belong together.

Moore is best known for her lively profiles of exemplary beasts— the jerboa, the plumet basilisk, the pangolin, the arctic ox (or goat)— for her tireless attention to the value and suggestiveness of natural fact. Precision is her passion; she sets herself indefatigably against error and misconception, making certain that things are called by their true names. The naturalist's delight in particularity and taxonony and the poet's delight in resemblance and synthesis combine as the dominant preoccupations of *Selected Poems*. But although Moore had majored in biology at Bryn Mawr (having been rejected by the English department), it was a decade before she began to bring her observations and experiments into the poet's laboratory. Her education in literary convention and decorum prohibited such adventures. The leading poetry of the day belonged to an exclusive, genteel realm of prescribed signs, forms, and meanings, which the imagination obeyed in order to be relieved of the disagreeable world. To bring the flux and relativity of the world into this carefully preserved quiet would be self-defeating, according to the prevailing aesthetic. Moore's earliest poetic efforts attempt to conform to the niceties of the genteel tradition (which she would shortly grow to "dislike"). During and immediately after college she wrote a number of short, sweet, symmetrical lyrics in which the symbols are known quantities and the rhythms premeasured. There is considerable virtuosity in these lyrics ("Ennui" was selected by a classics professor at Bryn Mawr as a model of classical form), and even a subversive tendency, but it is difficult to recognize the mature Moore, with her carefully crafted but idiosyncratic forms and images, in these small set pieces. One of the most interesting of the early poems is "Talisman" (*Poems*, 9), first published in *The Lantern*, 1912, and later in *The Egoist*, which T. S. Eliot ascribed to the influence of H.D., but which is more likely built from the same classical models that had inspired the "imagiste" (Moore and H.D. went to college together and remained friends after graduation).[1]

> Under a splintered mast,
> torn from ship and cast
>   near her hull,
>
> a stumbling shepherd found
> embedded in the ground,
>   a sea-gull
>
> of lapis lazuli,
> a scarab of the sea,
>   with wings spread—
>
> curling its coral feet,
> parting its beak to greet
>   men long dead.

The poem is sluggishly elegaic in comparison with Moore's related later work ("No Swan So Fine," "A Grave"). The images are stock and inexact, the sentiment, as Eliot observed, is "commonplace." Moore herself rejected the poem after *Observations,* perhaps because of its acceptance of conventional symbolism. But while the poem fits too comfortably into its formal and rhetorical frame, it bears a certain resemblance to later work in its challenge to heraldry. The talisman outlives its context of meaning, but meaning is not so much erased as revised by the new context. The object remains a symbol of endurance, but not in the assumed manner. It greets no proud generation for whom it symbolizes power and prosperity, but a humble shepherd, for whom it is a symbol of mortality.

Moore was influenced by prose ("its precision rather than its purple," as Eliot observed) as well as poetry, and this influence, along with others, was moving her toward a discursiveness, a descriptive precision, and a syntactic complexity uncommon for the day. Alongside her simple songs Moore was beginning to write witty epigrammatic poems controlled by argument and modeled more on the stately Horatian epistle than on the watery Georgian lament. Yet for all their complex intellectual maneuvers, these poems never seem abstract or dispassionate. Eliot, writing of Moore in an essay called "Observations," paid her the same compliment he paid Donne, that she "fuses thought and feeling."[2] Moore was sufficiently pleased with the essay to borrow Eliot's title as her own in 1924, and to thank him later under the image of the apteryx (after Eliot's pseudonym) in "The Mind is an Enchanting Thing." The coincidence of Eliot's remarks on Donne is significant, for the images in this second group resemble those of the metaphysicals rather than those of the symbolists or imagists.[3] They trace an image in order to present or explore an idea rather than to evoke a mood or sensation. But Moore approaches the process of analogy with a special self-consciousness that marks her as a modern.

Moore fuses thought and feeling by admitting into her emblems the particulars that have been worn down by repeated acts of representation—the occipital horn of the snail, the thorns of the rose. Her objective in this is not simply to assert the otherness of objects that have been appropriated as symbols of human values (a motive that would become stronger in later work), but to deepen or revise our sense of those values. Automatic thinking is bound by catchwords and emblems. Moore invigorates and challenges thought by reversing and revitalizing the analogies that direct thought.

Moore's poems enter a long and varied tradition of emblematic literature in which images are juxtaposed to ideas or morals with which they have little natural but primarily an abstract connection. Moore's later descriptive poems are really an extension of this tradition, attaching objects to ideas but detailing the image far beyond its representational function. In the earlier poems the images remain generalized and abstract but Moore creates a lively tension between the image and its conventional association, constantly checking our expectations, in order to toughen the emblematic process and awaken the mind to fresh thought.

Moore does not discard symbolism and association themselves, then, as Pound and Williams were inclined to do, but only the conventional uses of symbols and the conventional ideas with which they are associated. She persuades and argues not by nurturing our complacencies, giving us familiar signs and meanings in prescribed shapes and sizes, nor by abandoning the symbol, but by surprising us, by turning those symbols and their values upside down, showing us their error or the deeper meanings in them we have missed for our attention to surface. As always in Moore, these poems argue against the grain. For her, representation steers dangerously toward prejudice (black is evil) and needs constant revision. She introduces her unconventional ideas by unconventional approaches to conventional symbols. In some of these poems Moore is primarily concerned with challenging a meaning assigned to an object; in others she goes further to replace the old meaning or value with a new one. But even in the second instance, in which the literal object has little significance, it is the recalcitrant features of the image that allow her to revise or refute the standard conception connected with it. Indeed, her final points are often made exclusively through image, reasserting the power of things to guide the imagination. In these poems Moore is an observationist of style and attitude, not of natural fact, and yet her insight into the manners she observes is continually sharpened through analogy.

Metaphor is perspective. We consider a this in terms of a that. But because Moore likes to see a thing from all sides (both the subject and the analogous object), the "statements" of her poems are often ambivalent or ambiguous. They are usually addressed to someone, but they also react to something said previously—an opinion commonly held, an unjust reputation, a statement to which she takes exception, a criticism where praise seems justified. Moore proceeds by resistance and reversal, undermining absolutes, favoring the relative and the flexible in manners just as she favors the particular and the recalcitrant in nature.

Moore often celebrates the very objects in nature that have been appropriated as "catchwords" for the negative social or aesthetic values with which they have no natural connection (as in "A Fool, A Foul Thing, A Distressful Lunatic" and "Injudicious Gardening"). By redeeming such objects she is also, of course, making a larger point about the prejudice implicit in our impulse to symbolize and classify. In other poems she accepts a conventional symbol but extends its meaning and reverses its value. In "Roses Only" it is not representation but interpretation that is in error. Symbolism can be turned against its users; heraldry taken to its logical extreme (solipsistic mania for power) defeats itself—a symbol of power inadvertently becomes a symbol of suicide in "To Military Progress" and "To Statecraft Embalmed." Moore delights in dead metaphors, resurrecting them by importing forgotten details and associations in "Pedantic Literalist" and "To a Steam Roller." In "To a Snail" and "To a Strategist" images of praise are formed of condemnations, virtues are seen in what others have called weakness and vice. Again Moore sharpens the inversion of aphorisms and their attendant values by an inversion of symbolic representation. Analogy is an instrument of meditation as well as persuasion, and in "Black Earth" and "A Grave" Moore explores at length the subtle and varied meanings beneath the simple surfaces of symbols. These poems turn the structures of metaphoric doubleness and inversion inward, creating subtler gradations and revisions. They work, that is, by challenging assertions which they either refute or prove true in surprising ways. As meditations, they are constantly trying to become declarative, trying to convert an associative process into a rational one, a subjective understanding into an aphoristic truth. But metaphor is both their means and their conscious limit. The genuine remains outside of speech, influencing the dialogue of the imagination with itself and the world. As in the shorter poems, reason outwits itself, to reveal "the beautiful element of unreason under it."

One of Moore's first challenges to conventional symbolism was "Masks" (*Contemporary Verse*, January 1916) in which she redeems three creatures appropriated as disparaging symbols. The poem is slight, but it indicates a tendency that will become stronger and more complicated in later work.

> "Loon". . . ."goose". . . . and "vulture". . . .
> Thus, from the kings of water and of air,
> Men pluck three catchwords for their empty lips.
> Mock them in turn, wise, dumb triumvirate!

You, gander, with stout heart tooled like your wings of steel,
What coward knows your soul?
"Egyptian vultures, clean as cherubim,
All ivory and jet," sons of the burning sun,
What creatures call you 'foul'?
And you, nature's own child,
You most precocious water bird,
That shouts exultantly among lone lakes,
You, foremost in the madman's alphabet—
Laugh in superb contempt at folly's catalogue!

Moore not only defends these creatures by recalling their neglected virtues, she begins to reassign meaning, stripping off the false "masks" and revealing the "truth" of their proud natures. She points toward a new symbolic system: the gander as courage, the vulture as beauty, the loon as intelligence and wisdom. But the style of the poem lacks the appearance of spontaneity she calls for in its statement. Moore revised the poem and included it in *Observations* under the title "A Fool, A Foul Thing, a Distressful Lunatic." But the second version is very different in style and tone. Whereas the first is righteous and fiercely rhetorical in its anger against falsely assigned values, the second is left in questions meant gently to lift off appearances and alert the reader to the thoughtlessness of his assumptions and prejudices. The language, too, is less ceremonious.

With webs of cool
      Chain mail and his stout heart, is not the gander
   Mocked, and ignorantly designated yet,
To play the fool?
      "Egyptian vultures clean as cherubim,
      All ivory and jet," are they most foul?
And nature's child,
      That most precocious water bird, the loon—why
   Is he foremost in the madman's alphabet;
Why is he styled
   In folly's catalogue, distressful lunatic?
                              [Observations, 18]

"Injudicious Gardening" (CP, 81) is similar to "A Fool, A Foul Thing, A Distressful Lunatic" but much more complex in its message and much more immediate in its address. The poem challenges a particular instance of representational prejudice and examines the situation with more ambiguity and irony. The poem responds, as Moore's note to it discloses, to observations by Robert Browning:

> Letters of Robert Browning and Elizabeth Barrett (Harper, 1899), Vol. I, p. 513: "The yellow rose? 'Infidelity,' says the dictionary of flowers." Vol. II, p. 38: "I planted a full dozen more rosetrees, all white—to take away the yellow-rose reproach!"   [CP, 275]

But the bidirectional movement of the poem—a conventional sense of decorum and symbolism opposed to natural response, and natural response in turn opposed to respect for privacy, that respect for privacy tinged with sarcasm—is clear without the note. Moore had originally thought of calling the poem "To Robert Browning in His Act of Vandalism" but withdrew the reference from the poem proper. The poem turns, typically, on a conditional sentence, the conditions of which Moore ambiguously accepts but defeats. At one level, she sides with the outcast, the yellow rose, accepting the consequences of her alliance. At another level, ambiguously inside and yet outside the conventional symbolism, she identifies with the yellow rose (demonstrating her fidelity to spontaneous feeling), sharing its stigma precisely because she is unfaithful to the symbolism that labels it "infidelity." Typically, Moore creates the illusion of standing on both sides of the argument. The ambiguity presses further in the second stanza, in which Moore incorporates the respone of her adversary. The lyrical clarity of the first stanza may privilege it rhetorically, but grammatically she achieves a balance of contentions. Bernard Engel and others are correct in believing that the force of this poem is on the side of spontaneity, but in a sense both acts are spontaneous.[4] The ambiguity prevents the poem from settling into a simple opposition. The relative awkwardness of the second stanza can be read as a sign of self-restraint against the automatic response of the first stanza, or as a sign of sarcasm. Whose gardening is injudicious here? Like "infidelity," the word "injudicious" is assigned double objects which reverse double (negative and positive) meanings. Browning is injudicious in his acceptance of convention, the speaker in her defiance. But working in the opposite direction, "injudicious" is a negative word from the point of view of conformity, a positive word from the point of view of nonconformity. Both sides have their claims and their limitations. Moore will not create closure around either point of view. Grammatically dialectical and rhetorically ironic, the poem speaks from the shuttle running to and fro through its two stanzas.

Moore deepens ambiguity by leaving the subjects and objects implied in the second stanza. Whose ears are offended? Who is causing an effrontery to whom? How are passive and active roles aligned? By comparing the *Observations* version of this poem with that in *Collected Poems* and subsequent printings we can see these ambiguities more clearly. The earlier second stanza read:

> However, your particular possession—
> The sense of privacy
> In what you did—deflects from your estate
> Offending eyes, and will not tolerate
> Effrontery.   [Observations, 14]

If the "offending eyes" are the speaker's, they are "deflected" by her respect for Browning's privacy. There is even a third party involved, if we recall that the yellow rose issue was raised in an exchange of letters between Robert and Elizabeth. Browning's "fidelity" perhaps makes him intolerant of any "effrontery" to his wife's feeling, for which he might be "reproached." She is after all the conventional poet of the two, more likely to write in the style, if not the attitude, of the first stanza, whereas Robert Browning's verse is sometimes closer to the style of the second. The second version of the poem makes larger concessions to Browning's position. "Indeed might" and "need not" leave room for other points of view. Similarly, what is deprecated now is not the "offending eyes" of an iconoclast, but the "offended ears" of a traditionalist. The disapproval has been removed from agent to victim, but the ambiguity of who is who remains in both versions. Browning's privacy is, after all, a particular possession; he is not forcing it upon the world. The subjectivity is reinforced by the stanzas, the first written from the point of view of "I," the second from the point of view of "you." If the change in style (from graceful lyric to involuted prose), favors the "I," the sequence favors "you." While the tone is edged with sarcasm, it is a tolerant sarcasm.

Moore is usually viewed as a writer working outside of tradition, more idiosyncratic than original. But while she avoided the fierce frontal attacks by which Williams and Pound steamrolled their way through literary history, she deliberately positioned herself, during her formative years, in relation to predecessors. Thomas Hardy, Bernard Shaw, Ernest Dowson, Robert Browning, Thomas Carlyle, George Moore, Samuel Butler, William Blake, William Butler Yeats, Henry James, François Molière, Benjamin Disraeli, are only some of the writers she considers in her poems. Literary conversation is indeed her favorite field of observation, and many discursive and epigrammatic poems, while reaching beyond their occasion, respond in considerable detail to a prior text. These witty responses were for the most part written between the end of her college years and the beginning of her New York years. In the isolation of Carlisle, Pennsylvania, and Chatham, New Jersey, Moore constructed for herself an imaginary literary society. These poems sometimes have a peculiarly private air; we must construe their target from Moore's elegant repartee, but the sense of a dialogue is usually recoverable. Moore challenges received opinion, making a personal gesture toward redirecting the stream of literary tradition. And often she uses the form of direct address, after the Horatian epistles, taking a very particular sin of aesthetic judgment to task while implying much broader references.[5]

In "Roses Only" (SP, 42) Moore catches a symbol so advanced in its complexity as to seem almost decadent. Having made its way through love and beauty, frailty and transience, the rose symbol was a favorite target of modernists urging that traditional symbols be abolished. But once again Moore works within the establishment to create something entirely surprising and challenging.

Jean Garrigue has called "Roses Only" "a model of ambiguity" in which "a virtue is made of writing on two subjects as if they were one."[6] It works the other way around, as well; Moore writes on one subject as if it were two, and presents a unified but complex (ambivalent) attitude toward it. This poem combines criticism and praise, the same phenomena approached by volleying different points of view and, at each ironic turn, redefining the terms of evaluation.

> You do not seem to realize that beauty is a liability rather
>   than
>   an asset—that in view of the fact that spirit creates form
>   we are justified in supposing
>   that you must have brains. For you, a symbol of the
>   unit, stiff and sharp,conscious of surpassing by dint
>   of native superiority and liking for everything
> self-dependent, anything an

ambitious civilization might produce: for you, unaided, to
   attempt through sheer
reserve, to confuse presumptions resulting from observation, is idle. You cannot make us
      think you a delightful happen-so. But rose, if you are
      brilliant, it
   is not because your petals are the without-which-nothing
      of pre-eminence. Would you not, minus
thorns, be a what-is-this, a mere

peculiarity? They are not proof against a worm, the elements, or mildew;
      but what about the predatory hand? What is brilliance
      without co-ordination? Guarding the
   infinitesimal pieces of your mind, compelling audience
      to
the remark that it is better to be forgotten than to be re-
   membered too violently,
your thorns are the best part of you.

Garrigue does not name the two subjects, but she is presumably referring to the major inversion of the poem, in which the admiration is
transferred from the intrinsic virtues of the rose (beauty, intelligence) to
its inadvertent value as a moral example. Again Moore's irony is built
on a disparity and an inversion of perspectives. But she does not rest on
a single opposition between the rose's sense of how it is perceived, and
its audience's sense of its value. The language takes another turn, for
the perspectives of both rose and audience are themselves complex. In
the first turn, the rose's deep brilliance, of which the rose is privately
confident, is perceived in spite of her efforts to appear as "a delightful
happen-so"; in the second turn, the speaker surpasses the public point
of view, identifying the rose's real worth not as the rose imagines it, in
her "native superiority," but in the alienating effects of that superiority,
which prevent admiration from becoming envy.

At the level of the metaphor, Moore's irony takes similar turns,
through which she again both accepts and reinvents conventional symbolism. While her admiration transfers from the rose to the thorns, the
logic of the metaphor has already shifted to refute simple oppositions,
so that the rose and its thorns become identified, the rose even becomes
a symbol of its thorns, its self-conscious superiority, its unattainability.
Similarly "brilliance" is reassigned, not only from physical to intellec-

tual categories, but to moral ones. The ultimate wit of the poem rests in its tonal ambiguity. Typically, Moore goes beyond obvious forms of vanity to detect and debunk subtle ones, like the pose of humility itself when it disguises egotism. Finding brilliance that pretends a casualness about itself that it does not in fact feel, Moore retorts by acknowledging and then dismissing that brillance, preferring the true lesson of humility it teaches to the common world beneath it. Moore defeats her subject—exposing vanity disguised as humility—only to raise it again ironically on a new pedestal.

Moore's observations are almost always at one or several removes. This is true of her descriptive poems, which are collections and collages of facts and remarks presented by others—"flies in amber" she called them—and it is also true of her observations of social and cultural manners. She reacts to the reactions of others, often presenting the latter in quotation. She is most ingenious in responding to the inflexible, insensitive attitudes of critics, showing the triumph of spontaneity and wit through her statement and style. In several of these discursive and epigrammatic poems Moore deliberately borrows a dead metaphor (as if to lock her unimaginative subjects in their own manacles) and revives it by reintroducing suppressed elements, so that it regains its expressive power. Here Moore is not contradicting the import of catchwords but revealing their particular aptness. There is no ambivalence in "To a Steam Roller" (first published in *The Egoist* in October 1916), though its surprising extensions of analogy make it resemble "Roses Only." In general the shorter, epigrammatic poems have more certain, if no less complex, stances with respect to their subjects. Persepctive ranges but attitude is consistent.

The steam roller smothers his subject with his categorical judgments. As a poet of the ad hoc and the spontaneous, rejoicing in the deviant, the irreducible, the unique, Moore rallies her wit in a charming repartee against impersonal judgment. Metaphor is the sharp edge of her weapon, gleaming unexpectedly in the sun. She defeats by momentarily dazzling her over-rational subject.

Moore aims her wit at critical absolutists like Lawrence Gilman, whose sterile remarks on Ornstein's music she had recorded in her reading diary: "We have endeavored . . . to be clinical, strictly impersonal—momentarily ignoring the fact that an impersonal judgment in aesthetic matters is a metaphysical impossibility."[7] The tone of the poem is less ambiguous than that of "Injudicious Gardening," and the inversions are not dramatic, but ambiguity and inversion are here, working subtly to trip the steam roller on its own flat ground.

The four sentences of the poem seem to develop in a consistent direction—detailing the portrait of the steam rolling mind. But the poem does more than describe and criticize its subject, it also discreetly usurps it and finds, in the extreme of a position, the proof of its opposite. Moore manages this inversion of results by reversing the point of view. Whereas the sparkling chips of rock are relatively passive, subordinate entities, the butterfly (an original, entirely separate from the parent block) first *attends* the steam roller. The major irony of the poem is that the steam roller would destroy the very thing it was evaluating. But the irony works the other way as well, for a true "congruence" of the natural butterfly's complement would be spontaneity—the steam roller would be overthrown by this delightful presence, metamorphizing from a pedantic literalist to a literalist of the imagination. But his steam rolling ways preclude his even perceiving the genuine, which would provoke such spontaneity. The "congruence of the complement"—steam rollers matched to butterflies as imaginary gardens to real toads—is, of course, the metaphysical impossibility referred to earlier. Moore sets the unimaginative mathematics of the steam roller against the ideal, inspired mathematics that could find the complement of the butterfly's compliment. Such a mathematic is the intuitive wisdom of "half-wit" (an inverted catchword, like Moore's later "bird-witted"), not of those steam rolling rationalists who lack it.

The style of Moore's poem also answers to her subject. Her condemnatory manner gives way to a spirited tone that seems distracted by the fluttering presence it has conjured. She allows the literal to obtrude on the figurative as a steam roller of decorums would not. She lets image refute argument by importing details that the interpreting mind cannot reduce. Her poem is, in a sense, half reason and half wit, that is, half logic and half imagination. The logic of metaphor can go beyond the logic of argument. And the particular, in which this poem abounds, will never be pinned down.

Such surprise endings, in which argument yields to gusto and the general to the particular, are typical of Moore's epigrammatic poems. They overthrow all assertion and draw the reader into their sparkling originality. It is not only for the sake of argument, but for our "spontaneous delight" that the peacock's broad tail unfurls at the end of "To the Peacock of France," a poem about Molière. For Moore, the function of reason is to discover its own limit.

Through a dense network of ironic reversals in the logic and metaphor of "Pedantic Literalist" (published in *The Egoist*, June 1, 1916; CP, 37) Moore exposes the suicidal implications of a fault that seems, on the surface, relatively harmless. The pedantic literalist would seem to attract no blame to himself. But in taking his duty so literally, and in going about it so insensitively, he provokes the wrath of wit.[8] His fate is to be undone by his own literalness, and in a further irony, to have his literalness prove him insubstantial.

The train of metaphors that begins the poem—all illusory objects that dissipate on contact—prefigure the structure of the central metaphor, an elaborate play on the cliché of a "wooden character." The poem again moves through a series of ironic reversals until it achieves the paradoxical identity of opposites: the hard-core literalist proves the most rotten. So insubstantial is this character that he is only identified through a parallel character: "the meditative man with the perfunctory heart." The phrase "carved cordiality" pivots the poem's analogy, pointing back to the "perfunctory heart" and forward to "the inlaid and royal immutable production." To his woodenness is added his superficial decorum, his air of authority, his pomposity, his flourish. The poem then turns the metaphor around to reverse the meaning of "immutable" and make it accountable to the initial claim that he "invites destruction." Moore manages this ambiguity by a brilliant manipulation of metaphor that reminds one of Donne's satires. Pushed to its extreme, the metaphor reverses its initial meaning. Buried within "immutable" is "inflexible." A living tree bends and sways. This wood decays (withers) and eventually turns to stone (loses all spontaneity), which is immutable but also dead, thus destroyed. Within a single trope Moore has pursued several paradoxes: the pedantic literalist's polite evasions (his "carved cordiality ran to and fro") betray rigid, automatic responses, and in turn his moral rigidity reveals an emotional anemia. Immutability produces the opposite. The figurative takes revenge on the literal. His own efforts to delude others, to disguise his motives (saying unkind things with kindness, then pretending they are not painful), become the cause of his destruction. Like Dante, Moore loves to fit the punishment to the crime. The pedantic literalist's sins, as it were, come home to roost.

Moore sports in her satires on critical pretension. When the social consequences of the sins are graver, her deprecations are more severe, the reversals less taunting than admonitory. Abuses of power arouse Moore's bitterest wit. "To Military Progress," (*Others*, 1917; CP, 82) for instance, offers an ironic portrait of suicidal vanity. Playing on the metaphor of the body politic, Moore sees the destruction of that ideal model of cooperation in a head that gloats on its power even while the body perishes, and conversely, a body that cries for its lost head. Moore makes a similar point through inversion at the end of "To Statecraft Embalmed," (*Others*, 1915) about the need for authority and justice to exercise mercy and flexibility in response to "life's faulty excellence." Here again Moore attacks absolutism by ironic inversions that prove its self-defeating character.

We have seen poems in which Moore dismisses symbolism, and poems in which she turns heraldic symbols against themselves. Often Moore will reverse the value of a symbol, making a point of admiring values that have been slighted or condemned, using the very same images that had been used to criticize, but bringing out new aspects that invite praise. Just as there are drawbacks to being a rose, there are advantages to being a snail or a chameleon.

To Shakespeare the snail was an emblem of oversensitivity and withdrawal. Keats was fascinated by the image, and in a letter to J. H. Reynolds he quotes Shakespeare's lines from Venus and Adonis (11. 1033–1038):

As the snail, whose tender horns being hit,
Shrinks back into his shelly cave with pain,
And there all smothered up in shade doth sit,
Long after fearing to put forth again:[9]

But for Moore the compactness and precision of the creature make him an emblem of stylistic virtue. "To a Snail" is Moore's central epigram of praise and also her most self-reflective poem, not only because it demonstrates the general and specific virtues it describes, but because it deals with a source hidden but determining outward form.

Moore's use of metaphor here has all the virtue of the snail. The image is not the adornment of meaning, but its extension, so that the two terms of comparison cleave together to create a peculiar but efficient doubleness in the language—insistently literal and yet always figurative. The occipital horn proves the poem even further: it is the one part of the snail that eludes symmetry, as it is the one part of the poem where no corresponding abstraction can be discovered. In man the occipital bone is the place where head and body connect—metaphorically, that place between ideas and things. It is the *je ne sais quoi* of art as it is the nuance of the snail's shell. Thus it both is and is not an analogy for something else.

Looking at an early draft of this poem in the Rosenbach, we again see how the intrusion of the image into the thought helps toughen the thought. Originally, the idea controlled the poem and the image was simply used to illustrate the idea, and then discarded:

> If "compression is the first grace of
> Style" you have it. The absence of feet and your occipital horn
> Are perfectly in keeping with the philosopher's
> Definition. Contractility is not a virtue but modesty is
> A virtue, and that you instance both aesthetic and
> "real" virtue
> Is as true
> As that virtue "is." It is not the
> Acquisition of any one thing that is able to adorn—
> It is the incidental quality that occurs
> As a concomitant of things that are hid, and that is present
> only in
> Conjunction with things that are infinitely more worth
> while than style
> Is worth while.

Even allowing for Moore's characteristically convoluted style, this is wordy and confused writing. The poem lacks the "compression" it celebrates, and therefore doubly lacks "grace." It is also conceptually different from the published version. In the draft Moore maintains a superficial distinction between aesthetic and real virtue, between form and content. By returning to the image, which is far more dominant in the later version, she alters this familiar attitude, discovering an essential unity between form and content. She lives up to this discovery by making the "vehicle" indispensable to the "tenor." The poem is, of course, not essentialy about a snail at all but about poetry, and about this particular poem. But by allowing the image to check the easy flow of analogy, she has learned something she did not know before. The version of "To a Snail" published in *Complete Poems* (essentially unchanged from *Observations*) includes a note on only one of the quotations. "Compression is the first grace of style" is noted as " 'The very first grace of style is that which comes from compression.' *Demetrius on Style*, translated by W. Hamilton Fyfe (Heinemann, 1932)." We see that Moore has felt free to revise the language somewhat, holding it to the standard of compression it recommends. The notes to *Observations* attribute the quote to "Democritus," though Moore later corrected the reference. In fact the quotation comes from an article she filed in her scrapbook, signed "C." The article is a review of a translation. The other quotations in the poem, "a method of conclusions," and "a knowledge of principles," are not noted at all in *Complete Poems*, though Moore does attribute them briefly to "Duns Scotus" in *Observations*. The full source is noted in her reading diary as *Medieval Mind*, II, 516: "Is theology then properly a science? Duns Scotus will not deny it, but thinks it may more properly be called, a *sapientia*, since according to its nature it is rather a knowledge of principles than a method of conclusions."[10] While Duns Scotus distinguishes two kinds of thought, Moore identifies them as one in "To a Snail." His thought may lack contractility, but hers does not. She may have liked the choice of words, but she differs somewhat as to how their meaning should be ordered, just as she fused Yeats's opposition "too literal a realist of the imagination" into "literalists of the imagination."

Who this wonderful snail is, Moore never says, and the omission makes the local seem both universal and personal. But Moore may have had someone else privately in mind. She was an admirer of William Cowper's poetry, and quoted his poem "A Snail" in her essay "Humility, Concentration and Gusto." The quotation on style is from a review of translations from the Greek, and Cowper's poem is a translation of a Latin poem by Vincent Bourne. Moore's mother had given her a copy of Cowper's poems in 1910 (it is now in the Rosenbach archive) which she annotated and "corrected." The book is marked on the page on which "A Snail" appears. But even if the poem is a covert address to Cowper, it is also self-referential, in keeping with the spirit of Cowper. It is precisely the close tie of the poem to its maker that Moore admired in Cowper's poem, which ends:

> Who seeks him must be worse than blind,
> He and his house are so combined,
> If finding it, he fails to find
>   Its master.

For Cowper, as for Moore, outward appearances suggest hidden sources. For Cowper, the desperately shy "castaway," and for Moore, the most discreet, most self-protective of poetic animals, the "master" is certainly, among other subjects, the poet's self. Moore praises Cowper by imitating his disguises.

"Radical" (*Poems*, 21) resembles "To a Snail" in its emblematic tension between image and conception. But Moore omitted it after *Poems*, perhaps because it does not adequately engage us in its image, the growth of a carrot, and presses its theme, defiant freedom, too discursively. And yet the punning of tenor and vehicle, initiated in the title, makes this a delightful poem.

> Tapering
> to a point, conserving everything,
>> this carrot is predestined to be thick,
>> The world is
>> but a circumstance, a mis-
>>> erable corn-patch for its feet. With ambition,
>>> imagination, outgrowth,
>
> nutriment,
> with everything crammed belligerent-
>> ly inside itself, its fibres breed mon-
>> opoly—
>> a tail-like, wedge-shaped engine with the
>>> secret of expansion, fused with intensive heat
>>> to the color of the set-
>
> ting sun and
> stiff. For the man in the straw hat, stand-
>> ing still and turning to look back at it—
>> as much as
>> to say my happiest moment has
>>> been funereal in comparison with this, the con-
>>> ditions of life pre-
>
> determined
> slavery to be easy and freedom hard. For
>> it? Dismiss
>> agrarian lore; it tells him this:
>>> that which it is impossible to force, it is
>>> impossible to hinder.[11]

Observation here is heavily weighted on the side of ideas. The world of particulars is indeed "but a circumstance." And yet the image is not strictly emblematic, as it is in poems like "To a Snail" or "To a Steam Roller." Moore tries to pursue the illusion of continuity between the ideas and the images, to make the pun on root and radical more than a verbal link.

In its heroic rendering of a simple physical process, the poem recalls Cowper's description of the growth of a cucumber in *The Task*. Moore knew Cowper's work well and we can find evidence of his influence throughout her poetry. In a draft of "Humility, Concentration and Gusto" (in the Rosenbach archive) Moore drew on *The Task* "as an illustration of how feeling really can be induced to rise to the occasion." She liked the poem, she said, for its "self-amused benignity," a quality of which there is certainly evidence in all of Moore's descriptive poems. As in Cowper, the language that represents the nurturing process, while insisting on the specificity of the agrarian scene, ranges far beyond it and includes, in its course of association, the act of writing itself. Again, as the metaphor becomes more conspicuous, the language becomes more self-conscious. In its tapering syllabic stanzas, Moore's poem is "a tail-like, wedge-shaped engine with the / secret of expansion." The physical properties of the carrot, the moral properties that revise the farmer's lore, become exampled in the poem's aesthetic properties. The human recipient of these meanings is placed within the poem, marking the contrast between freedom, represented in nature, and slavery, represented in man, but also suggesting a continuity between the ideal and the real. Moore may have dropped the poem as too ready to "dismiss agrarian lore," too bold in its reinterpretation of fact.

"To a Strategist" (*Observations*, 16), which Moore omitted after *Observations*, is similarly self-referential. Woven into Moore's defense of Disraeli (attacked for his shifty political tactics) is a self-defense.[12] Her own style of reserve and indirection, her preoccupation with masks and disguises, and her preference for subtlety, relativity, and flexibility over assertiveness, dogmatism, and prejudice all converge in the figure of the chameleon, which she uses frequently as a sign of her approbation. The poem's primary inversion is simple: a transformation of value effected by a careful cleaving of image to abstraction, as in "To a Snail."

> You brilliant Jew,
> > You bright particular chameleon, you
> > Regild a shabby fence.

They understood
Your stripes and particolored mind, who could
    Begrudge you prominence

And call you cold!
But when has prejudice been glad to hold
    A lizard in its hand—

A subtle thing?
To sense fed on a fine imagining,
    Sound sense is contraband.

"Brilliant," "particular," "chameleon," "fence" (as in fence sitter), "cold," "subtle," "stripes," "particolored," are all puns binding image to idea, the grace of one causing us to reevaluate the other. In the final lines of the poem Moore carries the metaphor one step further, so that not only are the chameleon and Disraeli yoked, but the poem itself becomes integrated as reference.

The final lines create a reversable ambiguity that collapses together the two perspectives in the poem (the speaker's and the public's), as if to insist on the relativity of value. We expect the lines to modify the perspective that immediately precedes them, but in fact Moore has inverted the perspective so that we are now looking not at the lizard in the hand of prejudice but at "sense" in the hand of Disraeli. The inversion extends into the syntax of the last sentence. Are "sense fed on a fine imagining" and "sound sense" opposed or apposed? They would seem to be opposed, but the context of the poem works against the obvious logic to equate sound sense with imagination, and to turn contraband into a virtue, which the naive reader (the public) mistakes for a vice. The ambiguity works not only to produce opposite values but to overdetermine positive values: sound sense is contraband because the public is foolish and wisdom must be smuggled, *and* because the practice of smuggling is good strategy. For the poet "fed on a fine imagining" the last line has a final, crowning ambiguity in which "sound" and "sense" belong to both mind and ear. And indeed, meaning is smuggled through form in this discreet rhyme.

In a few early poems, particularly "Black Earth" and "A Grave," Moore uses an image to explore rather than to challenge or vindicate a subject. These meditational poems follow a course of association within the range of an image in order to move away from an initial view of a subject and toward fresh moral insight. The image becomes a path for the mind to follow in its search for moral and ontological conclusions. The expectation of definition persists, but the experience of the poem is constant revision and ambiguity, suggesting that human observation is never definitive.

"Black Earth" (published in *The Egoist*, April 1918; SP, 43–45) has elements of the metaphysical poem, turned toward reflection rather than persuasion or defense. Like the metaphysicals, Moore pursues an extreme logic of metaphor in an effort to resolve the dialectic of body and spirit. But an associative structure is woven into the logical one as subject and object, tenor and vehicle move apart and together and apart again, the result being, as in "Poetry," tautological but resonant meanings. Moore attempts to resolve a duality by pursuing a single image assigned contradictory meanings, thus offering the imagination a unity that reason cannot absorb.

As Bernard Engel has pointed out, the poem's later title, "Melancthon," means "black earth" in Greek but also refers to the Reformation leader who attempted to resolve the schism in the church.[13] (Moore's interest in Melancthon is corroborated by several copies she kept of the Dürer portrait of him. She also named an elephant wind-up toy after him.) The issue of the schism might be understood to center around whether Christ is metonymically or metaphorically present in the sacrament. In transferring this question into the larger question of the relationship between body and spirit, Moore elides it imagistically by moving freely between metonymic and metaphoric uses of her central image. In the poem the elephant is first an image of gross animal existence, but then an image of stoical unknowing. It is the exterior "skin" of earthy experience and primitive survival, then the mystery of the soul. Its trunk is both the circumference of mortal existence and the antenna from external to spiritual, immortal life. Even further, it is a metaphor of earth as a whole, and of universal soul, so that not only the duality of body and soul is incorporated, but that of self and other. "I" becomes the complex word that serves as the second term for the complex image of the elephant, but the unity of that "I" depends upon the elasticity of its analogies. Syntactically, Moore attempts to identify the tie between body and spirit by a series of chiasmic inversions. Thematically, she volleys between the limitations and the necessity of the empirical self, the obscurity but reality of the spiritual self.

We can see this elasticity in the first few sentences of the poem. Moore begins with an assertion of her "naturalness," her animal in-

stinct, through the comparison of herself with the alligator and hippopotamus (perhaps after Eliot's hippopotamus) climbing out of the river
to enjoy the sun.

> Openly, yes,
>   with the naturalness
>   of the hippopotamus or the alligator
>   when it climbs out on the bank to experience the
>
>   sun, I do these
>   things which I do, which please
>   no one but myself.

Man is like the animals in his physical pleasures. But he is distinguished
by his inwardness. Moore deals with this difference not through a simple opposition between the instinctual, hedonistic animal body and the
self-conscious, moral, human spirit, but by expanding the animal
image. It becomes metaphorical rather than metonymic and incorporates spirit. Within a few stanzas the images are beginning to operate on
a different level from the one on which they began, and their meaning is
accordingly altered. While the hippopotamus and the alligator are examples of instinct, the elephant is a more complex species: he is "like"
her in both a literal and a figurative sense—metonymically in body,
metaphorically in both body and spirit. Though she claims, at first, to
be acting "openly" from the body, by the end of the poem the body is
seen as an obscurity. R. P. Blackmur has made a similar point: "The
quotidian, having been shown as genuine, must be shown no less as
containing the strange, as saying more than appears, and even more, as
containing the print of much that cannot be said." To do this Moore
changes waters in midstream. The river from which the "I" emerges
is not the same one she shared with the alligator and the hippopotamus.

> Now I breathe and now I am sub-
>   merged; the blemishes stand up and shout when the object
>
>   in view was a
>   renaissance; shall I say
>   the contrary?

River and sun, which were at first examples of physical reality, are now also read spiritually: the river as time, the sun as illumination. The dunking is, in the new sense, a moving in and out of the light. The animal pleasure has become a baptism, though the "renaissance" (the reform of the self) that was aimed at has failed, simply reinforcing her sense of her "blemished" earthy nature.[14] It is her very earthiness that causes spiritual blemishes, symbolically expressed as outward blemishes since "spirit creates form." We are urged to answer no to the question of whether we can deny the flaws of nature, but Moore will revise this answer on further meditation. Typically, she will not dismiss her first, naive position, but will reaffirm it on a deeper level. The very blemish of bodily existence is an essential, even enriching (later beautiful) part of identity.

> The sediment of the river which
> encrusts my joints, makes me very gray but I am used
>
> to it, it may
> remain there; do away
>   with it and I am myself done away with, for the
>   patina of circumstance can but enrich what was
>
> there to begin
> with.

By introducing this new idea of "what was there to begin with" (typically left unnamed, but presumably the soul), Moore has complicated the simpler opposition between vice and virtue, nature and spirit, animal and human. At the metonymic level she is not the elephant skin but only "inhabits it." At a metaphoric level the history carved on the elephant's back is "a manual for the peanut-tongued and the hairy-toed." That is, she has incorporated the dialogue of body and soul into a dialogue of metonymic and metaphoric levels of a single image. This kind of self-consciousness is inevitably tautological (the elephant is a manual to the elephant). That is part of her point.

Moore now presses her complex image of the elephant even further, to deal with the complex word "power," which introduces a new duality, not only of body and spirit, but of self and other, all carried within a very complex sentence.

          Black
but beautiful, my back
    is full of the history of power. Of power? What
    is powerful and what is not? My soul shall never

be cut into
by a wooden spear; through-
    out childhood to the present time, the unity of
    life and death has been expressed by the circumference

described by my
trunk; nevertheless I
    perceive feats of strength to be inexplicable after
    all; and I am on my guard; external poise, it

has its centre
well nurtured—we know
    where—in pride; but spiritual poise, it has its centre where?

The ambiguity begins in the reading of "black," which can be taken as an emblem of evil (to be rejected) or obscurity (to be embraced) and as modifying back or power. In each case the meanings overlap. Moore will not simply reject external power and embrace spiritual power. There is always in her poetry a second movement back to embrace on a new level what has been rejected. Though the soul may dismiss fear, to the body which completes our identity external power is actual, and what is worse, "inexplicable," because motivated by other obscure (and possibly evil) identities. Of course if she is on her guard she is not doing things openly: she has revised her initial claims.

    Thoughts flow into one another rather than proceeding logically. As if to emphasize this, Moore works her grammar against the logic of her ideas. The final idea (beginning "external poise . . .") of the long sentence above sets another long sentence in motion, in which she focuses on the problem of self and other.

My ears are sensitized to more than the sound of

the wind. I see
and I hear, unlike the
    wandlike body of which one hears so much, which was made
    to see and not to see; to hear and not to hear;

that tree-trunk without
roots, accustomed to shout
    its own thoughts to itself like a shell, maintained intact
    by who knows what strange pressure of the atmosphere; that

spiritual
brother to the coral-
    plant, absorbed into which, the equable sapphire light
    becomes a nebulous green.

Here Moore puns together, in order to oppose, a metonymic and a metaphoric "trunk," one the limited self of the ego, which feeds on conscious awareness and whose mortality was measured earlier by its circumference, the other the more complete identity, which creates a continuum between physical and spiritual reality. The very awareness of the first trunk is a source of obscurity, for it creates the illusion of discrete identities, of your trunk versus mine (in the first printed version she called it "a cortex merely"). Meanwhile Moore is manipulating the elephant image so that the self has become an expansive term transcending discrete identity. It has become an ideal rather than a description of humanity, incorporating the entirety of the world, physical and spiritual, rather than simply the perimeters of the self. The "I" is appropriately dropped at the end of the poem.

                              The I of each is to

the I of each
a kind of fretful speech
    which sets a limit on itself; the elephant is
    black earth preceded by a tendril? Compared with those

phenomena
which vacillate like a
    translucence of the atmosphere, the elephant is
    that on which darts cannot strike decisively the first

time, a substance
needed as an instance
    of the indestructibility of matter; it
    has looked at the electricity and at the earth-

quake and is still
here; the name means thick. Will
 depth be depth, thick skin be thick, to one who can see no
 beautiful element of unreason under it?

But the poem concludes with a three-part image that describes a unity by parallel oppositions: the elephant consists of the skin (the indestructibility of matter), what is beneath the skin (the beautiful element of unreason), and the trunk, which extends out from the body (the conscious ego). But the reflection remains in questions (only equivocally rhetorical) because the self that manipulates language is only a small part of the totality it ponders. Like the six blind men of Buddhist legend who were asked to describe the elephant, Moore can only name it part by part. The whole eludes her.

Indeed, Moore has imbedded in the poem references to the limitations of the very activity she is engaged in. She confronts the narcissism of writing ("I do these things which I do, which please no one but myself"), its solipsism ("accustomed to shout its own thoughts to itself like a shell"), its vacillation ("like a translucence of the atmosphere"). In an artist who so often spoke poetic of form as a filter to light, the self-reference seems likely. The final line, like the final line of "In the Days of Prismatic Color," surrenders the effort to represent truth.

Moore omitted "Black Earth" from her *Complete Poems.* Though it remains one of her most profound and ambitious poems, she may have felt that she did not have all her many meanings under control. She does depend on a confusion of categories to make many of her connections. She was more satisfied with another meditative poem, "A Grave" (first published as "A Graveyard" in *The Dial,* July 1921), probably because, while it deals with equally elusive subjects, its ambiguities are introduced more gracefully and compactly. The element of unreason is discovered again through many ironic inversions, but the voice feels its way more confidently over uncertainties. This may be precisely because Moore distances herself somewhat from these reflections. While implicitly soliloquizing, she objectifies the issues by addressing "man looking into the sea." The poem was occasioned by an actual experience: "As for 'A Grave,' it has a significance apart from the literal origin, which was a man who placed himself between my mother and me, and surf we were watching from a middle ledge of rocks on Monhegan Island after a storm. ('Don't be annoyed,' my mother said. 'It is human nature to stand in the middle of a thing.')"[15] In responding to man's audacity, Moore moves through a series of ironic inversions, in which the dehumanizing force of death is encountered, evaded, and reencountered. While man's ego is deflated when the sea is recognized as a grave, the poet's ego must be in turn deflated, its metaphoric power seen as equally limited against unconscious reality.

"A Grave" (CP, 49) tests a conventionalized symbol and restores its source. In this case what is at stake is our tendency, in finding metaphors for death, to think that we have comprehended it. The issue is an extreme version of what all Moore's poems insist on, that language is a limited power, that it allows us to extend ourselves beyond our immediate realities, but only imaginatively. In this poem the analogy of sea to grave is shown to be a human projection, an attempt to circumscribe the sea's power by naming it, and an attempt to surround the fact of death with ceremony, as if to control it.

In a long discarded stanza Moore clearly shows the reader how futile are our attempts to define, as though definition were a means of control: "everything everywhere / yet nothing, because nowhere; infinity defined at last, still infinity because there / where nothing is." Moore's notebooks, full of passages about the sea, include one that seems to resonate with the poem: "Let who will pray for fair weather to bring him home Aristagoras who is buried here. The sea is the sea."[16] No matter what we impose on it, the sea is the sea. In the end the sea does become a grave; its very otherness and its indifference to the human world are as inscrutable as death.

> Man looking into the sea,
> taking the view from those who have as much right
>   to it as you have to it yourself,
> it is human nature to stand in the middle of a thing,
> but you cannot stand in the middle of this;
> the sea has nothing to give but a well excavated
>   grave.

The poem is not about the sea itself, but about man looking into the sea. Calling it a grave is his way of possessing it, but the ceremony that surrounds "the grave" on his side is obliterated on the other. Not able to look at death directly, we project modified versions of it; "the fir trees stand in a procession," the waves are "wrinkles" that "progress upon themselves in a phalanx." We "lower nets" and see the foam as a "network," but our ideas of order ebb as the "wrinkles" "fade breathlessly while the sea rustles in and out of the seaweed." The figurative language drops out at the end, the sea as an old man dies into its otherness, indifferent to human "lighthouses" and "bellbuoys."

There is something threatening about the fixed possessiveness of the man looking into the sea—for he projects his own image into the sea to the point at which the sea takes it, "quick to return a rapacious look." But as "observer *ab extra*" Moore is in the privileged position of presenting both sides of the line between self-reflection and annihilation.

> There are others besides you who have worn that look—
> ... the fish no longer investigate them
> for their bones have not lasted:

The man looking into the sea can approach questions of death only in humanized, ceremonious terms. Moore has projected an image of the fully dehumanizing reality. The colon has no clear grammatical function in the poem. But it does designate a line, create a pause, a "place" for what language cannot contain. For while Moore can make images for either side of the line she cannot describe the crossing. The sea is and is not a grave. Man can and cannot stand in the middle of it.

Nature is not the subject of these early observations, but is rather a book of symbols out of which various moral and social subjects can be read. To read the symbols right, to realize their full potential for signification, Moore attends to the particularity of the image. Moore became progressively concerned to pay tribute to the world, which offered such a rich variety of symbols. She returned to natural history as a way of discovering the original point of contact between image and idea and also as a way of reaffirming nature's autonomy. The camel sparrow of "He 'Digesteth Harde Yron' " is not just an illustration of an idea; his existence is prior to ideas. In longer descriptive poems Moore aims not only to discover the value of fact, to create a system of signs and an arrangement of sounds out of the variety of nature, but also to affirm the splendid independence of nature from our conceptual purposes.

3. The Capacity for Fact
Descriptive Poems

$\mathbf{M}$OORE SHARED her critics' uneasiness with the label "poetry," feeling, as she said in the poem of that title, that we do not yet "have it." What we do have, "in the meantime," are "observations." Thus in 1924 when Moore revised and expanded *Poems* she changed the title to *Observations*.[1] But the volume challenges the reader to ask what observation is, what *an* observation is. The word belongs to two ambiguous realms of usage which influence one another, just as we can speak of an impression made or received, a vision imagined or seen, a prospect expected or viewed, a view held or beheld. Even in the most descriptive of Moore's poems, we find considerable play in and exploration of the range of "observation." The mind is "enchanted" by the variety and particularity of the physical world, but also "enchanting" in itself, as it orders, interprets, and reinvents that world. Moore's poetry realizes both forms of enchantment, presenting objects that retain a life as discrete particulars, and at the same time making wide leaps of resemblance among particulars, composing the world into an imaginative order without seeming to disturb the natural order of things.

Moore's poems are not, finally, representations of things or statements of opinion. They are imaginative acts, efforts to reconstruct the world in language, and thus in relation to the self, to render the world harmless, and to give the self objectivity. These compositions conduct us through a dynamic and multiple but nonetheless unified act of attention, which claims no worldly authority but can provide the satisfaction and stability that the world denies.

While Moore's critics have varied radically in their judgment of the aims and aesthetic mode of her poems (a diversity of opinion that testifies to the richness, not to the vagueness, of her aesthetic), all agree about her affinity for facts. There is certainly evidence, not only in the poems themselves but in her reading notebooks, for her growing preoccupation with literal accuracy. For Moore, as for most modernists, exactness of presentation is a criterion of art. As she matured artistically, she went beyond the imagists, taking the notion of exactness literally, in the biologist's sense of getting the facts straight. She seems to be interested in recording the habits and features of sundry animals out of the naturalist's simple rapture at the variety and ingenuity of life. Marie Borroff's comparison of Moore's poems to feature articles describes perfectly their delight in and promotion of facts. At least one motive for her many notes may have been the urge for documentation. Her notebooks are filled not only with long, detailed presentations of "facts" but with quotations about the need for the factual in art. It is dangerous to construct an aesthetic theory from what Moore copied in her notebooks. I suspect that she often made notes as reminders of certain fallacies rather than truths. But certainly she was in sympathy with Yvor Winters's predilections when she jotted down a quote from him in September 1919: "There is a crying need for a Poet's Handbook of Science. W. R. Benet for instance should be informed that bats do not hang in barns at night, that they fly around at night and hang there in the daytime."[2] T. S. Eliot's influence on Moore was a decided one, judging from the extent of their correspondence.[3] Her title Observations was probably inspired not only by Eliot's own title Prufrock and Other Observations but by his comments on her work in an Egoist essay entitled "Observations." And later when Eliot remarked in "The Function of Criticism" that "a critic must have a very highly developed sense of fact," Moore made a note of it.[4]

But the question remains as to why factualness is so prized in modernist aesthetics, and how Moore in particular makes use of it. Hugh Kenner puts Moore in line with Ruskin, with justification since she recorded in her notebook and later in a Dial article the very passage Kenner quotes:

Hundreds of people can talk for one who can think; but 1000s can think for one who can see. To see clearly is poetry, prophecy, and religion all in one . . . Remembering always that there are two characters in which all greatness of art consists, first, the earnest and intense saying of natural facts; then the ordering of those facts by strength of the human intellect so as to make them for all who look upon them, to the utmost serviceable, memorable and beautiful.[5]

But there are important differences between this aesthetic and Moore's. For Ruskin, facts are the essential ingredients of realism in art. He assumes that facts connect us with reality and help us to resist subjective structures that will later fail. Facts are "useful" because they draw us out of ourselves and make us aware of external forces that affect our lives. But Moore is not very explicit about how "the genuine" is "useful" in this sense. Perhaps it is implicit. And yet she seldom directs our attention to scenes in which we are compelled to act. Her facts are seldom those of politics or love or economics. They are distinctly minor facts in the scale of things, and the meanings are artificially, not naturally, attached to them.

Despite the plenitude of fact in these poems, they do not seem to deposit us in the lap of nature, to "hand the thing over bodily." Moore's ideas are not drawn from primary experience, but from representations—in museums, films, drawings, books, magazines, pamphlets. The following passage from E. A. Newton's *Amenities of Book Collecting*, which Moore copied early on in her reading notebooks, may suggest her sympathy (though again, we cannot be sure) with the idea that the literature of the particular has little to do, directly, with physical reality: "give me those long descriptions of house parties, those chapters made up of dinner conversations, of endless hunting scenes, of editorials from newspapers [. . .] not in real life, but in the pages of Trollope."[6] Marie Borroff has helped to clarify Moore's use of particulars, emphasizing the second element in Ruskin's definition:

> Visual images of so high a degree of resolution, for all their authenticity, are far from realistic—they do not correspond to the selective and partially focused picture recorded by the seeing eye . . . Moore's surreal word photographs bespeak an *intellectual* curiosity as readily satisfied by the printed page as by visible phenomena themselves. The minutiae of external appearance serve in the poems as data, pointing toward an apprehension of the object in terms of essential form or emblematic significance.[7]

And yet, as Borroff's argument as a whole acknowledges, these details are not fully accounted for in terms of a developed argument of essential form or emblematic significance any more than in terms of an argument for verisimilitude. Indeed, particularly in the poems added to *Selected Poems*, Moore's data tend to crowd her interpretations. And the interpretations themselves seem to operate on a different order of reality from nature, actual or conceptual. The two characteristics that Ruskin outlines tend to pull apart in her verse, in dynamic tension, though both are indulged, sometimes to an extreme. To Moore there is a discontinuity between language as representation and language as an act of the poet. But she does not privilege either function consistently. Though Kenner begins with the Ruskin quotation, he ends by representing Moore's poetry in very different terms. Her poems, he says, develop separately as autonomous structures that resist our conversion of optical to psychic experience.[8]

We have, then, three distinct orientations toward the poem—as a vehicle for the clear representation of natural fact, as a vehicle for ideas, and as a separate reality of words. All of these functions are at play in Moore's poetry, converging and pulling apart in a drama of emergent, but secondary and dependent poetic order.

The world of objects is the pretext of the poet; it is from their existence that she derives her sense of being. Its variety, its density, its palpability permit her existence. As William Hogarth said in trying to explain the line of beauty, the love of pursuit is implanted in our natures. But the existence these construct for her is only implicit. It must become explicit, acted out, present in the world in its own right, an object for which she can claim ownership and grant authority, as she cannot (she is always reminding us) claim ownership of other things or grant authority to ideas. The act of forming something out of language has a value, then, beyond the "earnest and intense saying of natural fact." Beyond the need to see clearly or to hold ideas is the urge to complete the self in the creation of a text. The pleasure of exploring complex orders is fulfilled in creating them. The most basic reason for Moore's attraction to fact, I believe, is that it gives language a particularity and a variety that have compositional and textural value. The poet, and the readers of the poem, profit by and enjoy the experience of infinite variety brought under imaginative control. This is, foremost, why Moore copied out so many long passages, knew so many things that were not really "useful" in a functional sense. The creation of a text involves the further ordering of facts into generalities—affinities and resemblances that we can call "ideas," but which at a more primitive level are structures, recognitions of unities and gatherings against the flux of variety and particularity. Ideas, in Moore, take their place beside facts as elements in a composition, areas of bold, firm, epigrammatic focus, against the extension and plurality of description and list. Things and ideas are then the sources, not the end, of Moore's language structures.

Of course the poem does not separate itself entirely from its sources. It remains indebted to them and ultimately refers to them. The experience of reading provokes thoughts and sensuous imaginings. The poem becomes a theater for the mind to explore relations too rigidly defined in more "relevant" contexts. These poems are set apart, but are cognizant of the wider world which they cannot monitor. Their specificity, paradoxically, increases their abstraction, for while we are not drawn into the world of jerboas and pelicans, it is in the context of that world brought into the imaginary field of the poem that our orderings are accomplished. And since these orders are not pressured in the emotionally weighted realm of human situations, they provide a satisfaction.

At different stages in her career, Moore treated the pull between ideas and things and the gathering of poetic surfaces very differently. Particularly in her early work, influenced by the imagist movement, which tried to resolve idea and object into one inviolable presentation beyond formulated language, the images seem to have their reality nowhere but in the space of poetry, and conversely, meaning is seen as inherent in the image. While there is considerable particularity in the description, it usually tends toward a uniform evocation of feeling. There are, of course, considerable gradations and shadings within this aesthetic of fusion. In "The Fish" image dominates theme; "Like a Bulrush" is vague as to location; "Dock Rats" is very specific; but in all of these poems the imagery, diction, and style are relatively homogeneous. The facts are poet's facts. In her next phase Moore's images are more empirical while her meanings are more abstract. Progressively Moore worked toward the externalization of her materials and a heightening of the tension between fact and imagination—including more nonpoetic materials and words, technical data, highly particular unconventional images, quotation from nonliterary sources. The poems become longer and more temporal. This does not break down the boundary between poetry and the real world; rather it accents their separateness, reminding us that these objects are not properly connected with ideas, associations, and feelings, but are only appropriated on this occasion. By using highly specified subjects Moore marked her meanings as discontinuous and imaginary—her specificity *breaks* illusion. Whereas meaning is transfused through the objects in the earliest poems, in these poems— "An Octopus," "The Frigate Pelican," "The Jerboa," "Camellia Sabina"—particularity of a nonpoetic nature overwhelms association. Conversely, the mind is challenged to make identifications with the most trivial of facts, to read meaning into minute detail. These are the scientist's, the historian's, the reporter's facts, borrowed by the poet. The subjectivity and ingenuity of the meanings are more openly acknowledged as the sources become more "objective." The more specified the images, the more abstract and allegorical they become in the poem's imaginary logic. Even in later versions when Moore cut large sections of description out of "An Octopus," "The Jerboa," "The Frigate Pelican," "The Steeple Jack," "The Plumet Basilisk," and others, the effect of detail pulling against the hold of the theme remained. And as Moore increases the independence of image from concept, her poems also become more self-conscious, and more often explicitly self-reflexive. In *What Are Years* Moore continues her method of research, but despite the variety of their material these poems seem uniform and static in their orderings. "Virginia Britannia" is a fine poem in its way, but the conceptual terms of the experience are established at the outset and the mind is not kept alert as it is in "An Octopus" or "The Jerboa." Moore omitted "Walking Sticks and Paperweights and Watermarks" from her *Complete Poems*, but in its compulsive conversions of fact to value, and in its endless, delightful distractions, it resembles the work in *Selected Poems*.

"The Fish" (CP, 32–33) has been justly admired by critics, for the precision of its images (William Pratt included it in his anthology *The Imagist Poem*), for its skillful ordering of sounds and syllables (which Hugh Kenner has discussed at length), and for its poignant theme of defiance and endurance (which Bernard Engel elaborates in a close reading).[9] But how are these elements integrated in our experience of the poem? If the poem does not simply attempt to record the experience of the eye, what relation to the physical world do these images record? If the poem's aim is primarily thematic, why does Moore rely so heavily on images? And if the poem is an autonomous system of sounds and images, why does it nevertheless seem expansive in its range of references and associations? Like many of Moore's early poems, "The Fish" tries to achieve an integration of image and idea. It draws us into its unities and out to its diversity with an elasticity that seems never to let the surface break. But the poem depends on illusions of continuity that later poems will disrupt.

The first two-thirds of this poem detail an aquatic world for the mind to dive in. While it is clearly an imaginatively ordered scene it is not, conspicuously, interpreted. We experience a freedom of movement through its various currents. Whatever moral significance these textures and rhythms may have for their creator is kept at bay. Our experience is sensuous before it is intellectual or moral.

The Fish

wade
through black jade.
    Of the crow-blue mussel shells, one keeps
    adjusting the ash heaps;
        opening and shutting itself like

an
injured fan.
    The barnacles which encrust the side
    of the wave, cannot hide
        there for the submerged shafts of the

sun,
split like spun
    glass, move themselves with spotlight swiftness
    into the crevices—
        in and out, illuminating

the
turquoise sea
    of bodies. The water drives a wedge
    of iron through the iron edge
        of the cliff; whereupon the stars,

pink
rice-grains, ink-
    bespattered jellyfish, crabs like green
    lilies, and submarine
        toadstools, slide each on the other.

All the elements brought in might be justified as realizing this aquatic scene. But here Moore imported alien textures and images. Jade, ash, spun glass, fans, rice grains can only appear here as illusions, though we can easily restrict resemblance to the physical qualities of the scene. The piled-up mussels look like an ash heap, the shells like fans. The description is given immediate energy by the contrast of things moving (fish) and things static (jade), the slight movement of one mussel shell among many still ones, the subtle shifting of the shells, the light which can move into even tiny crevices, all minute differentiations. The syllabic and rhyme structure and the regularity of the poem's rhythm lift these images out of the utterance and give them an equality and independence in the line, running counter to the hierarchies of comparison or theme. The quiet differentiations in the lengths of lines and syllables repeat for the ear the textural rhymes and variation of the images. The mind can range along several lines of attention. These associations remain abstract and fragmentary, however, and are not organized to delimit "ideas" that can be extracted from the scene.

Why are these details appealing? The compared elements come with connotations, though the connotations are not advanced to the level of ideas. Black jade, ash heaps, injured fans, turquoise belong to a world of archaeology, excavation. Can we bring those associations to bear here or are they irrelevant? Perhaps the archaeological allusions draw attention to the temporal aspect of the scene, its multiple layers of history: fish of the present become fish of the past, recorded on the rock. We begin to excavate.

Even as we draw in archaeology, we can maintain aesthetic distance—these are, we think, artifacts. The allusions to the past do not subject the present to any immediate danger. These worlds are superimposed but they are not precisely fused or even simultaneous. The mussel shell itself is not literally injured, its movement only visually resembles the movement of a literally injured fan. But we take the comparison beyond the visual. They move us by their association with more familiar worlds, but because these associations remain implicit, the ideas infused in sensuous experience, they satisfy a curiosity that would be denied or shocked in a more emotionally structured setting.

A drastic modulation in tone, rhythm, and statement occurs in the poem about halfway through, which amplifies all the latent associations of violence in the first half:

All
external
    marks of abuse are present on this
    defiant edifice—
        all the physical features of

ac-
cident—lack
    of cornice, dynamite grooves, burns, and
    hatchet strokes, these things stand
        out on it; the chasm side is

dead.
Repeated
    evidence has proved that it can live
    on what can not revive
        its youth. The sea grows old in it.

What was observation of an innocent scene is now charged with
foreboding. The unharmed mussel shell is now itself subject to injury,
to becoming part of the ash heap, and the aesthetically pleasing "ruins"
become evidence of mortality. The subtle contrast of motion and stillness is now the bolder contrast of life and death. The lively, literal "sea
of bodies" portends a more tragic sea of corpses. We have a picture of
something that defiantly endures. The edifice's limited kind of power is
perpetually to expose a side to destruction without being totally con-
sumed. It can record the history of its abuse. By engaging our imaginations in the smaller world of shells and jellyfish, where the movements
between life and death are part of a rhythmic continuity, Moore soothes
the mind's associations with loss and time. But part of the excitement
of the poem is in having this meditation suddenly disrupted by harsher,
bolder contrasts. Nevertheless, these rhythms and associations are contained within a harmless world.

While the images of black jade and injured fans are only visually
justified in the immediate landscape, they reveal something latent in
that scene. Poets, unlike unconscious nature, are aware of history and
can thus imagine past mussel shells to their fate as ash heaps, can see
living bodies as future corpses. The poet can see the sea as a grave absorbing every modicum of life. But in another sense these comparisons

detract from physical reality and make association with questions of human value, the desire to "hide," the urge for defiance. But just as such words remove us from natural fact, the images draw us away from human fact. The endurance of the rock edifice has no real human equivalent; only in the imaginative space of the poem are such differences overcome. The poem places us in the privileged position of seeing what the fish cannot, a kind of displaced vision of our own mortality. Through the syllabic form, the internal and external rhymes, the visual and sound harmonies, the steadying rhythms and unqualified assertions, we experience a stability against the flux the poem thematically describes. But this imaginative extension remains a very distanced and ineffectual view of ourselves, not accomplished objectification. We are permitted to share the sun's spotlight perspective on the barnacles, but we cannot put ourselves in the spotlight at the same time.

The fictional scene offers a theater for the mind to explore and solve questions it cannot confront in a human context. We are not interested in the sea as such, but in the modulations of feeling and perspective accomplished in its description—the minor variations between stillness and motion heightened to violence and defiance; the quiet, hypnotic rhythms amplifying the bolder, harsher ones; images of helpless passivity set against images of strength. All of these qualities are drawn into a moral context, but the context is left broad by the very specificity of the fictive scene.

That these modulations and identifications occur in a fictional field is stressed not only by the conspicuous artifice of the poem but by a mutely suggested analogy with writing.[10] The poem itself is a kind of chasm: its steady rhythm bears a varying texture of elements that "slide each on the other" in a blending of images. It is also a defiant edifice, a stability against the flux of life, but like that edifice, limited in power.

The success of "The Fish" rests in its dynamic integration of representational and thematic elements. Except for a minor revision in the syllabic structure, Moore kept the poem as it was first composed, through every subsequent collection of her work.

"Dock Rats" (*Observations*, 53–54) is more completely dominated by its image; it contains little of the associative metaphor of "The Fish," its few abstractions expressing emotional value rather than emblematic significance.

There are human beings who seem to regard the place
    as craftily
    as we do—who seem to feel that it is a good place to
    come
    home to. On what a river; wide—twinkling like a
    chopped sea under some
    of the finest shipping in the

world: the square-rigged four-rigged four-master, the liner,
    the battleship like the two-
    thirds submerged section of an iceberg; the tug
    dipping and pushing, the bell striking as it comes; the
    steam yacht, lying
    like a new made arrow on the

stream; the ferry-boat—a head assigned, one to each com-
    partment, making
    a row of chessmen set for play. When the wind is from
    the east,
    the smell is of apples, of hay; the aroma increased and
    decreased
    as the wind changes;

of rope, of mountain leaves for florists; as from the west,
    it is aromatic of salt. Occasionally a parrakeet
    from Brazil, arrives clasping and clawing; or a monkey
    —tail and feet
    in readiness for an over-

ture; all arms and tail; how delightful! There is the sea,
    moving the bulk-
    head with its horse strength; and the multiplicity of
    rudders
    and propellors; the signals, shrill, questioning, peremp-
    tory, diverse;
    the wharf cats and the barge dogs; it

is easy to overestimate the value of such things. One does
    not live in such a place from motives of expediency
    but because to one who has been accustomed to it, shipping
    is the
    most interesting thing in the world.

Critics who have noticed this poem at all have treated it as "a colorful celebration of sensory delights."[11] It seems more limited than other place poems ("The Steeple Jack," "Virginia Britannia," "New York") in that its thematic contours are not delineated. The "theme" seems to be entirely specific to the setting: "shipping is the most interesting thing in the world." (The word "interesting" was a change from "congenial" in the earlier, *Poems* version.) Pleasure is its principle, and at one point Moore exclaims this outright: "how delightful!" "One does not live in such a place from motives of expediency," she tells us, coming as close as she will come to thematic statement, and we can infer further that one does not write about such a place from motives of instruction. But if we trace the lines of fascination that organize the poem we find the same contrasts and variations that in other poems are given moral dimension. This pleasing composition no more follows the logic of nature than does "The Fish." Its modulations of tone and focus bear the distinct marks of Moore's imaginative presence.

While the human subject (around which all meaning ultimately gathers) is only a witness, not an agent in the composition, he is there implicitly, in the image of the boats (making this poem in many ways similar to Williams's "The Yachts"). We are distracted from the significance of the boats by the aesthetic presentation, and yet that significance is introduced, by the contrast they make to the sea. Similarly the parrakeet and the monkey are amusing as parodies of human behavior (as we saw in "The Monkeys"). When we begin to study the alignment of images in this "delightful" scene, we see a moral imagination at work very much like that in "The Fish," though more reticent. In the first image the motion of the water is contained in the river, which twinkles "like a chopped sea," but with less force than the sea itself. The relation of dominance between man and nature is steady: the water is *under* "some of the finest shipping in the world." (We should remember that this is the era of the grand ocean liners and their grand disasters.) The second stanza goes on to celebrate these mighty structures which seem to possess the majesty of nature (one is like an iceberg) and the power to subdue it ("the steam yacht, lying / like a new made arrow on the / stream"). But the analogy of the chess game quietly mocks these pretenses, and as the poem continues and the mind's eye moves out of the harbor and into the sea, the relations of dominance reverse. "There is the sea, moving the bulk- / head with its horse strength; and the multiplicity of rudders / and propellers; the signals, shrill, questioning, peremptory, diverse."

These orders remain "delightful" just as the initial modulations in "The Fish" are "delightful," because they remain aesthetic. But they can easily be moralized. Moore has selected the motive of pleasure here, but the motive of judgment is almost always, in Moore, copresent with that of pleasure.

Who are the dock rats who indulge in these pleasures? Those idle fellows can always be seen loitering around docks, "rats" in that they are aliens, lurk in corners, appear and vanish. But the "we," unidentified in the poem, suggests possible self-reference, as well. Moore's family used nicknames from *Wind in the Willows* in their abundant correspondence and Moore was always identified as "Rat." She certainly can be said to regard the place "craftily." Is not the pleasure at the docks like the pleasure of poetry, which draws the variety of the world into its microcosm, which carries scents and suggestions of far-off places? Poetry, with its correspondences, its arrivals and departures, is, indeed, like shipping. No wonder, for Moore, "shipping is the / most interesting thing in the world."

But while the image in "Radical" is all too "expedient," that of "Dock Rats" is perhaps too "congenial." Moore rejected it after *Observations*. She also ultimately rejected "Like a Bulrush" (SP, 105), which first appeared in *Others* in 1917 (in three stanzas) and which she retained with changes in the setting through *Selected Poems*. In this poem she had tried to reveal the essential significance of her subject by what Louis Zukofsky called "the economy of omission" rather than by distortion. The subject is particularized through a series of comparisons, but never identified. The poem has, as Moore said of Gertrude Stein's writing, "an air of having meant something to the person who wrote it" (MMR, 171), but that meaning does not coalesce as statement. Nevertheless, the associative range and artistic challenge of the poem make it well worth our attention.

Like A Bulrush

Or the spike
of a channel-marker or the
moon, he superintended the demolition of his image in
the water by the wind; he did not strike
them at the
time as being different from
any other inhabitant of the water; it was as if he

were a seal in the combined livery
of bird plus
snake; it was as if he knew that
the penguins were not fish and as if in their bat blindness,
      they did not
realize that he was amphibious.

Louis Zukofsky admired this poem as a rare example of "objectification" in poetry, because authorial intention was entirely realized in "historic and contemporary particulars." The poem, he said, attained a sculptural presence in contrast to sincerity, ("a portrait of the author's character intent upon the subject"), which appeared as a "line drawing".[12] But there are some basic fallacies and confusions in Zukofsky's theory that may reflect difficulties in Moore's poem, and explain her own discontent with it. Zukofsky tries to fuse two modes of objectification—that of the presentation and that of the artifice—into one. He asks words to be at once absolutely transparent (using the metaphor of the lens) and opaque (using the metaphor of sculpture). Either way, whatever psychic structures the poet introduces must be entirely resolved into this unified "objectification." But these various urges—of representational poise, of formal poise—remain in an uneasy relation with each other here.

The poem seems to move toward the articulation of a particular scene, and yet to do this it generates a series of comparisons. One veil reveals another. Since we are not told to what object these comparisons are assigned, they are apprehended individually (not resolved into a picture). Similarly, the grammatical units marked by "as if" are freed of their function and gather in a nonsemantic coherence. But our impulses to imagine a picture and to construct a meaning draw us away from the poem's autonomous presence. Both impulses involve restless mental activity. At one level the poem becomes a kind of riddle from which we generate possible solutions. (Is it a man standing in the water looking at his reflection? Is it a frog? A heron? Probably a heron, but Moore's reticence resists the conversion of image to reference.)[13] At another level, too, the poem is restless. Because the similies are not assigned to a specific, literal second term, they are, in a sense, auctioned off to associations. It is a curious phenomenon of imaginative works that the absences they describe have a presence as indisputable as the elements avowedly present. The poem may stay, in Williams's sense, "close to the nose," but the nose discovers distant scents, and sense here. The pretext of these images may be to specify an object, but the metaphors expand the scene. We are not, supposedly, looking at spikes, bulrushes, channel markers, or the moon, but they do run across the page. Moore discards one image after another in an attempt to get to the essential one, but we never do arrive at the real, and she invests as much interest in those husks as in the hypothetical center. In the elaborate layers in which a man is compared to a seal which is in turn compared, insofar as he is like the man, to a hybrid of "bird plus snake," the images do not leave their trappings behind to locate a "finite object." I would suggest that the pleasure of this poem, even on a sensuous level, is not so much its accuracy with respect to a specific object or the rested totality of form, but its multiplied approximations.

Williams liked Moore's poems because they "avoided metaphor," a device of rhetoric, of illusion, and looked straight at "the thing itself." "To Miss Moore an apple remains an apple whether it be in Eden or the fruit bowl where it curls . . . The apple is left there, suspended. One is not made to feel that as an apple it has anything particularly to do with poetry or that as such it needs special treatment: one goes on."[14] But even as we do "go on," the associations are quietly accumulating. "Bird," "snake," "moon," even "channel marker" mean more to us than meets the eye. The "he" that is in fact *not* like these in a literal sense may resemble them in a figurative sense. These images have literary heritages that loosen objects into signs, even if the scene as a whole does not. If "crude symbolism," as Williams says in *Spring and All*, "associate[s] emotions with natural phenomena," there is a bit of crude symbolism in this poem.[15] Moore is never innocent of those generalized emblems which history has abstracted from nature; on the contrary, her insistence on detail is pointed, both resisting and invoking history. Though her apples are still apples, they are also, and more importantly, special ones. She lets the reader know why she values certain natural objects even if she maintains their seat in fact. The general pronouns, metaphoric verbs ("superintend"), and resonant nouns ("blindness") loosen the texture of reference and let in the flow of association; we think not only of this creature but of man in general, how he combines the earthbound and the skybound, how he is, indeed, "amphibious" in a metaphoric sense, how he is distinguished from nature by consciousness and self-reflection. However, these associations are made without assumptions—they resonate from the scene; they do not circumscribe it. For wherever facts seem to speak, Moore knows, we find human projections.

Moore's "sincerity" in this poem is her acknowledgment of illusion in the repeated "as if." She has not represented this scene in its authentic reality. But neither has she separated her subject from that reality. "As if" is the border of two worlds. And "as if" acknowledges the secondary, absent nature of imaginative works. Her poem is conspicuously written in the *past* tense, the story of how things *seemed*, where the "as if" is known as such. She acknowledges the inevitable temporal distance between an empirical self and an expressed self. Later in her career, in "Elephants," the situation of writing will seem gloomy: "as if, as if, it is all as ifs, we are at much unease," but her irony here maintains rather than subdues her gusto. Though providing a formal structure, the repetition of "as if" in the poem threatens any stable representational or thematic structure. But just as the multiplying comparisons begin to threaten any sense of conclusion, the poem resolves its elements epigrammatically, with "he was amphibious," a phrase encompassing the poem's ambiguities. Like the clean, brief, definitive words at the end of "The Fish," these three words provide the poem with a firmness around which its ambiguous references can circle. But as the poem's only real affirmation it is perhaps insufficient.

As the comparisons declare the fiction of the poem, its assertions lean inward and become self-reflexive. The action and the imagery of "Like a Bulrush" are not arrows to the author, but in the course of the poem they do accumulate significance which includes, specifically, the author's activity. It is hard to imagine a poem about *reflection* that would not. Poetry is indeed "amphibious," of the sensuous and the abstract. With the repeated rhetorical alternatives she offers (the or, or, or, as if, as if, as if,) Moore indeed "superintends the demolition of her image" (with a marvelous play on intention), delighting in its buoyancy, its resilience. I would not suggest that this demolition is the point of the poem, or even that Moore had it in mind when she began to describe the scene; only that when trying to describe, as when looking into the water, one's attention is drawn eventually to the surface, to self-reflection. Moore's associations are made valid not by insisting on the genuineness of the image they use, but by bringing them to bear on the act of writing, as the genuine experience out of which they flow. The poem is tantalizing; we never do *possess* its subject statically. We can confirm, however, the *genuineness* of the poem as an act of mind.

Presumably what attracted Zukofsky to "Like a Bulrush" was its attempt to fuse the representational, formal, and associative functions of the poem by eliminating adjectives or references that would shade off or separate an "I" from a "thing." But for Moore such ambitions are opposed to the very nature of language. A poem is necessarily a restless totality, in which the push and pull of self and other are continually felt over its forms and statements. In "An Octopus" (CP, 71–76) Moore exploited the tension between words and things, poem and world, more explicitly, working that tension into the texture of the poem, even making it her subject. "An Octopus" compares with "Like a Bulrush" in overlapping its representational and associative functions, which is why Zukofsky chose it as another example of objectification. But it does this by inclusiveness rather than by omission, by following a wavering course of imaginative movement rather than by remaining stationary.

We are drawn immediately into the quicksand of this poem. As in many of Moore's poems, the title is also the first line, denying us any preview or orientation.

An Octopus

of ice. Deceptively reserved and flat,
it lies "in grandeur and in mass"
beneath a sea of shifting snow dunes;
dots of cyclamen-red and maroon on its clearly defined pseudopo-
             dia
made of glass that will bend—a much needed invention—
comprising twenty-eight ice fields from fifty to five hundred feet
             thick,
of unimagined delicacy.
"Picking periwinkles from the cracks"
or killing prey with the concentric crushing rigor of the python,
it hovers forward "spider fashion
on its arms" misleadingly like lace;
its "ghostly pallor changing
to the green metallic tinge of an anemone-starred pool."

As in "Like a Bulrush," the representational subject remains unnamed, so that the initial comparison obstructs rather than enhances the illusion of a scene. No explicit thematic or narrative orientation helps us resist the flux of image and perspective. Our only source of identification is an abrupt, unidentified "you" as hypothetical witness.[16]

The poem continues to hurl us through its weltering depths and surfaces, and though we discover where we are (the glacial Mt. Rainier, which Moore calls Mt. Tacoma) Moore never permits us to settle into the scene or to construct the comfortable dwelling of an idea or a perspective. The only thing we are sure of for eight pages is an experience of reading—not just of tracing type, but of admitting sensations, of being tempted to draw conclusions about them, of being carried through a plurality of attitudes arranged concentrically around an image. But what, if anything, makes this "descriptive" poem, which does not plainly objectify landscape or relay an idea, more than labyrinthine nonsense? What in the poem demands our attention and makes us continually willing to adjust it?

Looking closely at the first few sentences (which cover many lines, and break all Moore's rules of concentrated writing) we are unnerved primarily by the drastic, eerie shifts the poem makes. We read "an octopus of ice" and look for the resolution of terms, since an octopus is usually associated with fluid movement, ice with rigidity.[17] Instead we are faced with another contrast in the opposite direction: the octopus seems "reserved and flat," stable, but lies "beneath a sea of shifting snow dunes." The disorientation is not overcome when the images cross purposes as they do with "dots of cyclamen-red and maroon on its clearly defined pseudopodia." It is easy enough to cope with the idea that red flowers on a glacial mountain look, from a distance, like red dots on the legs of an octopus, but the ease of that distinction is lost in incongruity: we have red flowers on the feet of an octopus. The fact that the feet are "*pseudo*podia" and that this term has a secondary reference to psychic illusion as well as a primary one to a zoological phenomenon heightens the uncertainty. A certain quantum of power comes simply from the verbal disorientation identified with visual disorientation. The reader's experience is further complicated by the idea that not only our perspective but the glacier itself shifts. At this point we are provided with a unified image to describe the action, a "much needed invention." But "glass that will bend" contradicts our ordinary experience of glass. The focus of the poem splits again: "comprising twenty-eight ice fields from fifty to five hundred feet thick, / of unimagined delicacy." The ice-octopus moves on, challenging our comprehension, "picking periwinkles from the cracks" or "killing prey with the concentric crushing rigor of the python." Now the analogy has spread to include not only "an octopus of ice" but pythons, spiders, ghosts, and glitter, and its visual ambiguity has become animate.

But even when we have identified the shifting language as based on a shifting focus and object, we cannot tolerate the turbulence for long. We need a viewpoint. Our attention is held with the introduction of a stable image by which we can achieve a focus, however ironically.

> The fir trees, in "the magnitude of their root systems,"
> rise aloof from these maneuvers "creepy to behold,"
> austere specimens of our American royal families,
> "each like the shadow of the one beside it.
> The rock seems frail compared with their dark energy of life,"
> its vermilion and onyx and manganese-blue interior expensiveness
> left at the mercy of the weather;
> "stained transversely by iron where the water drips down,"
> recognized by its plants and its animals.

Edmund Burke pointed out in his *Inquiry into the Sublime and Beautiful* that a prolonged series (he used the example of columns) can produce a sublime effect.[18] But the alien, disorienting effect of the ice-octopus and the endless columns of fir trees is replaced by images of human power and a look at the natural world according to human standards, however magnified. The final "recognized by its plants and its animals" has an inauthentic ring after the grandiloquence of the "American royal families." There is something mock-heroic about this humanized sublime.

The next passage increases our impression of the glacier's human attributes:

> Completing a circle,
> you have been deceived into thinking that you have progressed,
> under the polite needles of the larches
> "hung to filter, not to intercept the sunlight"—
> met by tightly wattled spruce twigs
> "conformed to the edge like clipped cypress
> as if no branch could penetrate the cold beyond its company";
> and dumps of gold and silver ore enclosing The Goat's Mirror—
> that ladyfinger-like depression in the shape of the left human foot,
> which prejudices you in favor of itself
> before you have had time to see the others;

As we had earlier, with the "interior expensiveness" of the rock, we see this scene too as if it were laid out by a human power for our human pleasure. And if the fir trees are more familiar than the glacier, the larches are yet more accommodating hosts, who "hang" their needles, who huddle against the alien glacial cold. The tourist-guide narrator relays the deceptiveness of the glacier's curves, but perhaps the deception goes further, into the very illusion of "polite" needles. The process of identification goes on to "The Goat's Mirror," which "prejudices you in favor of itself." We are not told why it is striking, but presumably implicit in it (though not clear to the tourist) is a deflected self-image: "that ladyfinger-like depression in the shape of the left human foot." The "goat's mirror" becomes our mirror, as we find resemblances to ourselves in its shape. Unwittingly, the tourist is drawn to his own image, not to natural grandeur, in his experience of the glacier. But a crescendo of natural detail wipes out the effect of this "gold and silver" framed flattery, the reflection. The landscape is not humanized, not tamed. Its glacierness subsumes the tiny "you" placed in its path. As readers we distance ourselves from this deceived "you" and this narrator, distinguishing the natural from the human projection.

> its indigo, pea-green, blue-green, and turquoise,
> from a hundred to two hundred feet deep,
> "merging in irregular patches in the middle lake
> where, like gusts of a storm
> obliterating the shadows of the fir trees, the wind makes lanes of
> ripples."

Here the language is "direct," not personified; indeed, the scene obliterates the grandiose "shadows of the fir trees." We expect the language to become more objective here, to focus on the alien realities of the wild: "What spot could have merits of equal importance / for bears, elk, deer, wolves, goats and ducks?" But again, it turns out, the merits are evaluated in human terms. The " 'thoughtful beavers making drains' " recall " 'the work of careful men with shovels' "; the "exacting porcupine" lives on land "preempted by their ancestors." There is something comic about our condescension here, since the bears "inspecting unexpectedly ant-hills and berry bushes" become parodies of our human "intimacy" with the natural scene.

As he is personifying nature, the tourist also aestheticizes it. Back at the "perspective of the peaks" the scene is to him a static, two-dimensional picture.

And farther up, in stag-at-bay position
as a scintillating fragment of these terrible stalagmites,
stands the goat,
its eye fixed on the waterfall which never seems to fall—
an endless skein swayed by the wind,
immune to force of gravity in the perspective of the peaks.
A special antelope
acclimated to "grottoes from which issue penetrating draughts
which make you wonder why you came,"
it stands its ground
on cliffs the color of the clouds, of petrified white vapor—

The goat and antelope (engraved) become surrogate figures that allow
us to see ourselves in the painting and to organize the flux of sensations,
against the turbulence in which the poem began. But again the poem
subverts this stability with implicit projections of disruption:

the sun kindling its shoulders to maximum heat like acetylene,
                                                        dyeing them white—
upon this antique pedestal,
"a mountain with those graceful lines which prove it a volcano,"
its top a complete cone like Fujiyama's
till an explosion blew it off.

Even at closer view the impulse to organize the scene according to a
symmetry directs the observation:

Larkspur, blue pincushions, blue peas, and lupin;
white flowers with white, and red with red;
the blue ones 'growing close together
so that patches of them look like blue water in the distance';
this arrangement of colours
as in Persian designs of hard stones and enamel,
forms a pleasing equation—
a diamond outside, and inside, a white dot;
on the outside, a ruby; inside, a red dot;
black spots balanced with black
in the woodlands where fires have run over the ground—[SP, 86]

The scene, made pastoral, in which every detail, under the control of
the eye, is subsumed in the composition, is threatened by the source of

the design, the forest fire, which suggests *loss* of control, wildness. Perhaps this is why Moore omitted these lines from *Collected Poems*.

As readers we are invited to feel superior to the tourist who domesticates the scene, who thinks himself "part of it" only to separate again and boast at home of the "wilderness" he has conquered:

> Distinguished by a beauty
> of which "the visitor dare never fully speak at home
> for fear of being stoned as an impostor,"
> Big Snow Mountain is the home of a diversity of creatures:
> those who "have lived in hotels
> but who now live in camps—who prefer to";
> the mountain guide evolving from the trapper,
> "in two pairs of trousers, the outer one older,
> wearing slowly away from the feet to the knees"

While we overhear the self-conscious tourist comment "they make a nice appearance don't they?" we seem to have a privileged, three-dimensional ironic view of the wild eagles "happy seeing nothing" perched "on treacherous lava and pumice" or indifferently posing on human signposts "which stipulate names and addresses of persons to notify in case of disaster," the tourists' way of having nature without consequence. We see the tourists' sense of adventure (riding ponies up the mountain) reduced to a scheme of "business men who / require for recreation / three-hundred and sixty-five holidays in the year." And until the *Collected Poems* version the business men were "totemic scenery." Later in this earlier version they were diminished by the blue-jay, their animal counterpart, who can go where they cannot.

> 'Hopping stiffly on sharp feet' like miniature ice-hacks—
> 'secretive, with a look of wisdom and distinction, but a villain,
> fond of human society or the crumbs that go with it'

In the contrast of "bristling, puny, swearing men / equipped with saws and axes," to whom the mountain is inimical, and "gentians, lady-slippers, harebells, mountain dryads," which are admired, we identify with the delicate. But what have we, really, other than an ironic view of the tourists' superficial sense of mountain mystery? We have no more faced the bare elements than they have; we need a point of view, and borrow theirs, even if we patronize it. We are subject to the added irony that we, after all, are only reading, and are controlled by an author's organizing mind. It is unlikely that the reader has been to this place, or cares to go. Our original experience of turmoil *was* a matter of language controlling us; we tried in turn to control the shifting words by stabilizing ourselves in superiority to a deceived viewer. But the language is not only shifting, in accord with a natural phenomenon; it is purposefully shifty. "Completing the circle, you have been deceived into thinking that you have progressed," mocks the poem, mocking our courage as readers, for language has created the perplexities we try to solve. We have only the wilderness of the page. The poetic image, like the image in The Goat's Mirror, is "obliterated" by gusts of storm.

Only metaphor can accomplish the dramatic changes of prospect that "privilege" our view. "The road 'climbing like a thread / which forms the groove around a snail-shell / doubling back and forth until where snow begins, it ends'," gives us the experience of distance and intimacy at once, but like the road, the poem ends where the snow begins. The language of description fails to circumscribe the viscous, inexpressible reality, and doubles back on itself.

Our attempts to gain control of the poem's shifting meaning are like the tourists' attempts to gain control of the visual shiftiness of the mountain. Often the lengthy and cumbersome sentences lose their syntactic hold on us. We forget the subject or antecedent in the tow of subordinate clauses. Colons and semicolons are suspended between groups without an easy sense of their relation. Appositions become subjects with their own appositions in turn. Participial phrases go on for several lines until we cease even to anticipate their subjects and simply enjoy the arrangement of words, the parts of speech, in the infinite variety language itself provides. We can always finally retrieve the structure, but not without a pleasurable strain.

When Moore discovers "gusto" in the work of other writers, it is primarily with regard to verbal excesses of one kind or another. And certainly if we try to transcribe any of her oddities they lose their vitality:

> Instructed none knows how, to climb the mountain,
> by businessmen who require for recreation
> three hundred and sixty-five holidays in the year,
> these conspicuously spotted little horses are peculiar;

Our first sense of this passage is that the horses are "peculiar" because they represent the tourist trade, are not part of the "natural" landscape

we hold against the tourist vision. But they are also "peculiar" by virtue
of their syntactic placement. The predicate here is trivial, even vacuous
in comparison with the modifying clauses which by ordinary standards
should be semantically subordinate. We right the structure by reading
vitality into the term "peculiar"; it gains power by what is piled onto it,
and by what follows. When we learn that these *"conspicuously* spot-
ted" horses are also "hard to discern," the emphasis on "peculiar" is
indeed an example of gusto. Modifying clauses are the characteristic
units of this poem; main clauses are repeatedly subsumed and reversed,
as are visual and ideational frames of reference; and any single focus is
certainly "hard to discern."

> hard to discern among the birch trees, ferns, and lily pads,
> avalanche lilies, Indian paintbrushes,
> bear's ears and kittentails,
> and miniature cavalcades of chlorophylless fungi
> magnified in profile on the moss-beds like moonstones in the
> water;

Up to this point the poem has focused entirely on the subject of
the glacier. Several perspectives are implied to be misleading, and questions of "prospecting" arise only as prospects are introduced. But the
descriptive focus is curiously jarred about two-thirds of the way through
the poem by a very precarious transition in which the bluejays paro-
dying the "swearing men" are contrasted with the Greeks, belonging to
a different realm altogether. Such extreme reaches are common enough
in the poem, but this one is extended to invert the relation of analogy,
to become, after a spatial break, the focus of the poem, to which the
glacier is secondary. The bluejay of the earlier version

> knows no Greek,
> 'that pride-producing language',
> in which 'rashness is rendered innocuous, and error exposed
> by the collision of knowledge with knowledge'.

The version in *Collected Poems* makes the move from the physical to
the conceptual mountain more abrupt, and to my mind less successful.
Without the bluejay the digression on the Greek mind is harder to take
in:

"Like happy souls in Hell," enjoying mental difficulties,
the Greeks
amused themselves with delicate behavior
because it was "so noble and so fair";
not practised in adapting their intelligence
to eagle traps and snowshoes,
to alpenstocks and other toys contrived by those
"alive to the advantage of invigorating pleasures."
Bows, arrows, oars, and paddles, for which trees provide the wood,
in new countries more eloquent than elsewhere—
augmenting the assertion that, essentially humane,
"the forest affords wood for dwellings and by its beauty
stimulates the moral vigor of its citizens."

This much we can contain within the issue of the tourists' vision. A sentimentalized notion of the woods, a kind of hard pastoral, is mocked. But the concerns of the passage extend beyond the mountain scene, into questions of language, and once that extension is made, our own sense of superiority to the tourists is in jeopardy. The "mind of mountain" like the "mind of winter" is an ideal: even irony can become complacent.

The Greek liked smoothness, distrusting what was back
of what could not be clearly seen,
resolving with benevolent conclusiveness,
"complexities which still will be complexities
as long as the world lasts";
ascribing what we clumsily call happiness,
to "an accident or a quality,
a spiritual substance or the soul itself,
an act, a disposition, or a habit,
or a habit infused, to which the soul had been persuaded,
or something distinct from a habit, a power"—
such power as Adam had and we are still devoid of.

Finding terms for the mountain's ruggedness must be as hard as climbing it. The Greeks turned over terms in a persistent search for accuracy, but knew, in their ceaseless search for knowledge, that they failed to achieve that Adamic power of naming correctly.[19] Our "permission in writing" to see the "genuine" mountain is tainted with the same "cool official sarcasm" that colored the tourist business.

For Moore accuracy is always an ideal. The writer struggling for it must, in failing, return to consider his own investment. It is according to this principle that Moore's poems always convert their subjects to self-portraits. It is not surprising, as the poem curves increasingly toward questions of language, that it should draw an analogy between Henry James, an anfractuous writer, with the fossil flower that the mountain's elusiveness "nurtures."[20]

> this fossil flower concise without a shiver,
> intact when it is cut,
> damned for its sacrosanct remoteness—
> like Henry James "damned by the public for decorum";
> not decorum, but restraint;
> it is the love of doing hard things
> that rebuffed and wore them out—a public out of sympathy with
> neatness.

Reading Henry James must be like climbing, like writing was for him, a writer who "liked smoothness." And Moore, in admiring James, imitates his precision, his "decorum, not decorum but restraint." By ordinary standards this holding back is a flaw, but the desire for precision, working together with a fear of finishing, here provides the gusto. "Idealism which was willing to make sacrifices for its self-preservation was always an element in the conjuring wand of Henry James," writes Moore in her essay on the novelist (*Predilections*, 23). Overconfidence never lets you "conquer the main peak of Mount Tacoma." At just this point the language of description gives way to the language of appreciation:

> Neatness of finish! Neatness of finish!
> Relentless accuracy is the nature of this octopus
> with its capacity for fact.
> "Creeping slowly as with meditated stealth,
> its arms seeming to approach from all directions,"
> it receives one under winds that "tear the snow to bits
> and hurl it like a sandblast
> shearing off twigs and loose bark from the trees."

The most striking thing about this passage is how the exclamation breaks the descriptive-discursive flow of the verse. It is the only time the poet's utterance is not addressed to some implicit audience or directed to some descriptive or ideational point. Indeed, the words immediately resume their directive function. But just where Moore begins to draw conclusions about inconclusiveness she must make her verse testify with language that, as she says of the spiritual man in "What Are Years," "accedes to mortality" and in its "imprisonment rises / upon himself as / the sea in a chasm." And, of course, "in its surrendering finds its continuing." We cannot conclude inconclusiveness. When description gives way to appreciation, our focus, which has until now been carefully deflected, is thrown onto the writer's energies.

"Neatness of finish" stands suspended in the poem between discussions of writing and discussions of nature, and since its referent is plural, it is repeated. The illusion is not broken, but neither is it completed. The mountain's neatness of finish requires our own, and the process must be infinite. "This" octopus (whose relentless accuracy we admire) is a metaphor, but for the glacier? The fact that it is a metaphor, not the glacier itself, lingers. The mountain's relentless accuracy is a trompe-l'oeil of the poem's own accuracy, its capacity for fact, always a little short of facts in themselves. The icy glacier is an emblem for the mind of winter, which offers no personal warmth but is all beholding and listening. The octopus's movement " 'creeping slowly as with meditated stealth, / its arms seeming to approach from all directions,' " is like the poem's, which invokes images from all countries of the mind, which gathers up "glacier like" whatever scraps of language come into its path. But even to say this is too facile. We don't "conclude" that the poem reduces to a metaphor for itself. Rather, at the point at which the poem becomes self-referential we see a correspondence between the reader and the poem and the observer and the landscape.

Moore plays with our sense of an ending, our assumption as to what an ending involves both rhetorically and thematically. But Moore, like Henry James, "seems to have been haunted by awareness that rapacity destroys what it is successful in acquiring" (*Predilections*, 30). She is not finished. In order to sustain the object beyond the words, she refrains from dominating it with her own conclusions (ironic or not), and that very restraint becomes an occasion for extension. Moore returns to description from this interlude of assertion with a gesture of accuracy even more relentless than before:

Is "tree" the word for these things
"flat on the ground like vines"?
some "bent in a half circle with branches on one side
suggesting dust-brushes, not trees;
some finding strength in union, forming little stunted groves
their flattened mats of branches shrunk in trying to escape"
from the hard mountain "planed by ice and polished by the
wind"—

the white volcano with no weather side;
the lightning flashing at its base,
rain falling in the valleys, and snow falling on the peak—
the glassy octopus symmetrically pointed,
its claw cut by the avalanche
"with a sound like the crack of a rifle,
in a curtain of powdered snow launched like a waterfall."

Having eluded formal closure Moore delightfully allows associative thematic closure. At the end of the mountain is a curtain of snow; at the
end of the poem—is a curtain of snow. This is not "the thing itself" but
"anticlimax," which Moore, through Longinus, claims "bears the
stamp of vehement emotion like a ship before a veering wind" (*Predilections*, 8).

It is characteristic of Moore's poems that while we have a clear
sense of what the terms of comparison in a given analogy are, we are
never quite certain of their relation. The relationship of passages repeats
the experience of individual sentences. The poem resists the search for
beginning, middle, and end. Impressions emerge and vanish in temporal coruscations. There is no framework predetermining the movement of the lines, and nevertheless they seem controlled, organically
necessary. At the beginning of the poem the language is directed to describing a glacier. Soon it is directed to questions of limited and rigorous vision, which in turn become questions of writing. What was originally the subject of writing, the glacier, becomes a metaphor for it. The
image of the octopus becomes the interface of these concerns, serving
simultaneously as an image for the glacier and an image for the poem.
Through it Moore can declare the nature and limits of her medium
without destroying our interest in its descriptive action. We are carried
through an experience of shifting emotions while being at the same
time aware that it is a rhetorical effect, that language has created it. The

image of the octopus is a good deal different from that of the white whale. Its parts do not collect into a circumscribing unity. Its concerns are not hierarchically arranged. We don't see mountain and poem at once, but intermittently, as we might see a trompe-l'oeil postcard that transforms an image according to the angle at which it is held.

The worksheets for "An Octopus" reveal an interesting period of gestation, in terms of Moore's impulse toward, and resistance to, analogy. From the beginning, Moore seemed to be interested in the relationship between the image of the mountain and the image of the octopus, but uncertain of what that relation might be. She worked on the poem for a long time, while writing others. It is impossible to reproduce here all the stages the poem underwent, but a simple contrast between two drafts will show how the glacier continually reasserts itself against Moore's efforts of interpretation. At one point the poem identified rather explicitly a contrast between aggressive emotion and aloof reality:

An octopus of ice
cool in this age of violence
so static & so enterprising
heightening the mystery of the medium
the haunt
of many tail-feathers
so cool—static emotionless

Moore rejected this passage, probably because of its too confident generality. In its next phase, the poem is immersed in the particular.

An Octopus
of ice
a snow crystal
226 enchanted peak
roots like writing serpents
roar of ice
topaz tournaline crystal robins egg blue water
valleys deep & narrow
quartz ledges encrusting valleys deep & narrow . . .
Lake Agnes—goats' looking glasses
shaped like the left human foot
brilliant ice fields
between the shadowy cliffs the liquid ice[21]

Moore goes on for many lines, practicing like this. But it is worth noticing that in her reassertion of the particular the shape of the vision as a
whole has changed. The glacier is not "static" now but, on the contrary,
demands rapid eye movement to keep up with the rush of detail. The
object eludes us not because it is impassive but because it will not stay
in place. Or is it the perspective of the poem that is unsteady, giving us
the feeling of unsteadiness in the object? We can see how Moore is
moving toward the final version.

In *A Grammar of Motives*, to which an essay on Moore is ap-
pended, Kenneth Burke defines metaphor as perspective, "a device for
seeing something *in terms of* something else. It brings out the thisness
of a that, or the thatness of a this."

> If we employ the word "character" as a general term for
> whatever can be thought of as distinct (any thing, pattern,
> situation, structure, nature, person, object, act, role, process,
> event, etc.) then we could say that metaphor tells us some-
> thing about one character as considered from the point of
> view of another character. And to consider A from the point
> of view of B, is, of course, to use B as a perspective upon A.

What is wrong, for Moore, with the tourist's vision is that it mistakes a
"perspective" for the thing itself. The Greek mind struggles for "poetic
realism" (Burke's term), which is the "collision of knowledge with
knowledge." Moore said to Donald Hall, "I like to see a thing from all
sides."

> It is by the approach through a variety of perspectives that
> we establish a character's reality. If we are in doubt as to
> what an object is, for instance, we deliberately try to con-
> sider it in as many different terms as its nature permits: lift-
> ing, smelling, tasting, tapping, holding in different lights,
> subjecting to different pressures, dividing, matching, con-
> trasting, etc.[22]

In this sense "relentless accuracy" can be called the strategy of Moore's
poem. But Moore never does establish the "character" of the glacier,
only something of the character of the poem. Given her paradoxes of
failure, "relentless accuracy" seems to be invoked for its own sake. She
never does "objectify" an image or use an image to convey an idea.
Abandoning the voice *of* things, she adopts a voice *for* things. Associa-

tion is a mode of engagement, and if viewed self-consciously, a mode of praise. Moore borrows objects for the sake of vivid effects based on association, while maintaining an earnest celebration of their otherness. Her bringing the poem back to writing represents a form of embarrassment about making observations, but it is also a way of authenticating those observations.

"An Octopus" collects "observations" that belie the interests of their speakers. The pretext of the poem is "relentless accuracy," but since the poem concludes as it does in inconclusiveness, what becomes its purpose? There is a certain amount of self-consciousness in Moore's "amusing" herself "with delicate behaviour / because it [is] 'so noble and so fair.' " In the varying movements of definition and description, disorientation and stability, long sentences and short, the desire for accuracy seems to give way to something like the pleasures of merely circulating. It is the limits of our attention, not the limits of the subject, that seem to determine the flow of the verse. It is Moore's self-consciousness about her direction and her practice, about what use a voice *for* things can be, that always brings her back to images of her own activity.

Curiosity is the motive and mode of attention of these poems. Curiosity is based on the sense of something attractive because like oneself, but different, not resolved into identity. Moore's mind follows likeness and finds difference, and again likeness, in the form of statements that are qualified, images that clash, rhymes that are interrupted, deviating detail, almost any kind of verbal differentiation. In the process she does not accomplish "objectification" (curiosity is not satisfied) but something more interesting: a composition that metes out likeness and difference, visual and aural as well as semantic. The composition has the rhetorical power both to make associations and to suggest its own limits, since these verbal differences are made to seem like the difference between the world and what we say about it. Moore's compositions are trails of associations which conduct the reader to the writer, their source. This identification occurs not only through our vicarious experience of her mental flux, but through her final, and distinct if subtle, self-portraiture. Moore begins by presenting an object apparently for its own sake, but in the process of describing it she borrows the object as a figure of her own activity. This self-portraiture is not the point of arrival of the poet's search for the thing itself, but a kind of parting embrace of words and things, a form of possession or appropriation that leaves the thing untouched while its ghost performs the function of analogy. Moore pursues the contours of objects for what she can discover of herself, but precisely because she learns about herself through observation of the external world, she can never declare her motive or speak of herself directly. "Imaginary possession" allows her to make associations without making assumptions. She never permits the idea to subvert the image. All her thoughts occur along the way to describing something visible. There are no static declarations or forms in her work. In this sense, the poem does not mean, but does. Her poems are actions, not reflections.

In *Selected Poems* Moore developed the kind of dense factualness and objectivity (by including scientific and historical data and by displacing poetic statement with quotation) that she had begun in "An Octopus." Such materials do not achieve an illusion of reality, but pull against the metaphoric frame that characterizes most of *Poems* and *Observations*, indicating the separateness of the empirical object from the poet's imaginary structures. The result, often, is a poem at once realistic and fanciful, literal and allegorical. While the subjects of Moore's long descriptive poems are more specific and local, the themes are in turn more abstract. But this basic duality between image and idea is overcome in the temporality of these poems, in the sense of them not as transparent representations or opaque sculptures but as dynamic compositions that record and stir acts of mind.

In "The Frigate Pelican" (CP, 25–26) the worlds of art and nature are brought together from the start, the question of priority between them dissolved into a series of instances and analogies. The frigate pelican is a living symbol, giving authenticity to the life of the imagination. By establishing a set of values in the natural order, Moore persuades us of their place in social and aesthetic realms as well. The poem argues the virtue of detached contemplation, against the criterion of purposive action. And in its final version this theme dominates the poem; the image of the frigate pelican serves primarily to give shape and objectivity to an idea. Our attention does not linger on the frigate pelican as an object in nature. Rather, we are drawn on the one hand into a series of comparisons and reflections, and on the other hand into the rhythms and sounds of the poem itself. The music of "The Frigate Pelican," while never of that persistent kind Moore disliked, prevails as the most immediate parallel and example of the structures described in the bird's flight. Moore's tendency to dramatize her subject in the action and form of her poem is at its strongest here, especially in the coda which rhythmically and imaginatively lifts the poem out of the descent of conclusion.

As it first appeared, in *Criterion*, July 1934, and as it was printed, slightly revised, in *Selected Poems*, "The Frigate Pelican" entered into considerably more detail about the object and its life in nature than it does in the final version. The bird's metaphoric value is clear, but it does not dominate the surface. In early versions this is still a descriptive poem, analogies arising out of a particularized surface.

> A marvel of grace, no matter how fast his
>   victim may fly or how often may
> turn, the dishonest pelican's ease
>   in pursuit, bears him away
> with the fish that the badgered bird drops.
>   A kind of superlative
>   swallow, that likes to live
>
> on food caught while flying, he is not a pelican. The toe
>   with slight web, air-boned body, and very long wings
>   with the spread of a swan's—duplicating a
>   bow-string as he floats overhead—feel
> the changing V-shaped scissor swallow-
>   tail direct the rigid keel.
> And steering beak to windward always,
>   the fleetest foremost fairy
>   among birds, outflies the
>
> aeroplane which cannot flap its wings nor alter any quill-
>   tip. For him, the feeling in a hand, in fins, is
>   in his unbent downbeat crafty oar. With him
>   other pelicans aimlessly soar
> as he does; separating, until
>   not flapping they rise once more,
>   closing in without looking and move
>   outward again to the top
>   of the circle and stop   [SP, 22–23]

The theme is more completely invested in the instance of the frigate pelican and thus more abstract. That is, we become more involved in

the visual and aural structures of the poem, in the range of movements
and perspectives that the subject of the frigate pelican sets in motion.
Indeed at the outset he is nearly identified with motion ("unless swift is
the proper name for him"). In the early version the frigate pelican provides a vehicle for the poet's eye, allowing her to introduce and expell
elements at will. While the exotic scene remains specific to the pelican,
it pulses with associations.

> It is not retreat but exclusion from
> which he looks down and observes what went
> secretly, as it thought, out of sight
> among dense jungle plants. Sent
> ahead of the rest, there goes the true
> knight in his jointed coat that
> covers all but his bat
>
> ears; a-trot, with stiff pig gait—our tame armadillo, loosed by
> his master and as pleased as a dog. Beside the
> spattered blood—that orchid which the native fears—
> the fer-de-lance lies sleeping; centaur-
> like, this harmful couple's amity
> is apropos. A jaguar
> and crocodile are fighting. Sharp-shinned
> hawks and peacock-freckled small
> cats, like the literal
>
> merry-go-round, come wandering within the circular view
> of the high bird for whom from the air they are ants
> keeping house all their lives in the crack of a
> crag with no view from the top. And here,
> unlikely animals learning to
> dance, crouch on two steeds that rear
> behind a leopard with a frantic
> face, tamed by an Artemis
> who wears a dress like his,
>
> and hampering haymaker's hat.   [SP, 24]

Like the poet, the pelican has the privilege of seeing outside the usual
limits of time and space to what is departing or arriving, what converges

or moves apart. The requirement of such perspective is detachment, "not retreat but exclusion." The turbulent world lacks a "view from the top"—it has no distance on its comings and goings. The artist, like the frigate pelican, frees herself from ambition and purpose in order to absorb the motion of the world. The immediate analogy of the poet enchanted with frigate pelicans while the world goes about its serious business is deliberately invited. Later in her career the pressure to say something useful overcame her and she wrote more expressly thematic poems. But around the time of *Selected Poems* Moore trusted in the poem as a primary unit of action. Description provided the best means of giving momentum to the imagination. Levity and strength are not the theme but the active principle of such poems.

"The Jerboa" (CP, 10–15) is, like Mt. Rainier, an elusive "untouched" creature, admired for defying every effort of possession.[23] "Course the jerboa . . . and you will be cursed." Moore delights in formal nuances just as she delights in the recalcitrant actions of the jerboa. It will not be subsumed by a single perspective, definition, analogy, but has its own, unified, unique identity. Moore puzzles over it and then rejoices in its mystery. Such changes from description to admiration are typical. "At a loss" to account for the origin of the monkey puzzle tree, for instance, Moore declares, "we prove, we do not explain our birth."

Moore's interest turns increasingly away from moral categories and toward aesthetic categories as "The Jerboa" progresses. Though she never changes subjects, as she does in "An Octopus," by concluding with art rather than nature, she at least equalizes the two.

> Its leaps should be set
> to the flageolet;
>   pillar body erect
>   on a three-cornered smooth-working Chippendale
>   claw—propped on hind legs, and tail as third toe,
>   between leaps to its burrow.

These are not simply gestures of representational accuracy, they abstract the subject. And because they abstract it to purely formal significance, they draw attention to the poem as an entity which has been displaying the very action it describes. The images dodge interpretation, the rhythms leap and pause against the pulse of expectation. Just as the jerboa "honors the sand by assuming its color," thus seeming invisible, so the poem honors the jerboa by assuming its actions.

By fifths and sevenths,
in leaps of two lengths,
  like the uneven notes

of the Bedouin flute, it stops its gleaning
  on little wheel castors, and makes fern-seed
  footprints with kangaroo speed.

As in "An Octopus," the uniqueness and independence of the jerboa become an opportunity for the poet's own "abundance" of language. In acts of description, the finite world becomes infinite because language is imprecise. Moore does not try to confine nature in art, as the Egyptians and Romans with their mimetic toys (described in the first half of the poem) had done. Rather, she makes nature a pretext for the creation of her poem.

"The Jerboa" is a complex poem, for while it celebrates the natural unity of form and function, the harmony of the desert rat with its surroundings, and while it implicitly criticizes human cultures for their will to perfect, transform, and possess nature in art, the poem's own activities seem to qualify that judgment. The Egyptians destroy the grace and order of nature with their geometries and parodies, elevating lowly creatures to the status of gods and degrading humanity to slavery. It is a world of perverse, unnatural configurations, wholly artificial. It is also a world fundamentally unsatisfied, for all its riches. Like the court rat, "its restlessness was its excellence." Even worse are the Romans, whose excessive will to conquest destroys not only the freedom of others, but ultimately their own freedom, and all aesthetic value with it.

In contrast Moore presents the jerboa, who does not impose on nature, but honors it by assuming its color. It is an adaptive rather than a possessive creature. It has a "shining silver house of sand" without altering the wilderness. It takes the shape of many animals without violating their autonomy. But this ideal creature represents something unrealizable by human culture. Moore knows that since the fall our relationship to nature is always incomplete and tense. Restlessness is our condition. We could not, since Adam, be the jerboa, had we the will. Moore's poem, with its careful measures and intricate rhythms, cannot really be compared to the natural simplicity of the jerboa. Indeed, the charm and ingenuity with which she presents the detail of Egyptian civilization, the precision with which she works an elaborate array of names and objects into her rhythmic patterns, suggests at least a measure of identification with that side of desert culture. She too has inverted and transformed the world to suit her human purposes, comparing the jerboa to a Chippendale chair, a Bedouin flute. But the Chippendale and Bedouin styles, and Moore's as well, are marked by restraint and spontaneity. Moore differs from the Egyptians in that she acknowledges the transformations as purely imaginary. Her associations make no claim to power or authority, but construct an imaginary theater in which the mind can restlessly pursue its own needs.

It is human to appropriate our surroundings by identifying them with what we already know. But for Moore, there are good and bad modes of appropriation. The narcissist superficially imoses his categories on experience and then is gratified to find them reaffirmed. Moore's poetry testifies to the futility of such self-projected delusion. A passage from the entymologist Henri Fabre she copied in her reading diary describes a scientist's criticism of the same naive, egocentric acts of interpretation: "Nowadays . . . men interpret everything w. glorious reassurance when they explain the lion's tawny mane as due to the color of the African desert, attribute the tiger's dark stripes to the streaks of shadows cast by the bamboos, + extricate any no. of other magnif. things fr. the mists of the unknown w. the same facility."[24] According to Moore's notes, after a long recollection of childhood dragons Fabre concludes: "mimesis, in my eyes, is a piece of childishness." For Moore, too, *mimesis* is a piece of childishness, but as a poet she is less censorious. We can indulge in acts of analogy and association, but know them as imaginative rather than real connections. "Imaginary possession" allows us to experience fully both the otherness of objects and the enchantments of our own minds.

For all the moral seriousness of their themes, "An Octopus" and "The Jerboa" show a whimsicality and creative autonomy unlike "The Fish" or "Like a Bulrush." They sport in a world of words, in which things glitter with associative value, and at the same time they acknowledge that it is not the phenomenal world of which they speak. "Camellia Sabina" is even more whimsical than these.

The pretext of "Camellia Sabina" (CP, 16–18) is the bustle and mystique surrounding the cultivation of hothouse flowers, fine wines, and food grapes. Its theme—"the gleaning is more than the vintage"— indicts the artificial and celebrates the natural. But critics have erred, I think, in seeing these as more than the pretexts of the poem. Donald Hall finds the poem's logic "a little cockeyed," but I think this is deliberate.[25] From the beginning of the poem Moore presents herself as a relentless and ingenious moralizer, finding fault in the most neutral of phenomena. But this campaign is entirely self-conscious and playful. It suggests a mind coping with the plenitude of fact by classifying it, by making distinctions. It is the ordering process that is imortant here, more than the specific terms (moral or aesthetic) of the classification.

Camellia Sabina

and the Bordeaux plum
from Marmande (France) in parenthesis with
A.G. on the base of the jar—Alexis Godillot—
unevenly blown beside a bubble that
is green when held up to the light; they
are a fine duet; the screw-top
  for this graft-grown briar-black bloom
on blackthorn pigeon's-blood,
    is, like Certosa, sealed with foil. Appropriate custom.

The ingenuity is underlined in the cumbersome style of the descriptive sentences and the pert abruptness of the evaluative statements. Once such an evaluative energy has been released almost anything could be turned in its machinery. Here presumably the "A.G." signifies the knowing condescension of the connoiseur, the foil and bubble signify confined life. Moore knows, of course, that glassblowing is innocent in fact; in fancy she can turn it to her pleasure. In the incongruity of the image and the evaluative meaning is a *jeu d'esprit:* "the French are a cruel race—willing to squeeze the diner's cucumber or broil a / meal on vine shoots."[26] Moore takes synecdoche to an extreme here, as she does in "People's Surroundings." She often openly leaps the logic of nature in order to make her associations, as when she brings together the darkness of the wine cellar with the effects of wine: "it makes the soul heavy."

In protesting the previous decorum of sophisticates, Moore works by indecorum. Critics have complained that the "Tom thumb" figure in "Camellia Sabina," the mouse who is "Prince of Tails," is out of place in the realistic vineyard. But such representational contrasts are entirely characteristic and outline the fantastic element in all her pictures. And the mock heroism of the figure (in which the small becomes large and the large small) is related to her constant play of perspective and orientation. If the detail in the Camellia Sabina is excruciatingly tiny, the picture of the mouse is blown to equally absurd proportions:

> Does yonder mouse with a
> grape in its hand and its child
> in its mouth, not portray
> the Spanish fleece suspended by the neck?

Ultimately it is we who are the object of such spoofs. By an ambiguous "you" Moore places us in the double vantage point of mice and men: "In that well-piled / larder above your head, the picture of what you will eat is / looked at from the end of the avenue."

In *Selected Poems* Moore made a place for "the genuine" in the independent life of particulars, the open artificiality of associations, the dynamic tension between observing and making observations. In *What Are Years* she pursued many of the themes (of freedom in restraint, of relentless accuracy, of imaginary possession) and many of the methods (inclusion of data, density of quotations, bold leaps of association, relentless evaluation of minor fact) she had developed in *Selected Poems*. But as a group these poems maintain greater interpretive control over the observations they record and press their meanings more earnestly. The images are less recalcitrant, the associations less openly subjective and less abstract. Thus for all their density of fact and detail and for all their imaginative connections, these poems seem less enchanted by the otherness of the world, and by the freedom of the imagination.

If we compare "Virginia Britannia" (CP, 107–111) and "An Octopus," poems alike in theme (criticizing human plunder and applauding nature's recalcitrance), subject (a landscape and its inhabitants), and length, we see the difference clearly.[27] The later poem is impressive in the range of facts in its moral perimeters, the controlled variety of its diction, but it is tamer and less exhilarating than "An Octopus." Its voice, style, viewpoint, theme, attitude, are somewhat static. The reader is not drawn into the drama of perception and association, except at the end, where the connection is thematic, not experiential.

Moore's "imaginary possession" of this Jamestown setting has less of the humility and restraint, less of the open subjectivity, and less of the moral complexity of earlier work. Her writing fits Susan Sontag's definition of photography as "an imaginary possession" of a "space in which [we] are insecure." "It means putting oneself into a certain relation to the world that feels like knowledge—and therefore, like

power."[28] In "Virginia Britannia," Moore denies the landscape its separate identity; she seems to want the security of having something to say
about it.[29] Writing more directly from books in "An Octopus," she
more openly acknowledges the difference between art and life. Though
the facts of Mt. Rainier are the pretext of the poem, "An Octopus" is
entirely invented. The opening stanza of "Virginia Brittania," while its
sentences still include multiple clauses and pile up adjectives and
nouns, is orderly and reassuring in its presentation of a scene and in its
syntax.

> Pale sand edges England's Old
> Dominion. The air is soft, warm, hot
> above the cedar-dotted emerald shore
> > known to the redbird, the red-coated musketeer,
> > the trumpet flower, the cavalier,
> > the parson, and the wild parishioner. A deer-
> track in a church-floor
> > brick, and a fine pavement tomb with engraved top, remain.
> The now tremendous vine-encompassed hackberry
> > starred with the ivy flower,
> > shades the church tower;
> And a great sinner lyeth here under the sycamore.

Despite the visual range of the images, there is nothing disorienting
here. There is none of the swirling immediacy of Mt. Rainier; our relationship to images is not textual or visual but firmly conceptual. The
nature/culture dichotomy is neatly balanced, and redundant (deer-
track/church floor; ivy flower/church tower). Though Moore will go on
to describe Jamestown as an "inconsistent flowerbed," it is really a
rather consistent pattern of native and imported elements. Moore
seems to stand outside the subject, and while there is much satisfaction
in the fine distance, we want to go in and be lost. The strength of the
poem is its indulgent mixture of Indian, American, and European
words and names—Mattaponi, Daniel Boone, Christopher Newport,
Madiera, and so on. At one point Moore considers language specifically: "Care has formed among un-English insect sounds." But the
theme remains tied to the scene and never becomes self-reflexive as it
does in other poems.

    The end of the poem describes the advance of evening, and thus the temporary and figuratively final obliteration of the scene and its dualities.

> The live oak's darkening filigree
> of undulating boughs, the etched
> solidity of a cypress indivisible
>> from the now agèd English hackberry,
>> become with lost identity,
>> part of the ground, as sunset flames increasingly
> against the leaf-chiseled
>> blackening ridge of green; while clouds, expanding above
>> the town's assertiveness, dwarf it, dwarf arrogance
>>> that can misunderstand
>>> importance; and
> are to the child an intimation of what glory is.

In "An Octopus" the obliteration of the image is connected self-consciously with the end of the text, but here Moore asserts a superiority of words over their subject by offering us a moral as consolation. In *Observations* and *Selected Poems* Moore would never have used allusion (here to Wordsworth's Immortality Ode) in this way or allowed herself such unqualified "poetic" solutions as the Wordsworth borrowing provides. This is presented as "truth," not as language. Such detached lyricism characterizes Moore's poetry of this period.[30] The title poem "What Are Years" has been admired by many for its grace and simplicity, but its graces are not, finally, satisfying, because the mind is not truly engaged in its sources and struggles.

One poem from *What Are Years* that does engage us in its imaginative action rather than confront us with prefabricated meanings is "Walking Sticks and Paperweights and Watermarks," (WY, 10–14) which regrettably Moore omitted from *Complete Poems*.[31] The poem is perhaps too cluttered and digressive in its associations to be finally successful; Moore struggled with it, and it went through several revisions from its first publication in *Poetry*. It is "an invisible fabric of inconsistency," but its inventiveness is sometimes dazzling. That the materials and the ideas they inspire are connected with writing and reading, making and receiving impressions, makes the poem that much more immediate. Again the theme of reciprocity is basic: "A device before it leaves / the wax, receives / to give, and giving must itself / receive." Moore plays with the old, fanciful etymology of sincere, *sine cera*, without wax, which Lionel Trilling tells us usually referred to objects and meant that they "had not been adulterated, or, as was once said, sophisticated."[32] For Moore, purity of gesture is derived from purity of effect—in poetry, in paperweights, as well as in sealing wax, "form dramatizes thought."

> Sincere
> unforced unconscious honesty,
>
> *sine cera*, can be furthest
> from self-defensiveness and nearest;
>   as when a seal
> without haste, slowly is impressed,
> and forms a nest
>   on which the raised device reversed,
>   shows round.

As objects that show a reciprocity of thought and form, paperweights, sealing wax, water marks (opposites but alike) are analogous to writing, though they retain their separateness. They are analogous to writing as well in that while they have turned something fluid into something solid and stable, they nevertheless reveal a flux and a vitality within their forms. The "hardened raindrop surface" of the paperweight "enlarges the / fine chain—lines in the waterleaf."

> The paper-mold's similarly
>
> at first unsolid blues, yellow-
> whites and lavenders, when seen through, show
>   leopards, eagles,
> quills, acorns and anvils.

These associations expand beyond writing to the subject of human error and uncertainty against ideas of stability and endurance. The most detailed image becomes the most abstract:

> Postmark behests are clearer than
> the water marks beneath,—than ox, swan,
>   crane, or dolphin,

than eastern, open, jewelled, Span-
ish, Umbrian
    crown,—as symbols of endurance.
And making the envelope secure, the sealed
wax reveals a pelican
       studying affectionately

the nest's three-in-one upturned tri-
form face. "For those we love, live and die"
    the motto reads.
The pelican's community
of throats, the high-
    way's trivia or crow's-foot where
       three roads meet, the fugue, the awl-leafed juniper's
whorls of three, objectify
    welded divisiveness.

As the poem draws random phenomena into its web of meanings, its artificiality (like that of the paperweight, the watermark, against the world they inhabit) is openly avowed. Symbols offer assurances where the randomness and brevity of life threaten. As images arise and are absorbed the poem so engages us in its reconstruction of reality that we accept its exhortation not to wisdom or knowledge or power but to process: "for those we love, live and die."

We understand Moore's poems best if we consider the movement of their composition, rather than the theme or the representational subject. Their motions range from description to definition, from fact to fantasy, from dense particularity to epigrammatic generality, narrowing down the image by an accretion of words, widening and abstracting the meaning but specifying the image. These compositions include a great deal of fact and a great deal of association, including self-reflection, but no single reference—perceptual or conceptual—controls their movement. The poems are offered as imaginative experiences, cognizant of the wider world, perhaps even obliquely useful in dealing with it, but separate, unique.

4. From Adversities to Conversities

Images of Sweetened Combat

W<small>E HAVE SEEN</small> how Moore's preoccupation with the genuine and her insistence on sincerity affect her methods of representation. The structure of her verse fluctuates as different levels of reference compete, perspective vying with perspective, the particular resisting the grasp of the general within a presiding design. Her predilection for tension and implosion in art is reflected in an imagery of combat, not surprising in a poet whose career spanned two world wars. Moore's interest in war and its ethical and aesthetic equivalents is clear from her reading and conversation notebooks as well as from the poems themselves. Her library included many books, articles, and brochures on the history of arms and armor, and she attended numerous lectures and exhibitions on these and related subjects. Her brother was a navy chaplain, and consequently war was a household topic, indeed an obsessive topic with her mother, who maintained a ready arsenal of protestant morality. Mrs. Moore's truisms of spiritual warfare run alongside the worksheets for many of the poems in *Nevertheless* and find their way into the poems themselves in a modified form.

Many critics have noted that armor is one of Moore's favorite motifs, and they have rightly identified the image with Moore's own aesthetic procedures. But they have misread the image and the related aesthetic by thinking of armor outside the important context of war, as a protective covering against the force and judgment of the world. In fact the imagery of armor is connected to a broader array of images of internalized combat, associated with the need for both power and restraint in art, as in life. One objective of Moore's art is to reactivate a war within, a principle of humility and openness whose lapse is the cause of external war. But the mind cannot sustain itself in constant flux and conflict. It seeks harmony and stasis through its assertive power. Moore's poems seek to stabilize without compromising the war within.

Art, for Moore, does not properly offer either advice or escape from temporal life. With its high tolerance for paradox and contrariety, its resolution of time and timelessness, it offers idealized reconciliations of difference, to which the imagination goes for sustenance and reassurance. Moore's strategies and images of armor are not intended as self-protective coverings. But neither is her aesthetic of collision meant merely as a reflection of the external reality. The poems incorporate conflict in order to resolve it on an imaginative plain.

Moore's poetry of combat, then, has two aims. To reclaim for the imagination the complexity, humility, and tolerance that action represses, and to restore for the imagination the experience of stability and harmony that experience disrupts. Neither objective is easily achieved, their path is cluttered with delusion and doubt, but Moore maintains an uncompromising ideal throughout her highly temporal, qualifying poems.

Moore was touched by Wallace Stevens's analogy between the poet and the soldier, an analogy developed "in the wake of an extraordinary pressure of news." What "matters most" for Stevens is that "the pressure of reality" might exclude "any power of contemplation."[1] Moore focuses on this idea in her 1943 essay on Stevens's poetry, "There Is a War That Never Ends."

> He is "the familiar man," the hero who "rejects false empire" and is "complete in himself despite the negations of existence." His affirming freedom of mind is involved in "war that never ends." He and the soldier are one. Mr. Stevens has summarized it in *The Noble Rider and the Sound of Words*, where he says that "as a wave is a force and not the water of which it is composed, which is never the same, so nobility is a force ... It is a violence from within that protects us from a violence without. It is the imagination pressing back against the pressure of reality." In the final poem of *Notes toward a Supreme Fiction*, the violence from without is summarized—the soldier who is preserving that

freedom of soul which gives rise to the violence within. Surely this is "the bread of faithful speech" for soldiers in the "war that never ends."[2]

For Stevens, then, the solution to "the storm" was to incorporate the structure of the problem into our imaginative lives, to find imaginative harmonies.

Moore makes a related argument in her "Comment" for *The Dial* on international peace, when she observes "complacency is not, as we know, an element of peace," and "the mere absence of armament is not necessarily peace."[3] Instead, since the cause of war is material self-interest, "true non-materialism is . . . itself a war on self-interest." Since the moralist was also an artist, the battle was fought on the ground of form as well as that of ideas and feelings.

During the war years Moore published two volumes of poetry, *What Are Years* (1941) and *Nevertheless* (1944), in which her observations are directed increasingly toward questions of possession, now explicitly in terms of combat, conquest, and graceful, vital survival. Ideas about armor had been implicit in her work all along, but gradually armor began to be one of the most dominant metaphors in her work, at times directly challenging a political ethos that viewed material possession, mechanization, and martial conquest as ultimate goals. "In Distrust of Merits" declares "there never was a war that was not inward." The irony of external war, she suggests, is that conquest can become enslavement because the conquerer is so convinced of his own power and righteousness that he cannot see beyond himself. But like Stevens she views the war among nations as "only part of a war-like whole." Ideal order is a balance of many counter-tensions. "Keeping Their World Large" has as an epigraph a quotation from the *New York Times*, June 7, 1944: "All too literally, their flesh and their spirit are our shield." The poem goes on to assert the importance of internalizing warfare: "they fought the enemy, we fight / fat living and self-pity." Both poems applaud what is the title of yet another poem about war, "Armor's Undermining Modesty," which is "a mirror-of-steel uninsistence."

But in Moore's best work the conventional wisdom of combat is converted by context into a fresh discovery of the power of art. The poems that pronounce about war and peace show too much the pressure of news. The moral intensity of war undoubtedly urged Moore away from the particular, which, like poetry itself, may seem irrelevant at times of crisis. But when she is truest to her talent and insight, pushing back with the force of the imagination, she does not use language to promulgate morality or ideology, but rather to enact the problems of observation and interpretation that are a source of war. Indeed, didacticism is a betrayal of the war within, even when that war is its subject. Moore's best poems observe struggle where it is free of preconceptions, where discovery can take place.[4] Concerned with art above all, Moore thought hardest, in crisis, about art. On the field of art she is often a stalwart soldier, preserving the freedom of the imagination against single-minded assertion. Indeed, in her comment on international peace she immediately draws on the analogy of art. Her quotations come from a discussion of architecture by Claude Bragdon, who condemns the skyscraper as "a thief of air and sunlight—a symbol of 'ruthless and tireless aggression on the part of the cunning and the strong.' "[5] Moore translates the problems of war into the problems of art and tries to solve them in that arena, making her work a healthy symbolic enactment of what is, in the world, a critical situation. As she records in her notebook, "opposed or opposing? that is life; that's art. And the aesthetic mind encompasses that struggle."[6] Moore's art reflects conflict in the existing world not only through its subject, but through its imagery, its diction, and the interplay of its sensuous elements. As always, the motive that justifies this aesthetic warfare is sincerity, the search for a true apprehension in the clash of partial ones. The imagination is never parochial or partisan; it thrives in the uncertainty that contending orders create, it finds its brilliances in the intervals of a storm.

Moore filled several pages of her reading notebook of 1932 with quotations from "The Principles of Film Form" by Sergei Eisenstein,[7] passages that articulate the concept of art as internalized warfare and parallel Moore's own convictions. Since many of Moore's poems introduce conflict not only as a theme but as a principle of form, a summary of Moore's notes from Eisenstein may help to illuminate her poems. Eisenstein's theory is based on a simple assumption that synthesis is constantly arising in the process of opposition between thesis and antithesis. Conflict is thus the essence of art, in terms of its social function and in terms of its form. Art awakens conflict in the observer, forging new perceptions in the dynamic collision of contrasted passions. Conflict exists too between "natural existence" and "creative impulse." A new dialectical art emerges from "the logic of Organic form" against "the logic of Rational form." Juxtaposition of different "ideographic signs" is, of course, a major organizational principle in Eisenstein's notion of montage. Moore notes several instances in which Eisenstein uses language as a model, and one in particular is revealing in terms of her work. Her note reads: "in speech [. . .] the liveliness and dynamism arise fr[om] the irregularity of the detail in relation to the rule of the system as a whole." We have already seen these principles at work throughout Moore's poetry, in her love of dichotomy and oxymoron, in her way of playing off visual and aural organizations, in her shifts of perspective, diction, manner, and in her basic play between image and medium and between object and perceiver. What is important here is the explicit association between these techniques and the idea of combat. Conflict among and within different levels of organization is the essence of dynamic art. All Moore's "restraint," on a moral and an aesthetic level, involves the collision of style with style and thought with thought.

Another important contemporary theorist for Moore was Kenneth Burke, a colleague and friend who had written about her as she had about him. Their many exchanges, at parties and in the offices of *The Dial,* are recorded in Moore's notebooks. Metaphors of combat abound in Burke's *Permanence and Change,* a book Moore had read and admired, and there are important similarities in the way these two writers incorporate such metaphors.[8]

Burke's theory of epistemology and communication has three basic stages. The first is a state of unrecognized error, in which partial statements or orientations are mistaken for complete truths, limited systems are thought infallible. From this state (comparable to the collapsing system in Stevens's lament), Burke moves to an intermediate phase of crisis, in which two or more orientations collide (like Stevens's competing nationalities), producing contradictions in statement. Anticipating a recovery, Burke calls this intermediate phase "perspective by incongruity," its expressive form "stylistic gargoyles." Burke's third phase is a "new apprehension," which avoids the single-mindedness of the first phase, but also the violence of the second. This final stage preserves what he calls a "principle of recalcitrance" in the structure of statement, and its model, not surprisingly, is the ambiguity of poetry. Moore's poetry is not developed according to standard logic, of course, but her thought evolves around very similar distinctions. Criticizing the "uncompanionable drawl of certitude," reminding that "an aspect may deceive," her poetry is shot through with verbal collisions, which she resolves in the form of paradox and ambiguity. But both Moore and Burke have trouble keeping the second and third phases apart, and there is, in both, a certain willfulness in moving from crisis to dynamic equilibrium.

Certainly we can see the likeness between Burke's gargoyles and Moore's tuateras, pangolins, rhinoceroses, which cannot be absorbed into symmetry, which shock rather than reassure, which are in these ways emblems of her compositions. For both Moore and Burke, the solution is an incorporation and stabilization of the problem. Like Burke, Moore seeks a model of action motivated by desire that is not imperial. Since conquest truncates experience, she seeks attainment without closure, a model of thought in which impulses are freed but do not expire in formulation. Thus, along with Moore's developing motifs of armor and war, which contrast external and internal battle, are more paradoxes of failure as a requisite of continuance: "A mirror-of-steel uninsistence should countenance / continence . . . / There is the tarnish; and there, the imperishable wish" ("Armor's Undermining Modesty," CP, 152); "When that we hoped for came to nothing, we revived" ("Elephants," CP, 129).

But both Moore and Burke equivocate on whether the battle of decorums is compelled by their sense of some transcendent whole, or whether it is generated by the writer's own "rage for chaos." Is the motive sincerity or gusto? Burke at least admits his mixed motives: "Other decisions made at times of 'Crisis' (which is but Greek for 'judgment'), characteristically also involve an *unsettling*, an attempt (or temptation?) to think in ways to which the deliberator was not accustomed."[9] Making Burke her example, Moore observes in "Poetry and Criticism" that what to some authors are difficulties, the artist welcomes as opportunities.[10]

But the mind seeks permanence as well as change. It is no accident that Burke speaks of decorum as "piety"; his whole argument is built on the arc of conversion. Though he predicts a breakdown in one form of piety, he celebrates a "new system," with a built-in humility, in which man's language is no longer viewed as self-sufficient. To distinguish the "principle of recalcitrance" in the third phase of his system from the crisis of the middle phase, Burke, like Moore, reverts to a mode of grace. His secular grace involves a reversal of focus from the particular orders in conflict to the process of interpretation itself. His third phase is "the poetry of action" because it moves from a focus on the forms in a comparison to an emphasis on the motion of comparison itself; but to effect this transformation Burke requires a "poetic perspective" like Moore's. In these terms he can "resign to struggle" without crisis.

There are questions that may be put about Burke's and Moore's use of art as a model for society, of composition as a model for civilization. Both try to resolve the problems of the part and the whole by grasping simultaneously a personal and an historic perspective. But at just this moment (where Burke's "resimplification" is required) they face an impasse. The third phase (statement which includes an element of doubt), sounds like a converted version of the second (the critical state of doubt). It can easily open up again the plethora of perspectives that follow the crisis phase. We have already seen some of the moments in which Moore's language multiplies perspectives in response to an experience of otherness. Is there not something self-consciously delirious about this concluding passage in Burke, in which association threatens to become confusion, in which anything may stand for anything else?

> To this end we sought to trace the tie-up among manifestations of the ethical or creative impulse, which we here list more or less at random: orientation, rationalization, motivation, interpretation, verbalization, socialization, communication, expectancy, meaning, "illusion," occupational psychosis, trained incapacity, means-selecting, attention, "escape," style, sense of what goes with what, piety, propriety, property (tools and "shelter"), custom, ingratiation, inducement, "hypocrisy," ritual, right, virtue, power, utility, analogical extension, "peripheral charging," abstraction, logic, "cause," purpose, will, metaphor, perspective, "conversion," method, "nudism," point of view, statistics, symbolism, situation, simplification, prejudice, censoriousness, vocation, sympathy, "egoistic-altruistic merger," ethicizing of the means of support, inferiority, "burden," obsession, "genius," guilt, doubt, symbolic and necessitous labor, "justification," education, evangelism, legislation, action, combat, participation, ultimate situation or motive, ethical universe building, "opportunistic revision," and recalcitrance. Let us call the whole complex: civilization.[11]

What Moore does with places and names at the end of "People's Surroundings," Burke does with concepts here. In *Permanence and Change* Burke demonstrates remarkable control of his rivaling terms throughout the book's development. But charted in this way the path looks like a maze. Burke seems to applaud variety as the spice of life, but the variety begins to obscure all flavor. If this is "permanence" it is as unsettling as change.

Thematically, Moore attempts to convert an ethic of external aggression and defense to an ethic of internal warfare, or warfare against complacency of thought and feeling. We find a similar conversion of combat occurring on a formal level in her poems. Metaphors and strategies of collision in her poetry hold out a promise of coherence, for which broken language clears the way. This promise is presented when the flow and texture of the composition create a collusion of images that are referentially opposed. While the referential logic of the poem presents conflict, then, the compositional logic encompasses and stabilizes diversity, making adversities into conversities. By drawing us into the immediate formal coherence of the poem, Moore attempts to extend this coherence to a unified reference that transcends apparent conflict. But here she depends, finally, on a notion of grace, an ideal grace of presentness and an immediate grace of art.[12] Just as she asks us, thematically, to accept the aesthetic unity of armored surfaces as a synchronic model for functional stability, she asks us to accept the formal balances of her poems as signs of the ultimate coherence of her vision. Art becomes a symbolic shield against, and model for, the unwieldly flux of internal and external forces.

Of the poems that deal metaphorically with the war on self-interest and find aesthetic solutions, "Nevertheless" is probably the neatest. Perhaps it is too neat, disguising a difference between functional resemblances and metaphoric ones. There is something similarly contrived about the equanimity and cheerful resignation celebrated in "Elephants." In "The Paper Nautilus," however, Moore maintains a dynamic relationship between form and function, composition and reference, in which a stable form becomes the "souvenir" (rather than the solution) of a struggle. In "His Shield," which like "The Paper Nautilus" deals with internalizing struggle and converting the energy of conquest to nurture, form is again symbolic of function, and symbolic action offers an alternative to aggression. "The Pangolin" is the most inclusive of the poems that employ the metaphor of combat. Like "An Octopus," it draws many subjects and images into its loose analogy, as it records a process of mind. Here, more directly than in the other poems, Moore imports a notion of "grace" to secure the parallel between the conversities of form and the adversities of function. But again, such associations are made self-consciously, as ideal and imaginative rather than experiential counterparts. In each of these poems, Moore explores the relationship between the look of things and the history of things. This is often a wishful connection which assumes the reciprocity of synchronic and diachronic structures. In the best poems, however, the connection is always recognized as symbolic rather than real.

"Determination with resistance" is a central theme in Moore's verse, written into the very title of her volume *Nevertheless*. And it is the principle of recalcitrance that guides the volume's title poem. "Nevertheless" (CP, 125–126) (originally "It is Late, I Can Wait") is about struggle and survival. Though it does not deal explicitly with issues of war, they were obviously in Moore's mind, and many lines of the poem come directly from Moore's conversations with her mother about the world situation.[13] In tracing the history of struggle Moore manages an overview that assures continuity and puts loss in a perspective of process. The very breakdown of one form is the source of another.

> you've seen a strawberry
>   that's had a struggle; yet
>   was, where the fragments met,
>
> a hedgehog or a star-
>   fish for the multitude
>   of seeds.

The principle of recalcitrance is the seed of survival and continuance. The strawberry is transformed, and one form is a consolation for the loss of the other. The seeds magically convert vegetable to animal. But why hedgehog or starfish? The difference between these and the strawberry is more than visual. While the strawberry suggests something vulnerable, the hedgehog and starfish bear a kind of natural armor. The transformation strengthens; the "struggle" of the strawberry becomes part of its new identity—it retains a symbol of its history.

The term "seed" suggests to Moore a notion of growth, and she digresses:

> What better food
>
> than apple seeds—the fruit
>   within the fruit—locked in
>   like counter-curved twin
>
> hazelnuts?

Oppositions here, as in marriage, are internalized to promote growth. The strawberry's struggle and subsequent transformation are part of a natural process, not to be regretted. As examples continue, each transformed object has an aspect of armor as a mark of survival: "carrots form mandrakes or a ram's-horn root some- / times," "a grape tendril ties a knot in knots till knotted thirty times—so / the bound twig that is under- / gone and over-gone, can't stir." The final slogan of the poem is "the weak overcomes its / menace, the strong over- / comes itself." Transformation is at one with survival.

But there is a large imaginative leap involved in seeing a distorted strawberry as a hedgehog or a starfish, a mutation in a carrot as a "ram's-horn." Analogy here creates an order not found in nature; this is only a myth of metamorphosis, depending on the observer's desire. Poetry is especially privileged in using transformation as a means of survival and stabilization. The world is less manageable.

Sometimes Moore's acceptance of conflict from a perspective of poise comes out directly as stoicism, as in "Elephants" (CP, 128–130) (also in *Nevertheless* and also inspired in part by conversations with her mother), a poem about humility and service.

> Uplifted and waved till immobilized
> wistaria-like, the opposing opposed
> mouse-gray twined proboscises' trunk formed by two
> trunks, fights itself to a spiraled inter-nosed
>
> deadlock of dyke-enforced massiveness.

This description is tense with oxymoron, and the scene it describes is appropriately one of creaturely combat, of "matched intensities." Throughout Moore's poetry we find such combat converted to images of reciprocity. Here what looks like combat is, we are assured, not "a knock-down-drag-out fight that asks no quarter" but "just a pastime." Combat is sweetened. The poem goes on to challenge our tendency to see power in terms of force, stressing a gentleness accompanying the might of the elephants. We have already seen such juxtapositions of power and delicacy in "An Octopus." It is made especially dynamic in "Elephants" since an image of man, as a kind of surrogate for the reader, is placed in the path of the battle. As in "An Octopus" our ethnocentrism is deflated when "the feather light mahout" is "asleep like a lifeless six foot frog" cradled by the beast.

The poem gradually turns its focus to another kind of struggle, a struggle for knowledge, taken up directly in terms of the action of the poem in its effort to describe. In the midst of the "warfare of imagination and medium" the poet exclaims: "As if, as if, it is all as if's; we are at / much unease." The elephant, however, accepts uncertainty, "serenity quelling his fears." At this point in the poem elephants become images of Buddhist or Socratic unknowing—the intellectual equivalent of physical restraint. In Moore's best poems such passivity is passionate, but here it is too wholly based on the negative virtues of quiet despair, defeat, and servility. "A prisoner of life, but reconciled." There is something too willful about Moore's admittedly witty pun on "Sophocles the Bee, on whose / tombstone a hive was incised, sweetness tinctures / his gravity." As she says herself (though without negative connotation) "equanimity's contrived by the elephant"—it is not, I would add, natural.

Moore's morality of armor has troubled a number of critics, particularly advocates of sincerity, who see the armor as a way of protecting the self against the conflict and judgment of the world. Indeed, lines like "a prisoner of life, but reconciled," or "deference will be my defense" or "his shield was his humility" do not (in isolation) convince us of the inner fortitude of the speaker. These seem to be negative virtues, retreats from the pressure of reality rather than counterforces. At worst the speaker's will seems to atrophy. But we need to identify the full complexity of Moore's idea of sincerity as armor, what she calls in "Walking Sticks and Paperweights and Watermarks" "sincere unforced unconscious honesty / *sine cera* can be furthest / from self-defensiveness and nearest." Often an apparent dispassion retains the energy of restrained emotion. Moore's best poems give the feeling of surging spiritual and emotional energy. This is precisely the quality Moore depicts in "The Hero" and "The Student." In the latter she writes that the student seems reclusive "not because he / has no feeling but because he has so much."

Moore's ethos and aesthetic of sacrifice ("precision," she notes, means "cutting before") usually manages simultaneously to imply substantial power. "If illusions of magnitude could be transmuted into ideals of magnanimity, peace might be realized." And she insists, "magnanimity is not a negative virtue."[14] It is not the loss of energy or power, but their conversion to a form in which they are never exhausted.

"The Paper Nautilus" is about such tense poise, achieved through restraint and magnanimity, not through surrender. Moore seems to agree with Claude Bragdon, whom she quotes in her "Comment" on international peace, that we need "the feminine ideal"—"the compassional," not "the forceful."[15] For Moore the female was not weak in expressing power by love rather than by aggression.

Maternity is the subject of "The Paper Nautilus" (CP, 121–122), and in comparing maternity to poetry Moore alters the conventional view of both. We conventionally think of maternal affection as a soft, graceful attitude, and Moore's poetry has been prized (with condescension), for its "relaxed ease."[16] But the poem describes the process of nurture as a struggle beneath an apparent gentleness. As always, Moore directly associates these issues of protection and struggle with problems of language and interpretation. Her ideal language announces its finitude in addressing infinite matters, offers itself as a vehicle not as a tenor, a shell in which our impression of the world can take shape without calcifying. "The Paper Nautilus" takes up this idea directly through the image of a shell as a vehicle, a "nautilus." The poem stresses the need in the end to release the object of thought from the structure that has borne it. The poem starts by distinguishing *kinds* of forms—those which are complacent or commercial, which "entrap" the writer as well as his audience, and some other, better kind. Appropriately, Moore will not "entrap" herself and her subject by telling us directly what this other kind is. Rather, after an initial reference to writers, she introduces a metaphor for metaphor itself. Language can never purely embody either the writer's feelings toward her object nor the object itself. It remains a "perishable souvenir of hope," a "thin glass shell," a sign of both subject and object and the trace of their contact. Though the paper nautilus is "hindered to succeed" in possessing the sea into which her offspring must finally venture, the shell in which she nurtures that offspring has a "smooth- / edged inner surface / glossy as the sea," which can suggest the world without.

The poem describes the creative process as a highly precarious restraint of energy. The health of the eggs somehow depends upon maximum power and maximum restraint. In the juxtapositions of "the ram's-horn-cradled freight," and a "devil-fish" and her eggs, of the shell's relative delicacy (like a wasp's nest) and of its strength (like Ionic columns and the force of Parthenon sculpture), we grit our teeth. The tension that occurs when we imagine holding back Hercules is clarified—but not relieved—in the notion of a "fortress of love." Here we have maximum impulse to action without the expiration of energy in action. The paper nautilus must "hide" her "freight" but not "crush" it, and so must poets.

The poem is about detachment as well as power. Both seem to be requisites of "freedom." Thus "the intensively watched eggs coming from / the shell free it when they are freed." Freedom requires differentiation. The imagination grows beyond the structures that nurture it. And yet the separation leaves a scar, a flaw in the shell that marks the former connection:

> leaving its wasp-nest flaws
> of white on white, and close-
>
> laid Ionic chiton-folds
> like the lines in the mane of
> a Parthenon horse,
> round which the arms had
> wound themselves . . .

White on white marks barely a difference, but a difference nonetheless. Insofar as the shell is a poem (and the reference to writers at the opening of the poem suggests this link) the flaw defines the "place for the genuine" that Moore is concerned to preserve. The shell is not interesting for itself, then, but as a souvenir of desire and struggle.

The ability "to relinquish what one would keep" is again the theme of "His Shield" (CP, 144) (in manuscript called "The Magic Shield"), and here the strength of humility is expressed in displays of untapped riches. The poem, borrowing from medieval legend, describes a utopia and its philosopher-king, who rules by restraining his power. Adapting a detail from the legend, in which this king is said to wear the fire-proof skin of the salamander, Moore bestows upon him all the elusive power of her other lizards, her basilisks and chameleons. "Presbyter John," the lizard-priest of the poem, is paradoxically the monarch of humility, and of power restrained:

> The pin-swin or spine-swine
>   (the edgehog miscalled hedgehog) with all his edges out,
>   echidna and echinoderm in distressed-
> pin-cushion thorn-fur coats, the spiny pig or porcupine,
>   the rhino with horned snout—
>   everything is battle-dressed.

Pig-fur won't do, I'll wrap
    myself in salamander-skin like Presbyter John.

Moore presents a dynamic utopia based on turning combat inward. Fire is a sign both for the lizard and for what he must endure: "A lizard in the midst of flames / a firebrand that is life . . . / asbestos-eyed asbestos-eared," can burn perpetually, fending off his own consuming ego. "His shield is his humility."

One kind of power involves self-imposing conquest, "greed and flattery," "envy," and "a measuring rod," which has no sense of otherness. But energy is also generated out of a perpetually perceived difference between oneself and the world, and the preservation of that difference. The former results in satiation, the latter in "unpompous gusto." Gusto, it seems, involves an "inextinguishable" energy and desire toward that which is "unconquerable."[17] But how do we stabilize this energy? How can such intense and unsatisfied desire be utopian? "The power of relinquishing / what one would keep; that is freedom." How can it be?

                    Though rubies large as tennis
    balls conjoined in streams so
  that the mountain seemed to bleed,

  the inextinguishable
    salamander styled himself but presbyter.

A presbyter's power is dispersed, invested in the community, and hidden. But we know of this power, which can potentially be collected and exerted toward conquest, through an aestheticized emblem of the effects of power. The mountain only *seems* to bleed, but in doing so it marks a potential encounter. Emblematized strength is perpetual, whereas exerted strength expires.

Humility for Moore does not mean the suppression or denial of power but the conversion of power from a conquest to an apprehension of the world. As Burke remarks, peace and war are continuous, and structurally similar. Life depends, as Stevens suggests, on a war that never ends, a balance of contention, in the world, in the imagination, and between these. As long as the contention is balanced, the mountain only *seems* to bleed. In peace the stream of blood is only the bloodstream, more than an emblem of vitality.

Moore admires the pangolin's armor for its usefulness and its beauty. Indeed, the language of "The Pangolin" (CP, 117–120) moves between these two aspects, sometimes attending to the efficiency and sometimes to the elegance of this protective covering. The task of the poem is to discover their connection. She finds it in any interplay between synchronic and diachronic structures.

> Another armored animal—scale
>> lapping scale with spruce-cone regularity until they
> form the uninterrupted central
>> tail-row! This near artichoke with head and legs and grit-
>>> equipped gizzard,
>>> the night miniature artist engineer is,
>>> yes, Leonardo da Vinci's replica—
>>>> impressive animal and toiler of whom we seldom hear.

The method and focus of this poem recall many of the earlier descriptive poems discussed in Chapter 3. The poem sets out to describe the combative qualities of an "armored animal," and these invite comparison with man's combativeness. The poem also confronts the problems of accurate perception, introducing rival categories of description and contending impulses in the observer of what to watch, of whether to describe or compare. In making an analogy between pangolin and man, the poem confronts several other conflicts: between sign and meaning, between the two terms of the analogy, between the limited perspective of comparison and the multiplicity of the objects compared—all of which finally suggest a more fundamental conflict between subject and object, between the observer-writer and the object of her attention. What Moore shows us in the struggle of the pangolin is repeated in her own poetic behavior. The problem the poem poses, in part, is how to stabilize the struggle, how to make it graceful, and the pangolin becomes the model for her solution.

The speaker of the poem rushes to identify the object before her, and immediately her attention is divided between the visual qualities of the surface and the *meaning* of that surface. The very act of calling the pangolin's scales "armor" interprets their qualities, but whereas armor ordinarily evokes ideas of aggression, the speaker immediately becomes interested in design, in the "spruce-cone regularity," the "artichoke"-like organization of the scales. Design suggests a designer, the "artist-engineer" Leonardo Da Vinci, so that the pangolin is seen as a replica both of the artist-struggler and of his symmetrical art. The poem opens with this deluge of descriptive images not yet unified.

We expect an analogy to develop between the pangolin and some aspect of man's life, but at this stage the poem seems more to oppose than to associate the two sides of the analogy. Man moves from dawn to dusk, the pangolin from dusk to dawn.

> Armor seems extra. But for him,
>   the closing ear-ridge—
>   or bare ear lacking even this small
>   eminence and similarly safe
>
> contracting nose and eye apertures
>   impenetrably closable, are not

Already Moore has placed not only metaphors but kinds of language, metaphoric and scientific, in uneasy conjunction. The poem is constructed of dichotomies and oxymorons. The pangolin is "a true ant-eater, not cock-roach eater." Though "serpentined about a tree" he is "unpugnacious," his "hiss" is "harmless." These are examples of power restrained. And as if to imitate this concept the speaker's aggressive acts of interpretation cease and she becomes careful to make distinctions before leaping forward too eagerly. As the pangolin "rolls into a ball" we sense that the creature is both literally and figuratively drawing into himself and that the speaker's "efforts to unroll it" are in vain. The language becomes curt and matter of fact; all analogy drops out, or seems. to. Apparently in the battle between subject and object (the speaker of the poem imposing the definitions and the object resisting them), the object has won the first round. Here the pangolin seems to be his unique self, not *like* anything else.

> strongly intailed, neat
> head for core, on neck not breaking off, with curled-in feet.
>   Nevertheless he has sting-proof scales; and nest
>   of rocks closed with earth from inside, which he can thus
>   darken.

Trying to find out what the pangolin "entails" the speaker finds it all the more "intailed."

As analogy ceases to function on one level it is restored on another: the interiority of the pangolin is both literal and figurative. Similarly the elaborate twistings and counterbalances earlier in the language of the poem made a design not unlike the wrought-iron vine the pangoline resembles. Now, as we look at the speaker looking at the pangolin, the animal's withdrawal becomes an emblem or analogy for the very breakdown of analogy (the retreat of the object into its individuality). In these terms the process of making analogies itself is the mode of attack the pangolin defends himself against. The creature will not be "set aside."

In the first section of the poem the speaker moved from testing out human comparisons and definitions of the pangolin to delighting in the sheer process of circumspection, the curves and counter curves of that study. But now that the pangolin has "darkened" himself and left the speaker literally speechless over his ingenuity, the speaker transfers her energy from description and definition to pure admiration. The poem and its objects are disengaged for a moment. It is a declaration of impotence, of the inviolability of things, but the tone is excited, not disheartened:

> Sun and moon and day and night and man and beast
>   each with a splendor
>   which man in all his vileness cannot
>   set aside; each with an excellence!

The "vileness" to which this stanza refers is not only man's martial instinct but also his intellectual one. The pangolin escapes both our physical and our interpretive grasp. But this is admiration not only of the pangolin, the apparent subject of the poem, but of all the images that have been brought in; "sun and moon and day and night and man and beast" were all part of the scenes described above. And curiously, man is on both sides of the concern, as intruder and object of intrusion. What has this ejaculation to do with the poem, a description of the pangolin? Perhaps it has some relation to acts of association and observation. To make analogy genuine, the speaker must go through a phase of self-examination, finding the example of man in his own behavior.

After the contraction, of the pangolin and of the language, comes another expansion. In the next stanza the speaker again sallies forth with description but with more images that suggest his own activity. From a temporary cheerful defeat, a temporary retreat into self-reflection, the speaker, like the pangolin, prepares for the next onset. The pangolin that was primarily an object of attack is now an advancer:

"Fearful yet to be feared," the armored
    ant-eater met by the driver-ant does not turn back, but
engulfs what he can, the flattened sword-
    edged leafpoints on the tail and artichoke set leg- and body-
                                       plates
    quivering violently when it retaliates
    and swarms on him.

Here we have not only a return to the description of the pangolin (and to the double armor-artichoke image used to describe him) but more images for the action of man and specifically for the writing of the poem, the tail reminiscent of the quivering pen, though nonetheless a tail. Like the pangolin, the writer "engulfs what he can," the form of his poem "quivering" as the recalcitrant details on the pangolin's reality "swarm on him."

           The giant-pangolin-
    tail, graceful tool, as prop or hand or broom or ax, tipped like
an elephant's trunk with special skin,
    is not lost on this ant- and stone-swallowing uninjurable
    artichoke which simpletons thought a living fable
        whom the stones had nourished, whereas ants had done
        so. Pangolins are not aggressive animals; between
        dusk and day they have the not unchain-like machine-like
        form and frictionless creep of a thing
        made graceful by adversities, con-

    versities.

Simpletons (and reductivists) impose their theories on the subject and err. Now the language of description, in an act of relative modesty like the pangolin's, approximates the observation; it is a "not unchain-like machine-like form." But like the pangolin, the poem is made graceful by adversities. The series of efforts and errors promises to leave a graceful pattern.

    It is difficult to establish a hierarchy of interests in this poem. No single principle of comparison seems to dominate. Rather, associative links are local and various, some sound-determined, some visual, some conceptual, and these do not immediately reinforce one another. The pleasure of the poem is in its overlappings, like the scales of the pangolin it sets out to describe. The notion of "grace," for instance, suggested by the pangolin's movement and appearance, divert's the speaker's attention to other modes of grace, specifically with regard to artistic creation:

> To explain grace requires
>   a curious hand. If that which is at all were not forever,
>   why would those who graced the spires
>   with animals and gathered there to rest, on cold luxurious
>   low stone seats—a monk and monk and monk—between the
>   thus
>   ingenious roof supports, have slaved to confuse
>   grace with a kindly manner, time in which to pay a
>   debt,
>   the cure for sins, a graceful use
>   of what are yet
>   approved stone mullions branching out across
>   the perpendiculars?

The transition from the grace of the pangolin to the grace of the church seems an unwarranted digression. On the slim axis of "grace" the poem inverts the terms of the analogy. The speaker has completely abandoned her original task of description and turned to another topic. And yet as she proceeds to quite another subject the same method of description recurs. The image of the pangolin is gone but its figurative and formal traces remain. Early the pangolin was compared to the Abbey gate. Now the poem focuses fully on the Abbey itself, recalling in its description the contours of the pangolin. The grace of the pangolin's scales and its graceful attitude are now the formal and moral grace of a human construction, the church. Is this the fulfillment of the implied promise of an unpugnacious human armor, offered earlier? Man's art is like the pangolin's form (a comparison already hinted at, playfully, not only in the Da Vinci analogy but in the repetitions of the term "artichoke"). The pattern of the pangolin's scales is like the repetitions in the stone mullions and relief sculptures on the cathedral. And just as the pangolin's scales are the shield he uses in his struggle to survive "from dusk to dawn," these architectural forms provide a kind of "shield" for man against the vicissitudes of time.

The "grace" of the cathedral is not purely formal and static. It is a "sign" of man's struggle and of intervening grace. The pattern of the scales becomes the factor of resemblance throughout the rest of the poem. It unites the grace of the architecture (patterned as "a monk and monk and monk") and the grace of the poem (with its pattern of repetitions). But what is initially a spatial metaphor becomes a temporal one as well. That is, the repetitions of the pangolin's scales and the church mullions stand for temporal repetitions, for a process. Now it is clearer why Moore continually played off temporal and spatial qualities. At the end of the poem we are introduced to the architecture of human history ("and new and new and new") played against the spatial arrangement of "monk and monk and monk." This encompassing "process" of adversity (human struggle) includes the struggle of creation, specifically that of writing. The sense of temporal struggle and the sense of spatial design are finally united in the poem when the speaker suggests that "that which is at all" "is forever." What is trial and error from a temporal point of view is symmetry from a spatial point of view, as each monk lives and dies and lines up along stone mullions. As we view these monks "branching out across the perpendicular" we are reminded that Moore's notion of grace is bound to the Christian paradox embodied in the cross as the intersection of time and eternity. But she writes entirely from the human perspective, in which the struggles of life are only *symbolically* resolved into harmonies.

Art provides a kind of double shield, for when we consider the imperfections of any human form we can imagine a process that may correct those imperfections, "time in which to pay a debt." Conversely, when we become exhausted with the sense of endless trial and error, of endless process, we can consider the pattern our lives have established, can imagine a spatial stability in repetition. Both perspectives imply a notion of grace, however, and grace is an ambiguous word here. Is it grace from without or grace generated by the patterns? In any case these are "ingratiating" forms.

As we read it becomes clear that the phrase "to explain grace requires a curious hand" is more than a suspended comment or superficial link; rather it is a governing principle of what has come before and what will come after. Both "grace" and "curious" are reciprocal words, providing a kind of connective link between the various orders of concern in the poem. The pangolin is curious to us and curious himself, just as the hand that defines the pangolin is itself observing and observed. Similarly "grace" itself has two meanings in friction with each other which are reconciled (two points of view, divine and human, which describe an alternating subject-object relation). The adversity between a writer and his object, a pangolin and his object, is reconciled in the pattern of repetitions that action itself produces when viewed as a whole. Grace occurs when that process can be conceived of as a totality. So the grace of the author becomes the grace of his product, given the grace of the reader in allowing that transmission. Subjectivity and objectivity become as two sides of the same coin, or two pangolin scales side by side defining a symmetry. So too the Abbey is both a symbol of man's limit (his need for intervening grace) and his power (as a graceful "artist-engineer"). He makes the best of conflict, he creates dialectical compositions. The mortal monks take their place among immortal stones. If we now recall the initial conflict of associations of armor and design in description of the pangolin scales, we can see that though these seemed to move in opposite directions, they are now reconciled.

We have seen the analogy of the pangolin with man pivoting in a description of a cathedral. Now the poem moves directly into the second term of the analogy, man and his struggles. As the pangolin embodied both synchronic and diachronic structures, the church architecture embodies the human version of synchronic ones, and Moore now turns to man in series, in history. But in shifting her weight to the second term of the analogy, she still totters.

A sailboat

was the first machine. Pangolins, made
for moving quietly also, are models of exactness,
on four legs; on hind feet plantigrade,
with certain postures of a man. Beneath sun and moon,
man slaving
to make his life more sweet, leaves half the flowers worth
having,
needing to choose wisely how to use his strength;
a paper-maker like the wasp; a tractor of foodstuffs,
like the ant; spidering a length
of web from bluffs
above a stream; in fighting, mechanicked
like the pangolin; capsizing in

disheartenment.

The rest of the poem will directly concern man, but the pangolin is transfused in the description of man just as man was earlier transfused in the description of the pangolin. Indeed, man is described in terms of the animal world: "there he sits in his own habitat." The poem itself has "capsized" its subject matter, but not in disheartenment. The expression of failure here provides the materials for success. This is a poem about trial and error:

> Bedizened or stark
> naked, man, the self, the being we call human, writing-
> master to this world, griffons a dark
> "Like does not like like that is obnoxious"; and writes error
> with four
> r's.

The "struggle" draws directly into questions of writing, of this writing, which is based on "likeness." But the sense of man's fallibility does not discourage the speaker because "among animals, *one* has a sense of humor." The central embarrassments of writing are met with this consolation: that we can stand aside and look at our errors even if we cannot avoid them in action. The poem does not conclude in precise definition or in resignation, only in the celebration of process. Similarly Moore celebrates the pangolin's adventures, for which his scales are a sign and protection, and the struggle of "monk and monk and monk" now "laid out across stone mullions" in a monument to their efforts and to intervening grace. Throughout the poem she assumes the possibility of some intervening force that can steady her in the flux of life and thought.

> The prey of fear, he, always
> curtailed, extinguished, thwarted by the dusk, work partly
> done,
> says to the alternating blaze,
> "Again the sun!
> anew each day; and new and new and new,
> that comes into and steadies my soul."

The poem opens and closes in exclamatory language, creating a kind of arc between. Though the speaker's work of interpretation remains "partly done," she can rejoice at the process of vision and revision she has pursued. (It is worth noting that this is a willful perspective whose opposite is "tomorrow and tomorrow and tomorrow.")[18] Finally life can be seen as a grand composition, and this becomes a "steadying" influence.

"The Pangolin" is a long circuitous poem with an elaborately disguised structure. My argument about it, in following its curves, has also been long and circuitous. It will be useful to summarize the relationships among some features of the poem, keeping in mind that they are not experienced reductively. Explicitly and implicitly the poem is about armor and about grace—its task is to find the union of these. In the image of the pangolin we find the union in seeing the scales at once as a sign of the animal's maneuvers and as aesthetically pleasing in themselves. We move to finding the maneuvers aesthetically pleasing, the adversities of combat repeating temporally the permanent pattern of the scales. Adversities are seen as conversities, and moral and aesthetic perspectives are brought together in a notion of grace. The double perspective on the pangolin is followd by an analogy with man, who must incorporate armor and art. Man's struggle through life (or with any specific effort) establishes a pattern which art encompasses as a monument to life. Temporal and spatial patterns converge in our experience.

But for Moore to make such an assertion complacently would be to deny the very process of assertion and contradiction she explicitly identifies as human at the end of the poem. She avoids complacency in several ways. She balances the equation of pangolin and man so that neither side of the analogy seems dominant. Man must determine her ultimate perspective, of course, but by inverting the analogy she leaves ambiguous our attitude toward man's efforts. He is simultaneously a graceful and an ironic creature. By variously making the pangolin analogy bear on her writing (on its action and shape) she includes herself in the group "made graceful by adversity, conversity." She does not settle for a dialectic of aesthetic and martial interests resolved in a figure that fuses them. We do not take the analogy of pangolin with man for granted. Rather, the dialectic forces its way into the very terms of the analogy so that even the bond between pangolin and man is revealed as a tentative, highly artificial one, making the assertions of the poem similarly tentative and contingent. But while the resemblance between man and pangolin is placed in doubt, the pattern of differences that formed it is maintained even by seeing them as rival orders. That is, the perspectives that prove the pangolin *unlike* man work in relation to those that prove him *like* man, to make a poem of counterbalances, just as the conflicts in the pangolin's adventures are told as a story in the scales, and the conflicts in man's adventures are told as a story in the design of his cathedrals.

In "The Pangolin" both the extremes of heroism and the extremes of tragedy are absent. The dichotomies in man's nature are not violent. Man has, after all, been described through the analogy of the pangolin, so that the paradoxes of his existence are lightened. The poem is not fully given over to the flux it celebrates, for beneath the rapid movement from one image or subject to the next there is a highly organized conceptual base, which is reinforced by unaccented rhyme, rhythmic repetitions, and syllabic form. Again, the formal harmonies promise to resolve the flux and contradiction within the referential function of the poem. Indeed, part of the excitement of poetry is this play between synchronic and diachronic structures. It is the only place where time and eternity are one and loss is gain.

All the poems I have discussed in this chapter deal with modes of combat, and all suggest ways of converting combat to a positive end, thus converting anxiety to gusto. As Burke suggested of his own work, "it is a book such as authors in those days sometimes put together, to keep themselves from falling apart." As Moore once commented in a reading, "art can't resolve human tragedy—it's a defense against it."

While Moore insists continually that the imposition of forms is in need of resistance, we see that they can also be the means of mitigating the experience of flux, can be the means of self-possession and self-location. Objects are thrown against our advance; it is through collision that we learn of them. Moore's ambivalence about conquest is revealed most clearly in her style, which presents a superficial appearance of flux and free association and disguises an elaborate thematic and formal structure. All the poems I have discussed here are inconspicuously rhymed, their stanzas ordered by syllable count. Antithesis, pun, parallelism, further unite formal and thematic structures. Certainly the principle of recalcitrance is everywhere alive in these poems, in guarding against too rigid a formal or thematic frame (through unaccented rhymes, inverted syntax, inverted analogies, and omitted connectives, for instance). But the recalcitrance is granted authority by the very demonstration of control in the poems' unities. Finding herself unable to order experience, Moore makes failures of order a life-supporting good and produces orders that both define this position and provide respites from it.

Moore made this relationship between struggle and harmony explicit in her comment on universal harmony in aesthetics, which I quoted in the first chapter.[19] While artists struggle with each other they are confirming a unified, enduring tradition, and while the artist struggles with his medium he is creating harmonious forms. "Determination with resistance," for Moore, always "results in poise," at least in art, for "wherever there is art there is equilibrium."

5. Fluctuating Charms
Images of Luminosity, Iridescence, and Metamorphosis

I F MOORE DISDAINS the showy brilliance of the suave young novices, the armor of her animals is no less shining. But as the war is turned inward, the glow is beneath the surface. The paper nautilus has a "dull / white outside" but "a smooth- / edged inner surface / glossy as the sea." Its light is inherent, not reflected. These creatures wear the armor of humility precisely because of the treasures they harbor. "Be / dull; don't be envied or / armed with a measuring rod" is the motto of that "unconquerable country of unpompous gusto" which contains "rubies large as tennis / balls." But the eye sensitive to the spark of difference can see the glow camouflaged in the apparent uniform dullness of the world.

In a lecture at Bryn Mawr (February 10, 1953), Moore quoted Wallace Stevens: "Poetry is a happiness . . . in which the intangible is more real than the visible." This is a surprising remark to be embraced by a poet famed for her real toads and relentless accuracies, but it confirms Stevens's suggestion that Moore digests "the 'harde yron' of appearance." Moore goes on in her lecture to quote Lawrence Binyon (also admired by Pound) on the Chinese masters: "art is a conquest of matter by spirit."[1]

But if "the power of the visible is the invisible," ("a message," she tells us in "He Digesteth Harde Yron," which is "missed by the externalist" (CP, 99), it is still only through the visible that we gain access to spiritual presences. Spiritual brilliances are "transformed / into an invisible / fabric of inconsistency / motheaten by self-subtractiveness— / now as outright murderers and thieves, / thrive openly" (WY, 10), are sensed in the stir and sheen of surfaces. Indeed, their concealment is part of their allure, as Moore's note from George Santayana suggests: "nothing absorbs the consciousness so much as that which is not quite given." Conversely, a shimmer across the surface of life can *imply* a source beneath it.

Moore is not the only modernist poet to use metaphors of luminosity to describe moments of transcendence. Pound's "luminous detail" and Williams's "radiant gist" are part of a similar imaginative configuration, which invests the natural particular with an infinite or eternal dimension and converts matter to energy. Such images are most conspicuous in the work of Stevens, though his figures lack the concreteness visible in Williams or Moore. For Moore, Stevens is "America's chief conjurer," in giving the familiar an unfamiliar air. Whether his words are divine revelation or inspired hocus pocus matters little. He makes the world more interesting, tears the veil of dejection. He does this, in part, precisely by veiling his subjects, creating an illusion of the infinite, or destroying the illusion of the finite: "a poet may be a wall of incorruptibleness against violating the essential aura of contributory vagueness."[2] Moore's description of Stevens's style fits the concealedness of her own creatures, whose armor—which includes various kinds of camouflage, metamorphosis, veils—not only protects but also tantalizes. Moore delights in the aura of vagueness that envelopes nature, an aura she inherits, clearly, from romanticism.

In the essay "A Poet That Matters" Stevens argues for reading Moore as a romantic poet.[3] He first proposed this theory in a letter to T. C. Wilson (March 25, 1935). "Miss Moore is endeavoring to create a new romantic . . . the thing in which she is interested in all the strange collocations of her work is that which is essential to poetry always: the romantic. But a fresh romantic."[4]

Moore's romanticism is not apparelled in celestial light. And she is not in quest of an impossible possible philosopher's man, only "piercing glances into the life of things"—butterflies, chameleons, jellyfish. They belong to an ambiguous genus, sliding freely between the natural and the supernatural, overlapping with the mythical strangeness of unicorns, dragons, and fairies. Moore approaches these enchanting creatures, which can be sensed but not touched, with a principle of negative capability defined by Kenneth Burke: "in this realm things reached for will evade, but will follow the hand as it recedes."[5] With Stevens she insists, "he that has only clear ideas is surely a Fool."[6] In style and statement Moore's poems of iridescence and metamorphosis maintain an "aura of contributory vagueness" about the level of abstraction at which they are operating.

Combat, as we saw in the last chapter, is intrinsic to the structure of Moore's poetry. An orthodox orientation of the mind to the world risks blindness and boredom. Sincerity leads to a crisis of interpretation, where multiple perspectives struggle for dominance and disrupt the flow of logic, producing a reaction of excitement and stress. But the mind cannot remain in this state of crisis—it must make an adjustment of some kind, find a poetic unity to replace the shattered one. The struggle is absorbed and legitimized in the figures of elusive natural creatures. We become less concerned with a conflict of perspectives than with fluctuation or oscillation as an inherent quality of an object we are observing. The indeterminacy of the object becomes less a problem to be overcome than an element of significance in identifying the object. Thus there is no longer a problem of plurality in the ways we can see or describe something, for this plurality centers around a single focus of desire, a creature (chameleon, butterfly, jellyfish) or an object (prism, flame, opal) that shimmers with varying color, or changes form at will. The mind is compelled to seek out the principle of unity that controls the diversity of the object, but fails and is "dazzled into a kind of stupor."[7]

Through the related qualities of luminosity, phosphorescence, iridescence, and metamorphosis (as the temporal equivalent of iridescence) Moore suggests the invisible power of the visible.[8] First, Moore's dialectic of presence and absence—flashes of appearance and disappearance, dithering luminosities—creates an ambiguity about the identity of her subjects—whether they are real or imagined, particular or abstract, natural or supernatural. This ambiguity is reinforced in Moore's delicate alternation of metonymic and metaphoric levels of representation. Second, the qualities of iridescence, and its temporal counterpart, metamorphosis, are figures for a multiplicity the rational mind cannot order. Third, iridescence and prismatic color, signifying a unity within apparent multiplicity, are usually associated, in Moore, with a sense of origins behind representations and derivatives. Fourth, Moore represents the resistance of these origins to our rational grasp with a pattern of recalcitrance in her figures and her form. Her elusive basilisks, chameleons, jellyfish, and the poems that reciprocate their movements, are the perfect analogues of Burke's third phase of orientation with its built-in principle of recalcitrance. Finally, the dialectic, of presence and absence, concealment and unconcealment, quickens the mind to attention and enthusiasm, or, as Moore puts it (and as Burke might have), "astonishment rather than enthusiasm, becasue the latter implies affirmation and prejudices in favor."[9] Moore is not a poet of monumental gestures, vistas, and emotions, but out of the shimmering minutiae of nature, she creates a version of the sublime.[10]

Of all Moore's elusive creatures, "The Plumet Basilisk" (CP, 20–24) is one of the most alluring. He inhabits the exotic border between the natural and the spiritual and teases the reader across, to find the unified identity controlling his various camouflages. The long poem represents a repeatedly thwarted effort to conceptualize the dynamic figure. Moore also wrote several short poems using similar figures, notably "To a Chameleon," "A Jellyfish," and "O to Be a Dragon," which, like her epigrams, bring the drama of this imaginative pursuit into sudden focus. "A Jellyfish," written in the second person, attempts to look at enchantment from a distance, as does "Snakes, Mongooses, Snake Charmers and the Like." But both of these poems suggest that enchantment is contagious. All of these poems describe the mind in pursuit of something a little beyond its grasp. But enchantment requires not only ambition but restraint and humility, as Moore suggests in "Sea Unicorns and Land Unicorns," "St. Nicholas," and "Spenser's Ireland." In all of these the imagination finds its satisfactions in a "supreme belief" beyond the possessive will of conscious fastidiousness. The enchanted mind can partake of original power without the proof of circumstance. Moore assigns the qualities of iridescence, luminosity, metamorphosis to a broad range of phenomena—in nature, in literature, in art, in music, even in the mind. Thus Disraeli is a "chameleon." A shining French brocade reminds her of "some lizard in the shade become exact" or a miniature painting of Sidney. The language with which Moore describes watching a Mozart opera on color television in "Logic and the Magic Flute" and the language she uses to describe the enchanting and enchanted movements of the mind in "The Mind is an Enchanting Thing" are almost interchangeable with her descriptions of nature. The enchanted mind, it seems, always hovers between the real and the imaginary, the concrete and the abstract, the visible and the invisible.

Luminosity is a metaphor of immanence in modern literature, of truth shining through its representations. And "truth" is connected with the thing itself. In Susan Sontag's words, "transparence is the highest, most liberating value in art—and in criticism—today . . . transparence means experiencing the luminousness of the thing in itself, of things being what they are."[11] But in Moore we find translucence, a veiled luminosity, so that the urgent "presence" is never entirely revealed. On the other hand, Moore shows no solid confidence in a reality outside the poem giving authority to her metaphors, leading beyond the translucence to an empirical or a transcendent goal. We are left with an awakened sense of something "beyond" the representation, but with no direction by which to account for that exxperience. Moore's poetry holds out the possibility that this magical presence is really the presence of the text itself, as a construct of the imagination. The Wizard of Oz may be just a man behind a screen. Quoting Joseph Conrad in her essay *Poetry and Criticism*, she equivocates on whether the "invisible world" is anything more than creativity itself: " 'Seeing, and saying;—language is a special extension of the power of seeing, inasmuch as it can make visible not only the already visible world; but through it the invisible world of relations and affinities.' The world of the soul? Difficient as it is to define the soul, 'creativeness' is perhaps as near a definition as we can get."[12]

From the ample fund of facts in "The Plumet Basilisk" one would expect to have a fairly concrete idea of the creature. We know its habitat, its markings, its behavior patterns, even its place in the broader family of lizards.[13] But the metaphors Moore chooses to characterize the basilisk tend to increase its abstractness. The more details are compounded, the more the creature seems to recede, until his empirical reality is altogether in doubt. The poem encourages us to follow the basilisk's scent, only to flout our efforts by revealing the metaphorical nature of that image, and thus the discontinuity between the image and what it represents.

From the outset problems arise in our attempt to visualize the lizard. The title of the poem announces the subject, but the sections focusing on the figure do not bear its name. Instead, a place name "Costa Rica" metonymically replaces it. But the sense of location remains ambiguous:

> In blazing driftwood
>> the green keeps showing at the same place;
> as, intermittently, the fire opal shows blue and green.
>> In Costa Rica the true Chinese lizard face
>> is found, of the amphibious falling dragon, the living firework.

The subject is immediately displaced, as though it cannot be introduced directly. The poem begins, that is, with a metaphoric substitution, suggesting the absence, and thereby enhancing the power, of the object. This becomes a pattern for the poem's movement. There are no connectives to aid us in locating the plumet basilisk, only juxtaposed images which are implicitly connected, by repetitions of the preposition "in." Flames are "in" driftwood in a special, fleeting sense, and only flashes of green appear in opal. Though in one sense the metaphor advances the visual impression of the basilisk, that impression is one of intangibility. Like Marvell's "Drop of Dew," this basilisk scarce touches where it lies, shimmering and ready to evaporate. Moore goes on to confuse more and less empirical orders of being, comparing the basilisk to "the Chinese lizard face"; she superimposes realms of natural and supernatural, implying that the basilisk is the incarnation of a deity. The language itself, shifting from science to legend, helps to blur these boundaries. While "the living firework" still seems at this point to be a metaphor for the natural basilisk, it later becomes apparent that the basilisk is just another metaphor for an intangible force. The image of burning driftwood introduces several associations which develop as the poem goes on. The opalescent quality suggests a play of color beneath a hard, filmy surface, a multiple, fluctuating identity held in a tense unity. Fire suggests again a fluctuation of form, but also the consumption of matter. Driftwood suggests water as well, which takes the form of its container, having no color or form of its own.

The second stanza introduces a moment of characteristic action which offers description, but also abstraction.

> He leaps and meets his
>   likeness in the stream and, king with king,
> helped by his three-part plume along the back, runs on two legs,
>   tail dragging; faints upon the air; then with a spring
> dives to the stream bed, hiding as the chieftain with gold body hid
>   in
>
> Guatavita Lake.

Much of the passage contributes to our idea of a natural object, but behind it, as though the eyes shone through from another world, is a mythical creature. As Laurence Stapleton has put it, such moments represent "the counterpoint of the legendary and the real."[14] The momentary union of the object with his reflected image draws attention to the separation, which can be read literally as lizard and reflection, but is also emblematic of a linguistic pattern. We shall see other such allusions to the symbolic action throughout Moore's verse. For now it is worth noting that the disappearance of an object is associated with the disappearance of its "likeness." When it reemerges, literally and figuratively, it is the magical powers that are emphasized.

> He runs, he flies, he swims, to get to
> his basilica—"the ruler of Rivers, Lakes, and Seas,
>   invisible or visible," with clouds to do
> as bid—and can be "long or short, and also coarse or fine at plea-
>   sure."

The poem has moved from the natural fluctuations within color and form to supernatural fluctuations between form and spirit. At this point, when the sense of unity in the identity of the basilisk figure is pressed to a fission, the section ends and the poem moves to another focus.

In the version of this poem that Moore sent to *Hound and Horn* in 1932 she included additional stanzas for the opening section, marked "could be spared," which develop the description of the basilisk. But these lines expand his legendary rather than his natural aspect; indeed, the natural itself is made to seem magical:

> With a
>
> modest quiver, he
>   ascends the bank on clinging tree-frog
> hands, and waits; the water draining, forms a lizard there, from
>   skin now looking a little newer than the log
> it rested on and the thick mass of verdure all about. This is the
>
> feather basilisk,
>   of travellers' tales, of which a pair stood
> bodyguard beside Confucius' crib: aquatic flying
>   lizard-fairy detested by such dragonhood
> as Michael fought. One has seen Kivu lizards fight, though
>   smaller and more
>
> harmless, brother matched
>   with brother, as if immune to pain;
> push, struggle and breathe hard; swell out and muster strength,
>   withdraw,

advance; and swerving, almost full—hoping to gain
the mortal hold and that some fang should pierce the marrow.
                                                When two plumet

    territories touch,
        the masters of them are dramatic
    without shedding blood, exerting charm as Chinese dragon-
        whiskers in a crystal handle charm; or as thick-
    flowering orchids gather dragons, in the East, by forming clouds
                                                    for them.[15]

The lizard's presence is marked only by tiny alterations in the look of
things. He is just "a little newer than the log." His real existence is a
matter of hearsay rather than experience, though the poet has a privileged intimacy with her subject. These creatures miraculously engage in
combat without shedding blood (an ideal of reciprocity for Burke and
for Moore), indeed their combat is charmed and charming. We are
fully in the realm of fantasy when they are compared to mythical dragons in flowering orchids, again an image of mysteries beneath natural
obscurities.

    With or without these stanzas the function of the first section is to
set the task of the poem: not to define something that has no location,
but something that has many, none of which contains it.[16] It is reserved
for the last section, which returns to the basilisk, to fulfill this task. No
substantive idea of the basilisk congeals there, but as he is chased into
the exotic boundary of the real and the mythic, we do get a sense of him
from quivering things that are signs of his presence. We know him by
hearsay.

    We begin to identify an object through classification, as we decide
that something is like X but different from Y. The poem moves now to
contrast "The Malay Dragon" to the plumet basilisk.

The Malay Dragon

We have ours; and they
    have theirs. Ours has a skin feather crest;
theirs has wings out from the waist which is snuff-brown or sallow.
    Ours falls from trees on water; theirs is the smallest
dragon that knows how to dive head first from a tree top to some-
                                                thing dry.

Floating on spread ribs,
    the boatlike body settles on the
clamshell-tinted spray sprung from the nutmeg tree—minute legs
    trailing half akimbo—the true divinity
of Malay. Among unfragrant orchids, on the unnutritious nut-

tree, *myristica*
    fragrans, the harmless god spreads ribs that
do not raise a hood. This is the serpent dove peculiar
    to the East; that lives as the butterfly or bat
can, in a brood, conferring wings on what it grasps, as the air plant
                       does.

The Malay dragon's identity is consistent and hierarchically organized. It is the aerial idealist of dragons, the timeless dragonfly. The nonsensuous creature is described in an ornate pattern of negatives, as the bird of dragons, the oxymoronic "serpent dove," a boatlike body without water, unfragrant, unnutritious, unsexual; it cancels out all its potentialities. The prefix connoting absence (un-) is contagious, "conferring wings on what it grasps." The early images of water and swimming are retained, but here in an evaporated form.

The tuatera, on the other hand, is the prince of the reality principle, and the logos of the stock exchange. He is presence as the Malay dragon is absence. He represents the condition of density, firmness, complacency, dormancy, tradition, time. And as with the Malay dragon, everything that enters his domain is infected by it.

The Tuatera

Elsewhere, sea lizards—
    congregated so there is not room
to step, with tails laid crisscross, alligator style, among
    birds toddling in and out—are innocent of whom
they neighbor. Bird-reptile social life is pleasing. The tuatera

will tolerate a
    petrel in its den, and lays ten eggs
or nine—the number laid by dragons since "a true dragon
    has nine sons." The frilled lizard, the kind with no legs,
and the three-horned chameleon, are non-serious ones that take to
                     flight

    if you do not. In
      Copenhagen the principal door
    of the bourse is roofed by two pairs of dragons standing on
      their heads—twirled by the architect—so that the four
    green tails conspiring upright, symbolize fourfold security.

From the point of the tuatera, the chameleon and the petrel are flighty creatures. But he is, nevertheless, of the same larger class. Like the basilisk, he has characteristics of both bird and reptile, a bit of the mythic as well as the real (though Moore relays the mythic in her typical matter-of-fact fashion). What seems to fascinate her here is the variety contained within a single larger genus. The tuatera, like the plumet basilisk, is a hybrid. As her note tells us:

> *The tuatera or ngarara.* In appearance a lizard—with characteristics of the tortoise; on the ribs, uncinate processes like a bird's; and crocodilian features—it is the only living representative of the order Rhynchocephalia. Shown by Captain Stanley Osborne in motion pictures. Cf. *Animals of New Zealand,* by F. W. Hutton and James Drummond (Christchurch, New Zealand: Whitcomb and Tombs, 1909).
>
>   [CP, 265]

But as mixed as their genes may be, their dominant traits define them as dragons. The Malay dragon and tuatera, then, are confined within their classes. One is sustained in the element of air, one in the element of earth, and everything that enters their kingdoms is subject to their conditions. But as a third category the basilisk has a special meaning, for it takes on rather than confers identity. The second basilisk section opens with an image of a fruitful tree (unlike the Malay dragon's unfruitful *myristica fragrans*). However, the tree does not drop its nuts on solid ground, but on a stream, a transient, shapeless substance. The basilisk is not of air or earth, but of water (taking on the shapes of its containers) and of fire (destroying the walls of every structure it enters). The Malay dragon and tuatera represent the absolutes of spirit and body, but the basilisk, represented in dynamic form, is a mysterious blend. And just as the basilisk disappears into the trembling surfaces of nature, so the verbal image is lost under the trembling surface of words:

the slight lizard that
   can stand in a receding flattened
S—small, long and vertically serpentine or, sagging,
   span the bushes in a fox's bridge. Vines suspend
the weight of his faint shadow fixed on silk.

The image withdraws behind the shadow of language as the S recedes in alliterative clusters.[17] Suddenly all we have left are the words themselves as traces of this unconquerable being.

The irony of the poem rests in our desire to fix a firm gaze on the basilisk, to make the poem freeze, to stop the moment of identification. The attractiveness, the gusto, of the basilisk (and the poem) is precisely its freedom from static forms. Placed on the hand the basilisk is "stiff and somewhat heavy like fresh putty." Moore was fascinated by the fact that the glow goes out of things when their freedom is gone (that is, when they are fully revealed). She copied a long passage from Isabel Cooper's "Wild Animal Painting in the Jungle" which points out several times the artist's chief difficulty: that the true beauty of her subjects is one with their elusiveness, their refusal to be fixed objects of study. When they become still subjects, their fire is literally snuffed: "Snakes' eyes extinguished by death—a dreadful mildew creeps up over the sparkling black pupil, . . . until the eye looks like a mouldering moonstone . . . There is a blazing green wood-lizard who becomes ashen in captivity—and remains so except when he is particularly enraged. When he flares up again into brilliant green—you can watch the waves of color flowing rapidly like a revolving spotlight."[18] Whether or not Moore had this passage in mind when she wrote "The Plumet Basilisk," the artist's dilemma is certainly close to hers.

Seen in terms of familiar, uniform decorums, in terms of the categories we have for comprehending things, the tail of the basilisk is "faulty." But it is precisely its virtue to be "extraordinary," recalcitrant to our symmetries in its "regal awkwardness." These differences are the signs of its sublimity. And this indeterminacy in the creature's nature creates a corresponding emotion of freedom in the viewer.

The basilisk's existence depends, in fact, on its fending off our comprehending gaze. In the daytime, categories are stable. We distinguish one form from another, one sense from another. But these categories are also the camouflage of the basilisk for those who cannot distinguish it from these superimposed forms. Ironically, form, which is usually the expression of a thing, is here its disguise, its camouflage. Camouflage is the perfect emblem of a confusion between metonymy and metaphor, for it creates the illusion of contiguity where there is actually separation.

> As by a Chinese brush, eight green
> bands are painted on
>   the tail—as piano keys are barred
> by five black stripes across the white. This octave of faulty
>   decorum hides the extraordinary lizard
> till nightfall, which is for man the basilisk whose look will kill but
>
>   is

> for lizards men can
>   kill, the welcome dark—

The reversion to musical imagery is important here, for it indicates the change in representation that is occurring. The physical presence of the basilisk is now less directly associated with its biological nature. Just as we cannot equate piano keys with music, so we can not equate the physical signs of the lizard with the lizard itself, though they cannot be entirely divorced. This is reiterated in the continuation of music imagery through the description of night. In the night our orientation is shaken; it is, in Burke's terms, the phase of logical purgatory in which all senses blend. In the night the usually distinguished categories of sensation come together in powerful incongruities and collisions. This is the stage of transition, rearrangement, disorientation, cacophony, synaesthesia from which mythology is born. Characteristically, the moment of transformation from natural to supernatural is obscured; the basilisk leaps out of the darkness.

> wide water-bug strokes,
> in jerks which express
> a regal and excellent awkwardness,

> the basilisk portrays
> mythology's wish
> to be interchangeably man and fish—[19]

The original context of the last three lines suggests something of their breadth of meaning. A first draft of "Ennui" which Moore sent to her family from Bryn Mawr, looked like this:

> I once heard him express a curious wish
> To be interchangeably man and fish—
> to fathom the sea, to inhabit the air
> He charged the unchangeable with despair.

The poem was later revised to look like this:

> He often expressed
> A curious wish,
> To be interchangeably
> Man and fish;
> To nibble the bait
> Off the hook,
> Said he,
> And then slip away
> Like a ghost
> In the sea.

We see Moore's typical camouflage of humility at work even in this family correspondence. In the letter accompanying the early draft of the poem she wrote: "These sporadic poems I don't work over . . . so I smile, (as if I had found a penny) when people tell me they like them and talking about writing poetry and so on as if it were gymnastics or piano practice."[20] It is clear that she worked over the words in secret with all the discipline of a pianist. This early poem has nothing to do with basilisks. In both versions it is about boredom and how to escape it. Boredom is the opposite of astonishment, of course, and so the enemy of poetry. The basilisk of the later poem is, in a sense, the natural coalescence of an unrealistic wish for changeful existence. We can see Moore moving toward the paradoxes of the "Plumet Basilisk" in the second version of "Ennui," which describes the desire to be a hunter and hunted at once, and further, to achieve both possession and freedom, to be both spirit and matter. Already the paradox is invested in a natural phenomenon—the way a fish flashes elusively under water as it swims away.

Returning to the poem in its final form, we see that out of the cacophony and disarray of night, as problematic as the complacency of day, comes a new "noiseless music" through which the basilisk can be known. Music becomes an appropriate metaphor for the basilisk because it involves a stabilized combat of elements none of which can be identified with what they together indicate. But like music, the basilisk is captive in that interaction, the composition, and has no presence without it, except for a slight decay. The poet's fingers follow the basilisk's movement through the image of the harpist, and the object ends where the figure for it does:

> traveling rapidly upward, as
> spider-clawed fingers can twang the
> bass strings of the harp, and with steps
> as articulate, make their way
> back to retirement on strings that
> vibrate till the claws are spread flat.
>
>   Among tightened wires,
> minute noises swell
> and change, as in the woods' acoustic shell
> they will, with trees as avenues of steel to veil
>
> black opal emerald opal
> emerald—the prompt-delayed loud-
> low chromatic listened-for down-
> scale which Swinburne called in prose, the
> noiseless music that hangs about
> the serpent when it stirs or springs.[21]

The subject recedes from tangible reality. Not only have the basilisk's traces been described in terms of music, but music itself is here "noiseless" and described in terms of poetry. Increasingly the basilisk is identified with abstractions. The passage is full of tensions, alternations, oppositions, in delicate control, as music is. But at the end we find the recalcitrant figure of the serpent, the principle of potential discord, whose power, like the basilisk's, is expressed only as slight disturbances on the surface of things. The poem leaves open the question of whether this "serpent" is the principle of sublime unity, or of chaos—whether the creature's value is hidden or created by the flux of surfaces.

According to Jorge Luis Borges's *Book of Imaginary Beings*,[22] a catalog of mythological figures, the basilisk is not only that creature whose look can kill, but also that creature who expires when someone holds up a mirror and forces him to confront his own image. The presence of the basilisk must be, then, hypothetical, since any witness to its life is immediately dead, and any precise reproduction of the basilisk's image means death to the beast. Like the serpent, the basilisk has a kind of untouchable power.

Since he "portrays mythology's wish," we are never sure whether the basilisk belongs to the realm of the fantastic or of the exotic. Moore makes these regions merge by continually pushing back the basilisk's "location." He can only be "represented" in the West, in a tower, symbolically, but not naturally. His natural existence, she says, is known diffusely; any sense of it depends on inference by contiguity, on an ability to imagine beneath surfaces:

> This is our Tower-of-London
> jewel that the Spaniards failed to see, among the feather capes
>
> and hawk's-head moths and black-chinned
>   hummingbirds;
>
> Thinking himself hid among the yet unfound jade ax-heads,
>   silver jaguars and bats, and amethysts and
> polished iron, gold in a ten-ton chain, and pearls the size of pigeon eggs,
>
> he is alive there
>   in his basilisk cocoon beneath
> the one of living green

The poet has the privilege of jumping ahead, beyond the contiguities of experience, to the point of view of the object she is trying to describe. But what she finds is a presence blocked by substitution, by layers of camouflage.

Finally Moore protects the rarity of her subject by denying it even the figure of the lizard she has seemed to be describing. It has a name, but to capture it there is to mistake it for its "cocoon," to mistake a thing for a name, or an energy for a thing. At this point the basilisk no longer belongs to material reality at all; he is more of a spirit. "Thus nested / in the phosphorescent alligator that copies each / digression of the shape, he pants and settles." The reality of the basilisk and his represented form remain slightly askew, as the repeated image of phosphorescence, most visible in darkness, reminds us.

The power of the basilisk depends on its innocence and rarity, its separateness from the fixed imagination. It literally defends that innocence:

> the innocent, rare, gold-
> defending dragon that as you look begins to be a
>   nervous naked sword on little feet, with threefold
> separate flame above the hilt, inhabiting
>
>   fire eating into air.

Again power and value are associated with an instability of form, with shimmering things. Here the container itself is highly unstable.

There is an equality of images in the last section on the basilisk, the sword no more illusory than the alligator skin the basilisk inhabits. As images accelerate toward the end of the poem we see the basilisk no longer as an animal at all but as a force running through various objects, like the water and fire with which it is associated. The container, the sheath, is the collection of images; the thing contained is the movement from one image to another, the power flow they record. Images (such as the sword) are swallowed up by others and reemerge in a fluctuating surface (the basilisk is an image swallower; swords are among his tricks). Moore's practice of leaving room between her associative links adds to the sense of magical transformation as the object keeps escaping its sheath.

The basilisk's appearance is as long as the poem's duration. He disappears with the last image, having no perceivable presence without it:

> his quicksilver ferocity
> quenched in the rustle of his fall into the sheath
> which is the shattering sudden splash that marks his temporary
>   loss.

As the last lines of the poem, these question the privileged view the poet has assumed. Our awareness of the lizard's movement is textually captive. The reflective power of the water is shattered. Just as he had at the beginning of the poem, the basilisk plunges into his own image (king with king), his identity, and disappears. According to the myth, the mirror held up to his uniqueness kills him, at least temporarily.

So as not to limit the identity of the basilisk, Moore scatters her metaphors for it. However, the sword emerges as the central one. It marks the principle of combat basic to the basilisk's power. This is the "innocent, rare, gold / defending dragon that as you look begins to be a / nervous naked sword." It wards off our glances "with a look of whetted fierceness." It refracts light, revealing itself but also protecting itself. Without the image we have nothing. Lurking in the poem is the possibility that the basilisk is only the principle of combat among the various metaphors of the poem, that the many perspectives do not support a substance but invent one. Finding herself divided in a world of multiple perspectives and interests, Moore projects the struggle onto a unified figure whose existence depends upon fending off all finite definitions. Having posited the reality of an "innocent, rare, gold-defending dragon," she can celebrate confusion.

The "armor" of the Plumet Basilisk is the language that marks his restlessness. His life in the poem depends simultaneously on signs of his existence and on the difference between those signs and his character. As a "myth" of substance inferred from coincidence and proximity, and from conflicting classes brought into juxtaposition, he is a coalescence of transformation itself, pure action, which various phrases and positions dramatically imply.

Scattered intermittently over worksheets for this poem are comments about Wallace Stevens almost identical to those which appeared in Moore's essay "Well Moused, Lion" in *The Dial*, January 1924. Moore was working on a medley of her remarks about Stevens at the same time she compoed the poem. After fragments of "The Malay Dragon" we find:

W. Stevens—a pride in unservicableness
    that is not syon. with the beauty of aloofness self~~sufficiency~~
the ~~fairy & the brute~~
a big ogre stalking toward one w a knobbed club
well moused, lion
Leigh Hunt—rhyme
Java peacocks argus pheasants toucan

        floes
arora borealis, ice ~~palaces~~ & hair seal needlework
Rousseau's paintings

> Stevens recoils from admitting the force of the basic emotions
> obliquely treats of it thru ~~the~~ interacting ~~vibrations of~~ allusive im-
> agery

The qualities she admires in her chameleons and lizards, and particularly in the basilisk, are precisely the qualities she finds in Stevens. And
in theme, organization, and imagery, the poem has much in common
with Stevens's "Comedian as the Letter C." In the guise of a descriptive poem, "The Plumet Basilisk" is another poem about the imagination.[23]

Donald Hall admired "The Plumet Basilisk" for its achievement
of "mystery," and I agree that in this achievement it is one of Moore's
major poems.[24] Laurence Stapleton is less enthusiastic, suggesting that
the poem may be too long and too various in its accumulation of fact
and reflection—a criticism that could be made of many of Moore's long
poems.[25] But if we read the poem as an imaginative pursuit—in which
the basilisk is first beheld, in which the speaker tries to define him by
classifications, in which he escapes and disappears—then the ranging,
stop-and-start manner of the poem is entirely expressive. Moore, like
Stevens, alternated between long and short poems, moments of concentration and moments of explicitness, of natural reticence and relentless accuracy. There are fewer short pieces after *Poems*, but Moore nevertheless saw the mode as an important counterpoint to the long poem,
collecting several examples in *O to be a Dragon*. The new poems in that
collection are trivial and tend to rely too heavily on conventional associations to bring about enchantment. The title poem has all the ingredients of sublimity—magical transformation, ambiguity of metonomy
and metaphor, identity and mask, fluctuating presence—but the poem
declares rather than achieves its felicities. But two other poems, printed
with "O to Be a Dragon" but actually composed before *Poems*, concentrate the fascinations that sustain "The Plumet Basilisk."

Like the longer lizard poem, "To a Chameleon" (CP, 179) belongs in the romantic tradition of natural supernaturalism. In
"Adonais" Shelley introduces "the green lizard and the golden snake"
who "like imprisoned flames, out of their trance awake," and in an un-
finished drama he describes a grapevine's fruit "like a sleeping lizard
under the Shadows." Like Shelley, Moore plays along the slim boundaries of elements, to suggest a further boundary of spiritual and elemen-
tal, inanimate and animate.[26]

The poem's title in *Poems*, "You Are Like a Realistic Product of an Unrealisitic Search for Gold at the Foot of the Rainbow," suggests its conceptual basis. The poem was perhaps originally offered in private praise of another artist, as were so many in *Poems*. But this sense was diminished by its republication in *O to Be a Dragon*. The simple, sustained message is that the grandest ambitions are realized in the simplest forms (a message wittily made in the incongruity between the poem and its original title). But the word "like" suggests that the chameleon is only an incarnation of a greater brilliance, beyond experience. Like the later dragon, he is "a symbol of the power of Heaven"—but as he consumes the spectrum, light becomes flesh. By contrast, the Dark King competes for sublimity, and light richochets from his ring. The chameleon is a figure, like the basilisk, for the infinite enclosed in the finite. And he is a figure for the irrational, as the first line of a draft in the Rosenbach archive makes clear: "the place where contrarieties are not equally true is nothing to me." In this sense Moore might have had Keats's "camelion poet" in mind. She had a copy of Keats's letters and might have known his remarks to Richard Woodhouse about Shakespeare, remarks borrowed from Hazlitt. Keats wrote:

> As to the poetical character itself, (I mean that sort of which, if I am any thing, I am a Member; that sort distinguished from the wordsworthian or egotistical sublime; which is a thing per se and stands alone) it is not itself—it has no self—it is every thing and nothing—It has no character—it enjoys light and shade; it lives in gusto, be it foul or fair, high or low, rich or poor, mean or elevated—It has as much delight in conceiving an Iago as an Imogen. What shocks the virtuous philosopher, delights the camelion Poet . . . A Poet is the most unpoetical of anything in existence; because he has no Identity—he is continually in for—and filling some other Body—the Sun, the Moon, the Sea and Men and Women . . .[27]

Moore's reticence, her preference for relative over absolute values, her style of indirection, are all supported by this passage. Moore's favorite compliment to another artist was to call him a chameleon. Thus, in her unpublished review "Concerning the Marvelous" (about a Museum of Modern Art Exhibition by that title in 1937) she writes that Arthur Dove "affects homeliness and literalness as disguises for the exact opposite . . . he is as accurate as a chameleon or cuttlefish in its adaptation of pigment to background."[28] And the chameleon qualities others had condemned in Disraeli are virtues for Moore in "To a Strategist."

In "To a Chameleon" camouflage is again the armor of humility, analogous to the poet's own efforts to make her language blend into the forest of everyday words and things. And again, these veils have a double aspect, hiding the reality of the object, but nonetheless providing its only expression. So metaphor both hides "the power of Heaven" and discloses it symbolically. The genuine, like the chameleon, has no single, tangible form, but takes on its identity according to its context. The chameleon is "hid" by twining itself around the stem of the foliage, and the poem similarly twines itself around the shape of the chameleon.

Moore's attraction to the "unforced passion of the Hebrew language" is just one instance of her interest in the sublime. Moore read Longinus early in her career, and his manual of sublime rhetoric was important to her as late as *Predilections*. In 1909 she composed a little poem about him.[29] The brief poem appeared on a page of Moore's English Literature Notebook (February–May 1909) around the same time she included an original draft of what was then called "Rhyme on a Jellyfish" in a letter to her family (16 March 1909). The latter poem (published in the Bryn Mawr *Lantern* in 1909) contains some elements of the sublime, quiet and self-contained as it is.

> Visible, invisible,
> A fluctuating charm,
> An amber-coloured amethyst
> Inhabits it; your arm
> Approaches, and
> It opens and
> It closes;
> You have meant
> To catch it,
> And it shrivels;
> You abandon
> Your intent—
> It opens and it
> Closes and you
> Reach for it—

The blue
Surrounding it
Grows cloudy,
And it floats
Away from you—[30]

When Moore returned to "A Jellyfish" in *Complete Poems* she replaced the last five and a half lines with:

> you had meant
> to catch it and it quivers;
> you abandon your intent.   [CP, 180]

But the sense remained the same. The "charm" of the jellyfish is almost
literal: the reader-observer is thrown into a trance. The power of disappearance is connected with the tantalizing translucence that allows us
to see but not touch, to observe but not possess. In this sense the jellyfish is another brother of the opalescent basilisk and the chameleon who
consumes the spectrum. He is also a figure for Moore's poetry, if we recall that she describes her quotations as "a collection of flies in amber."
The phrase primarily denotes the ordinary and temporal lifted into the
extraordinary and eternal, like all her luminous creatures. But it also
connotes a tantalizing denial of contact, here in delightful counterpoint
to the static rhyme.

The second-person narration of "A Jellyfish" allows the poet to
examine a state of enchantment at one remove. "Snakes, Mongooses,
Snake-Charmers and the Like" (CP, 58) begins with the third person,
but by the end of the poem the speaker herself seems to have entered
the imagination of her subject. As in "Poetry," what the narrator "dislikes" becomes an object of fascination (not surprisingly, since Moore
was personally a great admirer of snakes). The snake is a culmination of
the various slippery things that have appeared before.

> "The slight snake rippling quickly through the grass,
> the leisurely tortoise with its pied back,
> the chameleon passing from twig to stone, from stone to straw,"
> lit his imagination at one time; his admiration now converges
>   upon this.

The words are taken from a passage in *The Expositor's Bible*, which concludes, "the ideal is to bring them into sympathy with ourselves."[31] We have already seen the relationship between sympathy and enchantment in "The Plumet Basilisk" (and it is also the subject of "O to Be a Dragon"). Here sympathy is directly challenged by the extreme tradition of distaste surrounding the figure of the snake. But the trance is described much as earlier trances have been: a vision of origins overwhelms the power of analysis. Again the original presence is characterized as a translucent unity revealing an intangible depth and multiplicity:

> Thick, not heavy, it stands up from its traveling-basket,
> the essentially Greek, the plastic animal all of a piece from nose to
> tail;
> one is compelled to look at it as at the shadows of the alps
> imprisoning in their folds like flies in amber, the rhythms of the
> skating-rink.[32]

Like the basilisk, Moore's unicorn in "Sea Unicorns and Land Unicorns" (CP. 77–78) inhabits the nether region of fact and fiction, and is able to "disappear and reappear" like a bickering flame.[33] Its "moonbeam glow," so impossible to represent, inspires the sublime feeling of "agreeable terror" in its beholders. In "Sea Unicorns and Land Unicorns" "miraculous elusiveness" involves a principle of extreme and perpetual dualism. The paradoxical nature of the individual creatures in the poem, (who are "civilly rampant" or "mild wild") is compounded by the "fourfold combination" of lions and unicorns, on land and on the sea, who represent an astonishing "unanimity" framed by " 'polished garlands' of agreeing difference." These oppositions challenge the frame of the picture, but they also represent an ideal of dynamic reciprocity held out for the beholder. The poem contrasts the frustrated hunters obsessed with bringing back these wondrous beings and the happy "virgin" who matches the qualities of the unicorn and thus tames it through reciprocity. She is "a lady inoffensive like itself— as curiously wild and gentle." The word "inoffensive" is strategic here, for it suggests that a relation of pursuer to pursued has been replaced by mutual curiosity and uniqueness. In such a state the unicorn loses none of its power or freedom, even while it is fully beheld, and thus in a sense has surrendered its mystery. It is also worth noting that in identifying the virgin and the unicorn Moore presents an image alive with sexual tension.

But finally such mutuality is only represented, not experienced. The story of the virgin, the unicorn, and their encounter is based on hearsay. Indeed, at every stage the poem reminds us that we are dealing in fictions. "Upon the printed page, / also by word of mouth, / we have a record of it all." But after insisting in this way, she proceeds to move from teller to tale. In order to do this she passes from description to metaphor, releasing the genuine and accepting the consolation of symbols. While the poet mocks the antique historians who insist on the factualness of their fantastic stories, she enjoys a strictly imaginary possession of the miraculous.

It is just this kind of consolation that Moore implied in "In the Days of Prismatic Color," which put truth in quotation marks. Since the visible and the invisible no longer appear as one, she accepts surfaces and reproductions for the source, the presence, the originality they symbolize. Often we are several removes from the genuine, as in "Nine Nectarines," where in quest of the "spirit of the wilderness" we must imagine past the poem to the plate, to the nectarines imaged on it, to the real cultivated nectarines, and finally to the wild fruit.[34] Similarly, in "Four Quartz Crystal Clocks" the standard of exact time is crystal enclosed, and the world is full of slippage and error. Though "repetition should be synonomous with accuracy," it seldom is. Moore's comment on this poem in a draft of "Humility, Concentration and Gusto" (in the Rosenbach archive) suggests that accuracy can be as much a source of sublimity for her as grandeur: "One's imagination by the very nature of it needs the ground for it. FOUR QUARTZ CRYSTAL CLOCKS weren't large round clocks with gold hands, such as Cinderella might have timed herself by at the ball, but my interest managed to transfer itself to the phenomenal accuracy of the clocks." The play of words in the poem ("jupiter" or "jour pater") parodies the lapse from the original created in acts of verbal reproduction. And yet it may be the very difference between an ideal, singular original and its representations that excites the imagination most.

"St. Nicholas" (CP, 196–197) is a relevant poem in this context, for it is all about desires. But these desires are not aggressive ones, for the things the poet yearns for lose their value with their freedom. If Moore cannot have a chameleon, she will accept a substitute, but whatever it is, it should be a representation or an intimation of some greater power, not the power itself, which will disappoint in the very possession of it. This is the wisdom of humility.

> But don't give me, if I can't have the dress,
> a trip to Greenland, or grim
> trip to the moon. The moon should come here. Let him
> make the trip down, spread on my dark floor some dim marvel

Again, it is the "dim marvel," the "not quite given" that Moore enjoys the most. Moore's last and firmest request summarizes her attitude of imaginative awe:

> A thing yet more rare,
> though, and different,
> would be this: Hans von Marées'
> St. Hubert, kneeling with head bent,
>
> erect—in velvet and tense with restraint—
> hand hanging down: the horse, free.
> Not the original, of course. Give me
> a postcard of the scene—huntsman and divinity—
> hunt-mad Hubert startled into a saint
> by a stag with a Figure entined.

It is a characteristic moment of intensity, in which desire and restraint are in full tension, in which a pursuer is humbled by a luminous, original presence, an incarnation of spirit. As in the scene of the virgin and the unicorn, power is not absent but suspended. The knight kneels as the poet defers. (In a draft of "Snakes, Mongooses, Snake-Charmers and the Like" at the Rosenbach, Moore's "friend," who seems to be herself, is "Beaten to a / crouching position by the fact of such un / precedented subtlety." And also as in that scene, the presence is not known empirically but only through a representation, a "post card," in fact, a representation of a representation.[35] She must *imagine* the brilliant colors within the black and white copy. The state of St. Hubert, as of the poet, is a state of enchantment, in which we abjure our physical and rational power and are possessed by what we behold. Enchantment is a key word in Moore's poetry, and the subject of "Spenser's Ireland" (CP 112–114), in which Moore's "supreme belief" is again invested in acts of "relentless accuracy" and we are again reminded that the sublime can occur in minute differentiations as well as in giant forces. "Their pride, like the enchanter's, is in care, not madness." And the fairies, like all Moore's figures, protect themselves from "discommodity" by becoming invisible (in the old days this was not necessary). Their presence, like the basilisk's, is felt over the surface of nature. As usual, we know these figures only by hearsay. This is "the greenest place I've never seen." As in "Half-Deity," about the metamorphosis of a butterfly ("last of the elves"), "we are not permitted to gaze informally on majesty," large or small.

"Hindered characters / seldom have mothers / in Irish stories," Moore tells us, borrowing from Padraic Colum, "but they all have grandmothers," and grandmothers have a "native genius for disunion." Moore's heroes are denied the external possessions of parents, marriage, unity, commodity, certainty, in order to experience the power of the invisible. Again, disunion and hindrance—in writing as in life—are the preludes to vision.

The terms of enchantment are consistent in Moore's aesthetic, but the objects of enchantment vary a great deal. She moves freely among levels of concreteness. Thus she delightedly describes a color television set in terms similar to those with which she rejoiced at the chameleon. Both snap up the spectrum for food, both contain infinity within simple exteriors. In "Logic and The Magic Flute" (CP, 171–172), about watching the Mozart opera on color television, Moore pushes back layers of abstraction, to reveal each form as a mere vehicle of the illogic of spirit.

The poem moves through a variety of spirals and Piranesian ascents, leading out of sense. The language itself creates this sense of vanishing points, as each image is a metaphor for something else, and as illogical patterns wind through the text. The winding stair recalls the wentletrap, which in turn recalls abalonean gloom, which harks backward to ghosts and forward to catacombs. The images that offer metaphors for the music (in the first stanza) merge with similar images of the music's *environment* in the second stanza. These images locate the performance, but they rise out of the descriptive context. Time and Life become abstractions; the tantalizing patterns left by the skaters trace out the patterns of the music (recalling the image of unified multiplicity in "Snakes").

The poem begins in an ascent, a spiraling motion toward some elusive object. In counterpoint we have suddenly a demonic descent, a roaring question, perhaps echoing the speaker's own internal question, or expanding to find the nature of the initial pursuit. The "answer" is characteristic of Moore's circumlocution: laziness and aggressiveness are the antipodes of beauty and affection, which are realized illogically, magically.

In dodging logic at every juncture, and in switching from natural to artificial metaphors, Moore equivocates as to whether her sublimities are natural or rhetorical—whether it is the world or the mind that is enchanting. In "The Mind Is an Enchanting Thing" (CP, 134–135) she makes this equivocation her subject—the mind is both object and subject, enchanter and enchanted. And the mind, not surprisingly, has all the charm of the natural sublime, in which unities dissolve into baffling multiplicities, "like the glaze on a / katydid-wing / subdivided by sun / till the nettings are legion," like "the fire in the dove-neck's / iridescence" in which the senses are baffled by the challenge of synaesthesia.[36] In accepting the irrational, the "inconsistencies of Scarlatti," Moore transfers her attention from object to process so that confusion is not a frustration of unconfusion but an experience of significance in its own right, steadied, like the gyroscope, by its constant fall. This allows her to consume her own artifact, to bury her tracks as she goes, to allow metaphor and yet reveal its fictionality:

> It tears off the veil; tears
>   the temptation, the
> mist the heart wears,
>   from its eyes—if the heart
>   has a face; it takes apart
>   dejection.

Paradoxically, the veil the heart wears is the veil of unconfusion, of consistency. To tear the veil, for Moore, is not to reveal truth but to release it for the sport of the chase. The veil is also dejection, however, whose cause is dreary certainty, taken apart for the sake of gusto. In Moore's idiosyncratic alignments, tedium is the opposite of integrity. Aesthetic and moral values merge, sincerity and gusto are one and the same. Whether her goal is truth or enchantment does not seem to matter.

With this "power of strong enchantment" the imagination can delight itself even in a dull world. When difference is a source of gusto, when the concealedness of all things in their otherness excites the imagination, we do not need the heights of Mt. Rainier or the distance of Costa Rica to find the exotic.

6. Argument by Design
The Form of the Poems

Marianne moore took every opportunity to declare her aim of "plain speaking" in poetry: clear, simple statement imitating the movement of the speaking voice. Poetry, she seems to say, should not be differentiated, in form or function, from other kinds of language. As she wrote to Samuel French Morse in 1934, in reply to his queries about her style: "With regard to form, I value an effect of naturalness and feel that the motion of the composition should reinforce the meaning and make it cumulatively impressive."[1] But such arguments for the "expediency" of form and its subservience to statement need to be set against other assertions Moore made about her style and against her actual practice. In her letter to Morse she goes on to admit her fondness for "contrapuntal effects." Such effects, she admitted elsewhere, were a determinant of "The Jerboa" and "Nine Nectarines." The poem, she was fond of saying, should fall naturally, like drapery. But the "garment" of style does not always fall along the contours of the body. She considered the stanza, not the line, her controlling unit, but her stanzas seldom conform to the structure of sentences and paragraphs, the main vehicles of "plain speaking." And even when they do, the syntax of these units seems almost to hinder, rather than facilitate, simple statement, though we find ourselves pulled along by the magnetism of word clusters, sounds and images. If Moore intends form to reinforce meaning, then her notion of "meaning" goes beyond the straight-forward aim of presenting ideas and opinions. Moore made this clear in a lecture she gave at Bryn Mawr: "the message is part of the way the thing which is being done, is done."[2]

Wallace Stevens has a crucial insight into Moore's poetry when he writes in *The Necessary Angel:* "Considering the great purpose that poetry must serve, the interest of the poem is not in its meaning but in this, that it illustrates the achieving of an individual reality."[3] Moore makes the same point about T. S. Eliot in her essay "A Machinery of Satisfaction," where she says, "method is the main part of pleasure."[4]

Moore's poetry does not fit a strict representational theory of linguistic meaning, in which the elements of the poem are symmetrically organized to support some externally developed, direct statement about the world. She almost always proceeds by indirection. She revises the forms and structures peculiar to verse, stanza, rhyme, syllabic count, and so on, and those inherent in ordinary language, syntax, punctuation, and so on, to hinder the automatic flow of statement into established orders that may seem to be "natural" but are in fact language-bound. By making her forms work against the conventions of direct statement, Moore radicalizes our way of seeing.[5]

Through revolutions in form, Moore makes meaning dynamic and exploratory. Meaning is always, in this sense, in suspension in her poetry. As she said of e. e. cummings's poetry, "parts of speech are living creatures that alter and grow."[6] Setting the form of her poetry against the conventional forms of statement frees words from their subordinate place in a linguistic order and allows them to become free agents. Williams has the best statement of this effect:

> With Miss Moore a word is a word most when it is separated out by science, treated with acid to remove the smudges, washed, dried and placed right side up on a clean surface. Now one may say that this is a word. Now it may be used, and how?
>
> It may be used not to smear it again with thinking (the attachments of thought) but in such a way that it will remain scrupulously itself, clean perfect, unnicked beside other words in parade.[7]

Such a view of form as bearing a dynamic relation to meaning shows the multiple error in a notion of poetry that distinguishes form as the "outsides" of a poem. Moore's poems do not "contain" a meaning directed in turn to the "external" world. Geoffrey Hartman has conclusively connected Moore's preoccupation with the surfaces of animals to her own functional "outsides." We should recall that for Moore the outside coverings are only coverings to the externalist. Hartman writes:

It is not that she disdains the insides of things, but that, especially in a psychological age, the surface qualities are slighted. There is a peculiarly modern morality in this respect for surface: content or *fond*, said Valery, is only form in its impure state. Contemporary painters make everything a function of form; and in poetry, too, despite the obvious difference of medium, attempts are made to find a style in which aesthetic and didactic elements are inseparable. Marianne Moore is so much in this tradition of modern art that one reads her poems less for their message (always suffused) than for the pleasure of seeing how style may become an act of the living—the infinitely inclusive and discriminating—mind.[8]

Moore must be distinguished from other modernists and postmodernists in her experiments with form, however. Her poems have much of the tension and dynamism of poems by Pound or Williams, but she does not blow apart the familiar world in order to create her own energetic system. While she reactivates meaning by loosening form from statement, she never violates the rules of composition. This allows her to rebel without culpability or offense—to create an individual reality without losing her reader's confidence. Moore's method is to appear to be simply getting it said, like everybody else, to appear unconscious of the fact that her way of getting it said, and consequently what gets said, are often extraordinary and unconventional. Moore's syntax is impeccable, if not cooperative, and her poems will always yield eventually to paraphrase. Williams understood, while he did not share, Moore's sense of the possibilities of freedom and exploration within available rhetorical forms. In a letter to Moore, responding to some comments she had made on his work, he makes the distinction between their styles:

> Perhaps you are right in your adverse view of my sometimes obstreperous objections to decorum. I must think more of that. But each must free himself from the bonds of banality as best he can; you or another may turn into a lively field of intelligent activity quite easily but I, being perhaps more timid or unstable at heart, must free myself by more violent methods. I cannot object to rhetoric, as you point out, but I must object to the academic associations with which rhetoric is hung and which vitiate all its significance by making the piece of work to which it is applied a dried bone. And so

I have made the mistake of abusing the very thing I most use.[9]

The vitality of Moore's art derives from the confluence of many levels of organization, rather than from the shattering of orders. She preserves a superficial coherence of statement, but the significant reference of all her poems is to the irregularity, the density, and the motion of life. The risk of such an aesthetic is high, and Moore's poems do not always succeed in communicating. She often strains syntax and makes associative leaps beyond a reader's patience or stamina. Pronouns become detached from their antecedents, references become drowned in the rapidity of the line. It is not always enough that she is "never consciously obscure to [herself]." But when Moore stays within the boundaries of sense while pressing against familiar frames, she achieves a dynamism of form which renews a reader's energy and appreciation.

Moore's rhetoric against formality and in favor of plain speaking seems to suggest a distinction between artificial and natural language. But as she elaborates this distinction in the poems it is clear that her real contrast is not between natural and artificial or plain and complex but between static and dynamic forms. "Novices" presents this distinction most explicitly. Moore condemns an art that is highly sophisticated, symmetrical, rational, and decorative, but the more "primitive" art of the Hebrew poets has its own asymmetrical mode of complexity, of "angle at variance with angle till submerged in the general action." It is just this mode of complexity that characterizes Moore's difficult poetry.

We have already seen the density and fluidity Moore achieves in her descriptive poems, in which effusions of detail fray the smooth borders of syntax and generality. In her poems of social and moral address, Moore pulls against the stasis of assertion, creating crosscurrents of meaning within the simple unit of the sentence. The compact frame of the epigram, in such poems as "To Be Liked by You Would Be a Calamity," "Nothing Will Cure the Sick Lion but to Eat an Ape," "To an Intramural Rat," and in a different tone, "Blake," allows her to create a chiasmic square dance of wit. Moore achieves her most tempestuous effects in poems of a third type, in which a wide range of conceptual and physical categories are drawn together by the discreet and tentative control of a central, abstract idea. The generating structures of these poems exert minimal thematic control over their materials. Moore chooses sistrophy, parataxis, association, over sequence, narrative, logical argument. The rhetorical signals become ways of encountering rather than reducing the world's variety. And the simplicity of these external structures gives the poems a velocity that requires extra exertion from the reader to take in the usually difficult, internal, conceptions and metaphors. "The Labors of Hercules" builds on one, infinitely repeatable clause, opened, complicated, and reversed by the other structural ingredients of the poem. In "People's Surroundings" the simple clause that sets the poem in motion is not even repeated, but only sustained as the implicit synecdochic principle running through several clusters of widely divergent objects and qualities. "England" and "These Various Scalpels" similarly carry the reader through a series of grouped qualities, though the degree of organization is increased by subtle subcategories of size and diction and by an implicit analysis of a whole in terms of its parts. "Marriage" and "Bowls" are associative poems, drawing together numerous, diverse anecdotes and images. "Marriage" builds around an "institution, or perhaps one should say enterprise"; "Bowls" around a principle of prompt precision. Each of these broad, simple thematic structures creates an exhilarating rapidity in the poem which works against the density of the lines, their conceptual and imagistic leaps, their complex syntax and punctuation.

Poetry draws on another set of structures, unrelated to standard meaning. In Moore the visual and aural organization of the poem often work against the flow of rhetoric. In her discreet rhymes of minor words, her syllabic stanzas, and her use of contrapuntal and other internal rhythmic effects, she again makes form a means of discovery, of keeping the poem open, of liberating words from the constraints of conventional statement.

Moore's method of quotation is perhaps the most distinguishing mark of her form. The dynamic relation, not only between the poet's statement and the orders of prosody, but between both of these and the external materials that make up the substance of the poems, needs thoughtful consideration. Her quotation is not, as she often said, simply a matter of deference, but it creates a dynamic play of inside and outside, which is a major source of energy in the poem. In all her hesitant remarks about her method, Moore revealed her ambivalence about form. But what appears as ambivalence in her comments becomes dynamic tension in her style. Between the urge to order words according to unique patterns and associations and the urge to make words facilitate statements about the world, we discover the wonderful crosscurrents of Moore's verse. The tension is like the imaginary garden with real toads, ideally resolved. But in the meantime, while our structures for "plain speaking" are inadequate and the forms of poetry seem detached, Moore presents poems of turbulent motion in which order presses against order in the search for the genuine.

The chief authority of Moore's poetry is its relentless verbal intelligence. Other poets strike us by their sensitivity, their lyricism, their force, their profundity. Moore's wit binds us in its invisible ropes, overgone and undergone, until we can't stir, and yet we feel strangely free. It was Moore's wit in the broadest sense that Pound admired when the called her work "logopoeia or poetry that is akin to nothing but language, which is a dance of the intelligence among words and ideas and modification of ideas and characters."[10] And who can tell the dancer from the dance? Through the turns and counterturns of irony, Moore performs a dizzying pattern within which she harbors her sources and ends. Sincerity here is paradoxically on the side of subtlety, indirection, discretion, flexibility, elusiveness, even irony. Gusto is the sudden victory of the ineffable, the irrational and spontaneous, against the defenses of conscious fastidiousness. Moore's wisdom emerges in the gyroscope's constant fall, in the poise of crosswinds. The genuine—the touchstone of the good, the true, the beautiful—is the absolute to which these verbal dances allude, but it is only visible in the spin, is, indeed, the enemy of all other forms of certitude.

The grammar, conception, and rhetoric of Moore's moral and social observations work on a submerged principle of inversion, registered at the surface in the form of direct or indirect address. Her precepts and aphorisms are all reversals of conventional wisdom and symbolism: "fear is hope," "restraint is freedom," a snake is no longer an emblem of evil but "by shedding its skin is a sign of renewal." As wholes, these poems work on a structure of overt or implicit chiasmus (the reversal of subject and object), creating an ambiguity of perspectives, values, and meanings. We have already seen this ambiguity at work in the conversities of the genuine that arise in Moore's poems on art, in her revisions of conventional symbolism, and in her descriptions. Moore's imagination works against the current without appearing to apply any pressure—quotations seem to condemn or usurp themselves, negatives yield intangible positives, conventional analogies turn up unpredicted conclusions. Moore's inversions are never one-fold; the antithetical structure of her thought is relentless and will not rest in simple oppositions. The effect, in every case, is a target kept in motion by the instability of language and reference—the flexible relation between words and meanings, grammar and rhetoric, image and idea.

A very simple example of ironic reversal occurs in an early poem about turning the other cheek, called "To Be Liked by You Would Be a Calamity" (Observations, 37), in which Moore disarms her opponent with the weapon of civility in style and statement. While the poem is perhaps too brisk and insubstantial, it provides a neat introduction to more complicated and more profound uses of similar techniques.

> "Attack is more piquant than concord," but when
> > You tell me frankly that you would like to feel
> > My flesh beneath your feet,
> > I'm all abroad; I can but put my weapon up, and
> > > Bow you out.
> Gesticulation—it is half the language.
> Let unsheathed gesticulation be the steel
> > Your courtesy must meet,
> > > Since in your hearing words are mute, which to my senses
> > > Are a shout.

Since the genuine has no indicative form for Moore and belongs to no single point of view, her wit is almost always reactive, often many times removed. The quotation in this poem is spoken by a Hardy narrator in *A Pair of Blue Eyes* (himself untrustworthy) after describing an incident in which a self-satisfied critic, Henry Knight, has devastated a writer, Elfridge Swancourt.[11] We are immediately struck by the incongruity between the subject's brutality and the speaker's civility. But in the fencing between "you" and "I," subject and object exchange places. Through the instability of categories gesticulation is also a sword, attack a courtesy, words mute, and silence audible, depending on the point of view, which the grammar doubles. The initial quotation, asserted on one level, then opposed, is embraced on a new level in which the terms of the statement have new references. The chiasmic square dance of meaning here is specifically designed to oppose a subject for whom meanings are rigid. The original title of the poem, taken from a cartoon by Oberlander which Moore had seen, was "To a Stand Patter."

Moore practices a similar but more complicated maneuver in "Nothing Will Cure the Sick Lion but to Eat an Ape," (CP, 86) responding to a remark by Thomas Carlyle. As in "Injudicious Gardening," someone else's criticism precedes the poem, but Moore's work as a whole would seem to support the opening point of view. "Novices," "Those Various Scalpels," "People's Surroundings," are only a few of Moore's poems that include attacks on the "masked ball attitude." But this poem will not accept a simple opposition of sincerity and artifice. Moore's irony penetrates layers of masks, to discover egocentric motives in apparent unselfconsciousness. She shows how sincerity itself can be a role in which self-regarding will overwhelms truth.

Even more at fault than the dilettantes is their critic, who throws up his hands in an excessive disdain that betrays his egotism. While on the one hand he claims to despise the futile enterprise of moral instruction, on the other hand his insistent resignation is itself overbearing. Moore's roving perspective again creates an ambiguity of accuser and accused, making positive values (fresh air) negative, and negative values (masks) positive. Another critic appears to pull the rug out from under himself.

In many of these poems not only Moore's attitude but the arena of her criticism is obscure. But her intention may be in part to draw us away from external reference and into the Gordian knot of the language that it occasioned. The "you" and "I" become counters and affect us as the linguistic play of opposition. Since this is one sentence, our effort is concentrated on ordering the restless phrases as we encounter them. We can therefore appreciate the poem without recognizing its references. But the sources of these poems do more than set them in motion. Moore retains a tension, not only between the figures and phrases in the poem, but between the poem and the external text that provoked it. In "Nothing Will Cure the Sick Lion but to Eat an Ape" we have only a remote clue, in a note, "Letters, Carlyle," as to the source of her quarrel. But the note is misleading. Nowhere in Carlyle's letters do we find the words quoted in her title. Moore's "quotations" are often in reality drastic summaries of something she has read; in this case she has condensed several chapters of *Past and Present*.[12]

The theme of *Past and Present* is that England (which Carlyle repeatedly refers to metonymically as the lion, after Richard Coeur de Lion) is sick of an ailment for which there is "no Morison Pill," no fashionable cure-all. It is spiritually sick, infected with self-consciousness and affectation. In a chapter called "Gospel of Dilettantism," Carlyle expresses his dismay at the insincerity in social intercourse, particularly as it has blighted language. Plain speaking is out of fashion, displaced by ornamental wit. "His poor fraction of sense has to be perked into some epigrammatic shape, that it may prick into me;—perhaps (this is commonest) to be topsy turvied, left standing on its head, that I may remember it the better!" He loves "honest laughter" he says, but "human faces should not grin on one like masks." (P&P, 151). Carlyle goes on to imagine the consequences of such affectation in a parable of Moses and the Dwellers by the Dead Sea, to which he refers several times later in the book. A tribe of men who dwelt on the shores of "that same Asphaltic Lake" had lost their sense of naturalness and fallen into feigning of various kinds. When Heaven sent them a prophet who of- fered " 'remedial measures' " they turned their noses up at him sardon- ically. "Moses withdrew; but Nature and her vigorous veracities did not withdraw. The men of the Dead Sea when we next went to visit them, were all 'changed into Apes.' " (P&P, 152–153). They had, ironically, been returned to their animal origins as punishment for their affected, unnatural behavior. Carlyle indulges for several sentences in the vision of this foolishly metamorphosed company, whose self-consciousness is now nearly unconsciousness, who having neglected their souls have lost them.

In the next chapter, called "Happy," Carlyle complains that our obsession with private material satisfaction takes the place of nobility. "The word *Soul* with us, as in some Slavonic dialects, seems to be syn- onomous with *Stomach.*" Carlyle continues with an anecdote of "a be- nevolent old Surgeon" and "a Patient fallen sick by gourmandising" who (ironically) complained of his loss of appetite. The doctor's re- peated cure for these absurd social "needs" is to repeat "it is of no con- sequence." The cure, once more, is unselfconsciousness. In the next chapter, "The English," Carlyle declares "Nay of all animals, the freest of utterance, I should judge, is the genus *Simia*: go into the Indian woods, say all Travellers, and look what a brisk, adroit, unresting Ape- population it is!" Again and again throughout these beratings, Carlyle holds up "Nature" as the test of Humbug and work as the best way to maintain contact with nature. But the next chapter, "Two centuries," ends in an image of man as nearly irredeemable. "Idle Dilettantism, Dead-Sea Apism crying out, 'Down with him [Labour]; he is danger- ous!' " The book goes on for several pages in this way, mocking the va- cuity and pretentions of sick society, summed up in the chapter called "Democracy," which declares how little men know or value the true meaning of "liberty." "Thou who walkest in a vain show, looking out with ornamental dilettante sniff and serene supremacy at all Life and all Death . . . and art as an 'enchanted Ape' under God's sky . . . doest thou call that 'liberty'?" Carlyle once again launches into a tirade against these "apes" of affection for whom "a thousand Moses would be but so many painted Phantasms, interesting Fellow-Apes of new strange aspect,—whom they would 'invite to dinner,' be glad to meet with in lion-soirees." Meanwhile they are spiritually "dying of hunger." (P&P, 218–220).

The poem is perhaps limited by the obscurity of its pretext. But with these passages from Carlyle in mind, the terms of the argument and even its form are clearer. Moore is in sympathy with Carlyle's diagnosis of society, but not with his attitude. The "sick lion," alludes generally to the moral emptiness of England and specifically to the "lion-soirees," the pretentious gatherings of the English aristocracy. An "ape" in Carlyle signifies a kind of soulless cleverness and cynicism, to which he sees his country hopelessly damned. An ape cure is perhaps a drastic confrontation with the consequences of neglecting the soul but more likely represents wit and satire, which Carlyle sees as insincere and causing the demise of soul. Carlyle gloats in his despair of human redemption. His correctives are all predicated on the assumption that we will not heed them. Thus in parading the virtues of naturalness and unselfconsciousness ("fresh air") he "smothers" his subjects with his moral superiority and ironically proves he is just as self-absorbed. The excesses of Carlyle's style, and his lack of humility in reprimanding his audience are the target of Moore's compact, understated wit. Indeed, through the indirect and discreet style of this and all her poems, she proves the potential advantages of masks. She does, indeed, perk her sense into epigrammatic shape, but it is her subject, not herself, who is left "topsy turvied." Her irony carries us beyond the clever inversion in which naturalness becomes pretentious and fresh air can smother.

"George Moore" is more ambivalent about its subject, disdaining the decadence of his tone and subject, but celebrating the energy in his narrative style. But Moore's ambivalence pushes beyond dualities, to suggest that the gusto of George Moore's style belies his show of cynical ennui.

> In speaking of 'aspiration,'
>   From the recesses of a pen more dolorous than blackness,
>   Were you presenting us with one more form of im-
>   perturbable French drollery,
>   Or was it self directed banter?
>   Habitual ennui
>   Took from you, your invisible hot helmet of
>   anaemia
>   While you were filling your little glass from the
>   decanter

Of a transparent-murky, would-be-truthful
"hobohemia"—
And then facetiously
Went off with it? Your soul's supplanter,
The spirit of good narrative, flatters you, convinced
that in reporting briefly
One choice incident, you have known beauty other than
that of stys, on
Which to fix your admiration.

The pretext of this poem is George Moore's "Vale," which later became part of his fictional autobiography *Hail and Farewell!* In her notes to the poem Moore quotes the line "we certainly pigged it together, pigs no doubt, but aspiring pigs." The line comes at the end of a long anecdote in which George Moore describes bohemian life as a series of squalid sexual encounters and dreary bouts of drunkenness. The final scene, however, shows the artist's friends (painters) at work, struggling to get the grace of nature onto canvas. "We certainly pigged it together, pigs no doubt, but aspiring pigs, who went out in the morning to the borders of the lake to paint, Lewis able to get down a large willow-tree in the foreground, retaining some parts of the view, rejecting others, fumbling with the beautiful outline of the shore."[13] Moore's ironic reversal shows the affectation behind the "hobohemian" pose of natural debauchery. The artist's creativity rises above the depravities of his spirit so that style supplants subject. In other words, what George Moore finds natural Marianne Moore finds artificial. It is in his art, not in his life, that he makes a place for the genuine.

Moore dropped "George Moore" after *Observations*. She may have felt, with some reason, that the poem was too difficult and not sufficiently tight, whereas "Nothing Will Cure" has a rightness and lucidity in spite of its obscure references. "Blake" never appeared in any of Moore's collections, perhaps because she felt it was slight, but it remains one of her loveliest and wittiest poems of praise.[14] There is no jewel like Moore's praise (even her praise of praise, as in "To William Butler Yeats on Tagore"), just as there is no weapon like her blame (even her blame of blame). Her campaign against absolutists is balanced by her celebrations and defenses of relativists like herself. Moore finds virtue, as she finds vice, in unlikely or hidden places, using metaphor as her Geiger counter just as she used it as her lie detector.

In Moore's poems of praise we find the same principle of chiasmic wit at work. "Blake" is one of the purest examples of this device;

chiasmus controls not only the syntax but the conception and image. The epigram is beautifully suited to its subject if we recall that Moore quoted Yeats naming Blake a "literal realist of the imagination." For one who thought almost entirely in polarities and found the imaginary world more real than this one, the congruence of the compliment is unquestionable.

> I wonder if you feel as you look at us,
> As if you were seeing yourself in a mirror at the end
>   Of a long corridor—walking frail-ly.
> I am sure that we feel as we look at you,
> As if we were ambiguous and all but improbable
>   Reflections of the sun—shining pale-ly.

The uncooperative, uncongenial, and elusive character of wit seems to have troubled Moore even when it was her most brilliant instrument. She always took her mother's opinions to heart, even when she differed with them, and when her mother criticized some of her "prized" work as "ephemeral" she absorbed the remark in self-criticism.[15] In May 1915 she published a private little poem in *Poetry*. But even for those who did not know that Moore and her mother called each other "Rat" and "Mole" respectively, the reticent self-criticism in "To an Intra-Mural Rat" is implicit.

> You make me think of many men
>   Once met, to be forgot again
>   Or merely resurrected
> In a parenthesis of wit
> That found them hastening through it
>   Too brisk to be inspected.   [Observations, 9]

In this rare glance within the walls of the self, Moore turns wit against its own devices. For the weakness of wit is its swiftness, but its strength is elusiveness. And wit that can turn so brilliantly on its own source is not ephemeral, even if it is brisk.

In longer poems Moore replaces these chiasmic strategies with larger counterstructures in statement and form. It is not the theme but its variations that impress us in "The Labors of Hercules" (CP, 53), appropriately so, since the poem's theme is the need to keep an open mind. Moore achieves this openness in her organization of the poem.

The unity of the poem, under constant pressure from the density of its internal relations, is defined in a single long sentence-fragment only completed by the title. Such a unit forces the reader to receive the poem's many words and images at a velocity exceeding his ability to assimilate these materials into familiar semantic structures.[16] That primary motion of reading is paced by the paratactic units of the poem, marked in a series of complex infinitive clauses over which the title is suspended and implicitly repeated. [It takes] "the Labors of Hercules," "to (prove, persuade, teach, etc.) to X (some noun phrase indicating closed-mindedness) that Y (some direct object phrase indicating spontaneity or naturalness). But these units are no firmer in their authority over the whole. Within this rhetorical structure are crossdivisions of punctuation, syntax, line, and word, which deviate from the sponsoring structure and resist subordination.

The asymmetries of diction and word category are perhaps the most striking. Moore bounds from literal to figurative, from abstract to concrete, from colloquial to formal without pause or connective, forcing the mind to exert more than its usual quantum of energy in making its way through the line. The poem is constructed on a series of clichés and dead metaphors revised and expanded out of recognition. This revitalizing of stock phrases is in keeping with the poem's theme, for we are forced to understand actively, rather than receive passively, these thought units. The labors of Hercules are, indeed, demanded by the phrasing, which presents, by elaborate circumlocution, simple ideas. Without such extreme measures, Moore implies, these ideas would not penetrate. Thus "to persuade the stubborn" becomes: "to popularize the mule, its neat exterior / expressing the principle of accommodation reduced to a minimum." The dead metaphor is enlivened by the special emphasis on both its concrete and abstract elements. Similarly, "to change those over-wary of wasting time" by the special concretions of "waste" and "time" becomes "to persuade those self-wrought Midases of brains / whose fourteen-carat ignorance aspires to rise in value, / that one must not borrow a long white beard and tie it on / and threaten with the scythe of time the casually curious." The images are not only yoked to abstractions, but are drawn from two separate realms, tied by the syntax.

The lines break according to yet another system of division, determined more by the rhythm of the whole, which sustains long breaths at first but comes to a gradual halt. Some of these lines carry a single idea, others several ideas, others only incomplete ones. Similarly the paratactic units vary in length and complexity (some clauses marked by "to" and "that" are syntactically subordinate to others), so that our reading in terms of these units meets resistance. Punctuation, too, deviates from, rather than reinforces, the paratactic unit. Minor and major clauses become confused because equalized in the line or in the unit of punctuation.

Taking their cue from Moore's own remarks about revision, critics have generally seen the changes she made in this poem for publication in *Collected Poems* as clarifications. But while she deleted a few lines after *Selected Poems*, she complicated the poem in other ways. Whereas initially a colon had marked out each major infinitive clause and paratactic unit, in the later version Moore's punctuation becomes irregular. What this revision indicates is that the paratactic balance is misleading: some units covertly dominate over others. While the infinitive units continue to divide the poem into short segments, the punctuation after "curious" suggests that the second half of the poem is one long digression on "creative power." Subtly inverting main and subordinate clauses, Moore has displaced "the labors of Hercules" with "creative power" as a controlling phrase. Thus the main sentence "it takes the labors of Hercules to persuade X that Y" contains one long subordinate clause, which gathers a momentum of its own: "one detects creative power by its capacity to prove to X that Y." The tone also changes here, becoming more severe as the syntax becomes more clipped.

In no obvious sense can this poem be considered an example of "plain speaking." While the content is simple, the utterance strains over a dozen crosscurrents, asymmetrically arranged. But these complexities work into the very fabric of statement—they are an essential, not ornamental, part of what is said, making the poem, like the piano, "a free field for etching."[17]

Closure is an inherent problem of paratactic structures, particularly when, as in this poem, deviation has already become a norm. Moore solves the probem in a variety of ways, here by a surprising simplicity and symmetry, of end-stopped indicative phrases, all sharing the same structure and rhythm. The final one-syllable word gives the perfect sense of closure, which works against the momentum of the list and the controlling phrase "one keeps on knowing" to create an effect of gusto so that the energy is compacted and recoils rather than expires in the line.

The "theme" of "People's Surroundings" (CP, 55–57) is really a minimal instruction for reading its variations: people's surroundings are synecdoches of their character. We are told "they answer one's questions" but the answers and questions are as infinite as humanity. To the extent that a poem is dominated by theme, its narrator intrudes on her materials. Under the rubric of "People's Surroundings" Moore has resisted statement almost completely, so that by the end of the poem the images overwhelm the syntax, which indicates little more than two columns into which an infinite range of nouns for people and places could be placed. The poem seems to release these words from the structures that have borne them, as if deferring to the stronger tow of dense reality.[18]

In the body of the poem Moore details several settings, and these intimacies, too, work against the pat, periodic formula, until the formula itself is inverted: "these are questions more than answers." We become lost in the variety Moore asks us to absorb. Seemingly random objects, bits of speech, attitudes, presented at varying length and with varying complexity, become expressions of character.

> The vast indestructible necropolis
> of composite Yawman-Erbe separable units;
> the steel, the oak, the glass, the Poor Richard publications
> containing the public secrets of efficiency
> on paper so thin that "one thousand four hundred and twenty
> pages make one inch,"
> exclaiming, so to speak, When you take my time, you take something I had meant to use

This surrounding speaks of efficiency and economy. The next passage presents quite the opposite, though in a similarly understated manner. All these items are decorative and superfluous:

> the highway hid by fir trees in rhododendron twenty feet deep,
> the peacocks, hand-forged gates, old Persian velvet,
> roses outlined in pale black on an ivory ground,
> the pierced iron shadows of the cedars,
> Chinese carved glass, old Waterford, lettered ladies;
> landscape gardening twisted into permanence

But why is the final phrase set off by a semicolon? Though this punctuation has no clear semantic function, it slows the rhythm of the stanza. This slowing draws attention to the last unit in the otherwise breathless list of images, and prepares the reader for a contrasting stanza, which is based not on efficiency or luxury but on directness. We go from "landscape gardening twisted into permanence" to "straight lines over such great distances"; and from the instinctive horizontals of the American West we move in the next stanza to the verticals of "Bluebeard's Tower above the coral reefs," where "sophistication, 'like an escalator,' 'cut the nerve of progress'." In each section, then, the perception of an essential form in a range of contexts suggests an essential character in a range of attitudes.

Moore's impulse to order things according to taxonomies determines the structure of "The Buffalo," "The Plumet Basilisk," and several other poems. This encyclopedic ambition is never realized since it always works back down to the particular. In one way or another most of these poems conclude with an image or form that defies category. Thus "England" (CP, 46–47), which turns out, ironically, to be about America, concludes of this country (after pigeonholing others), "it has never been confined to one locality." "England" is the best of these paratactic poems not only because of its "and" connectives have a cumulative effect but because its density and understatement do not defeat the reader, as sometimes happens in "The Labors of Hercules" or "People's Surroundings." In each cluster of national trademarks Moore includes an abstract word toward which the image-filings discreetly gravitate:

> and Greece with its goat and its gourds,
> the nest of modified illusions: and France,
> the "chrysalis of the nocturnal butterfly,"
> in whose products mystery of construction
> diverts one from what was originally one's object—
> substance at the core: and the East with its snails, its emotional
>
> shorthand and jade cockroaches, its rock crystal and its imperturb-
> ability
> all of museum quality

The charm of Moore's national stereotyping rests in the surprising details she invokes. Have we ever thought of Italy's "equal shores" as the symbol of its "epicureanism from which the grossness has been extracted," or of England's "baby rivers" as more than accidental, in fact as meeting "the criterion of suitability and convenience"? The imagination that sees such significance in the outline of dead fact believes passionately in the inherent order of things, but is also wary of imposing order prematurely. The warning at the end of "These Various Scalpels" stands as Moore's motto: "why dissect destiny with instruments more highly specialized than components of destiny itself?" The poem's procedure, as testimony to this complaint, is to parody the Renaissance convention of the blazon of beauties, creating drastic incongruities between the parts of the natural anatomy and their baroque appearances. Moore's leaps of association are a devastating weapon of wit: "your cheeks, those rosettes / of blood on the stone floors of French chateaux, / with regard to which the guides are so affirmative." But as if to guard against her own reckless dissection, she allows her images to gather a momentum of their own:

> your other hand,
>
> a bundle of lances all alike, partly hid by emeralds from Persia
>   and the fractional magnificence of Florentine
>   goldwork—a collection of little objects—
>   sapphires set with emeralds, and pearls with a moonstone,
>   made fine
>   with enamel in gray, yellow, and dragonfly blue; a lemon, a
>   pear
>
> and three bunches of grapes, tied with silver

The "message" here is that her jewels weigh down her hand just as the details weigh down the sentence. But Moore also indulges, as she does often, in the rhythm of the list for its own sake.

On the surface, "Marriage" (CP, 62–70) is Moore's most loosely structured poem—a collection of flies in amber. It stands out among her poems, too, for its streamlined appearance over many pages, which speeds up the train of associated epithets and mottos. But Moore hinders the relentless pace of the catalogue (this is her longest poem) not only with her usual convoluted sentence structure, but with a pattern of ironic counterpoints and tonal contrasts. As the language rises and falls, strokes and bites its subject, as Adam's view of Eve is set against her view of him, the poem's dialectical structure shuttles across its linear advance.

I wonder what Adam and Eve
think of it by this time,
this fire-gilt steel
alive with goldenness;
how bright it shows—
"of circular traditions and impostures,
committing many spoils,"
requiring all one's criminal ingenuity
to avoid!

Our impulse is to privilege the demystification, the prosaic over the lyrical, the contemporary over the nostalgic, but sentiment regains its buoyancy in the poem. Verbal irony gives way to a deeper, more tragic irony here:

Below the incandescent stars
below the incandescent fruit,
the strange experience of beauty;
its existence is too much;
it tears one to pieces
and each fresh wave of consciousness
is poison.

Elsewhere the irony lapses as Moore looses the imagination into detail for its own sake.

a crouching mythological monster
in that Persian miniature of emerald mines,
raw silk—ivory white, snow white,
oyster white, and six others—
that paddock full of leopards and giraffes—
long lemon-yellow bodies
sown with trapezoids of blue.

In her conclusion Moore describes an institution not only ironic and absurd but also dynamic and enticing in its balance of contentions.

One sees that it is rare—
that striking grasp of opposites
opposed each to the other, not to unity,

which in cycloid inclusiveness
has dwarfed the demonstration
of Columbus with the egg—
a triumph of simplicity—

When Williams observed that Moore achieved her effects by rapidity rather than fragmentation, he was thinking of "Marriage," but
his remarks are even more pertinent to "Bowls."[19] The poem's rapidity
is perfectly in keeping with the subject, or more accurately, with the associative principle—prompt precision. The extreme difficulty of the
poem is due in part to the abstraction and reticence of its central idea,
which draws together images and anecdotes with no practical connection—bowling, Chinese painting, etymology, magazine correspondence—all in two sentences. Among Moore's poems "Bowls" most
closely fits Pound's notion of *periplum*, which he defines under the
analogy of a ship moving swiftly along a coast and gathering glimpses of
exotic landscapes as it passes them. The images are not absorbed by
their natural context but develop into a new, dynamic relation in the
poet's, and in turn the reader's, imagination. The line breaks do not aid
our interpretation of "Bowls" but complicate it by varying syntactic
value. The many lines beginning "and," for instance, are not equal in
their grammatical status. The poem's white-water surface may finally
drown interpretation. The sarcasm, for instance, in Moore's prompt response to imprecise questions remains largely submerged. But the
structure and rhythm of the poem are so fitted to its subject and image
that we tend to accept its obscurity on a first reading as the necessary
blur of the landscape from a fast-moving vehicle, which draws to a neat
epigrammatic halt and final focus.

Geoffrey Hartman's casual notes are again the single best summary of the relationship of form and meaning in Moore's verse, and are
particularly descriptive of poems like "Bowls":

This mind, or rather Miss Moore's, is "an enchanting
thing"; it takes us by its very irrelevancies. Here too everything is surface; she talks, so to say, from the top of her
mind and represents herself as a gossip on the baroque scale.
But secretly she is a magician, and distracts on purpose.
While her message eludes us through understatement, the
poem itself remains teasingly alive through overstatement of
its many tactics, till we accept the conventional rabbit,
glorified by prestidigitation. Yet the magic of language be-

comes intensely moral on further acquaintance and her crazy quilt of thoughts, quotations and sounds resolves into subtler units of meaning and rhythm. The free (but not formless) verse helps break up the automatic emphases of traditional syntax, and respects the more dynamic shifts of the inner, and not merely spoken voice . . . Her technique is not uniform, not abstractly applied; it depends on the movement of the whole poem.[20]

We have been attending to those subtler units of meaning; the units of rhythm also call for comment. Moore gives some clues as to her view of the relation between rhythm and meaning in "The Accented Syllable," published in *The Egoist* in October 1916. The article begins: "For the most part, in what we read, it is the meaning rather than the tone of voice which gives us pleasure. By the tone of voice I mean that intonation in which the accents which are responsible for it are so unequivocal as to persist, no matter under what circumstances the syllables are read or by whom they are read." But the tendency of the article as a whole is to emphasize the importance of "tone of voice." Though "intonation must have meaning behind it to support it, or it is not worth much," meaning with a dull intonation fails to delight. Most of her examples prove the latter point. And her final example, of language which "isn't worth much" because of its vacuity, nevertheless points up how close many of her own lines are to pure rhythm. It was the throbbing force of the line that drew Moore to the Hebrew poets, and it is often the rhythm, integrated with the rhetorical structure, that determines the movement of her poems. Moore's alternations between long and short sentences and clauses, between lists and epigrams, is primarily a function of rhythm. The rhythmic effect of her catalogues is variety in repetition. The asymmetries of syllable length, of phrases against single words, make this list from "The Steeple Jack," for instance, a pleasure to the ear as much as to the eye:

> the trumpet vine,
> foxglove, giant snapdragon, a salpiglossis that has
> spots and stripes; morning-glories, gourds
>   or moon-vines trained on fishing twine
> at the back door:
>
> cattails, flags, blueberries and spiderwort,
>   striped grass, lichens, sunflowers, asters, daisies—
> yellow and crab-claw ragged sailors with green bracts—toad-plant,

        petunias, ferns; pink lilies, blue
                ones, tigers; poppies; black sweet-peas.   [CP, 5–6]

We do not visualize these items so much as relish their sounds, and the general impression of variety. Similarly, the brevity and compactness of the epigram are more striking than its content. We hardly ponder the *sententia* at the end of "Bowls." Set against the accelerating rhythm of a list or a compound sentence it provides a dramatic finality that makes the poem rebound. The same is true in "Four Quartz Crystal Clocks." The thematic conclusiveness of the word "punctuality" works beautifully against the velocity of the sentence:

                        And as

        MEridian-seven one-two
    one-two gives, each fifteenth second
        in the same voice, the new
    data—"The time will be" so and so—
        you realize that "when you
            hear the signal," you'll be

    hearing Jupiter or jour pater, the day god—
        the salvaged son of Father Time—
    telling the cannibal Chronos
        (eater of his proxime
    newborn progeny) that punctuality
        is not a crime   [CP, 116]

       Moore's fondness for contrapuntal effects, reinforced by internal rhyme, alliteration, and assonance, is so dominant in some poems as to defeat the conventional rhythm of the sentence. But most often it creates an effective tension in the line, pulling against the automatic movement of syntax. Such a tension can immediately revise our learned responses to words. In "Nine Nectarines" the contrapuntal effects convert prosaic objects and statements into lyric grace:

        Fuzzless through slender crescent leaves
            of green or blue or
            both, in the Chinese style, the four

pairs' half-moon leaf-mosaic turns
out to the sun the sprinkled blush
of puce-American-Beauty pink
applied to beeswax gray by the
uninquiring brush
of mercantile bookbinding.   [CP, 29]

The ping-pong of syllables frees the ear from the advance of the sentence and the reduction of meaning. Sometimes Moore's rhythms will reinforce a view she is taking of an object—the Swinburne-like low down-swing of the plumet basilisk, the nervous half-note hop of the jerboa. It means little, however, to say that image is controlling rhythm, since the animals are so often allegories of aesthetic qualities. Image and rhythm develop mutually. The sustained climax achieved in the several long stresses against short stresses of "The Frigate Pelican" are beautifully reinforced by the image of a bird riding on the channels of the wind: "These, unturbulent, avail / themselves of turbulence to fly—pleased / with the faint wind's varyings, / on which to spread fixed wings" (SP, 25). These are just minor instances of a control of rhythm so pervasive as to be the major determinant of the poem, but so integrated as to be hardly noticed.[21]

In descriptions of her poetic practice Moore always deemphasized her control over materials. "Nature's laws of motion have to be obeyed," she observed in a lecture at Bryn Mawr.[22] The starch and bustle of meter and regular rhyme were, to her, too confining and too noisy. "In the Days of Prismatic Color" parodies meter as a monster: "In the short-legged, fit- / ful advance, the gurgling and all the minutiae—we have the classic / multitude of feet. To what purpose!" "In the absence of feet" she offers "a method of conclusions, a knowledge of principles." But that method is not so hidden as she suggests in "To a Snail." It would be a mistake to ignore the careful prosodic design of Moore's poems. Moore herself was always down-playing her influence over them. Poems emerge, she said, as a "felicity of words or combinations of words which seem to demand that other words be written around them." To Donald Hall she remarked "words cluster like chromosomes." But she practices genetic control from the start, shaping the lines of the first stanza out of rhymes she discovers in it. The nature of chromosomes is to reproduce themselves. While Moore's first stanza may indeed emerge out of the internal rhythms of a statement, the shape of the poem as a whole will often follow the initial pattern of the syllables. Since aural effects are more dominant than visual effects in the surface of language, Moore's syllabic method is perhaps more discreet than metrics, interfering less with the utterance. But it is no more spontaneous. Syllabic measure works independently of statement, allowing statement its own order while establishing a new order in which words are liberated from syntax.

Moore's equivocation about her syllabic method is one of many instances of her ambivalence about form. We see a similar mixedmindedness in "No Swan So Fine," which has the sonnet's fourteen lines, but which is otherwise free verse. The poem's theme, similarly, describes this ambivalence. In her interview with Hall she often gives an irritated response to his queries about form. For example, Hall asks, "How do you plan the shape of your stanzas? I am thinking of the poems, usually syllabic, which employ a repeated stanza form. Do you ever experiment with shapes before you write, by drawing lines on a page?" And Moore replies:

> Never, I never "plan" a stanza. Words cluster like chromosomes, determining the procedure. I may influence an arrangement or thin it, then try to have successive stanzas identical with the first. Spontaneous initial originality—say, impetus—seems difficult to reproduce consciously later. As Stravinsky said about pitch: "If I transpose it for some reason, I am in danger of losing the freshness of first contact and will have difficulty in recapturing its attractiveness."
>
> No, I never "draw lines." I make a rhyme conspicuous to me at a glance, by underlining with red, blue or other pencil—as many colors as I have rhymes to differentiate. However, if the phrases recur in too incoherent an architecture—as print—I notice the words as a tune do not sound right.[23]

During a reading at Harvard University in 1963, Moore objected to the words of a critic who had "accused" her of being a rigid writer of syllabic verse. "Syllabic verse," she said, is an "ogre" and a "misdemeanor." However, she went on to say that "for practical reasons we like to know how well one stanza matches another, how nearly identical it is."[24] What these "practical" reasons are, she never explains. Moore never felt entirely at ease with her prosodic practice. Poems like "Peter," "When I Buy Pictures," and "To a Snail," originally in matched stanzas, she later converted to free verse. But she was no more comfortable with the notion of "free verse" and as often rejected that label. Moore never dropped the practice of syllabics, for while it confined language in one sense, it freed language in a number of ways. "The Jerboa," she observed in a lecture, should actually be one continuous poem rather than a series of stanzas, but read as one block the effect seemed "heavy."[25] By attending to the properties of language as free as possible from syntax, Moore opened her poems to imaginative renewal while providing the satisfaction of something said.

Moore equivocated in the same way about her method of quotation; she insisted that her motive was deference and humility, but she practiced considerable independence in her borrowings. I have been exploring some of the ways Moore places a poem's various orders in a dynamic relation. Her poems also stand in a dynamic relation to the richness of language outside their boundaries, from which they are constructed. It is not to things that her poems refer, but to ordinary language, to the meanings we frame for everyday use, which the poem rearranges and challenges. Moore's poetry emphasizes this inevitable linguistic mediation of experience, by using quotation. Just as by setting one form against another she tries to liberate the poem from static form, so by reordering the statements of others in her own linguistic system, she tries to involve the reader creatively in a unique act of ordering.

Probably no other poet kept such careful track of the world as it is mediated by the printed word. Moore's diaries are not personal records, or even commonplace books, in the sense that others use these terms. Moore immersed herself in a world of words. We can say, of course, that these words refer *to* things, but given her selection and use of these notes, she seems to have at least as much interest in their nature as linguistic constructions, kinds of representation, as in their subjects. Indeed, Moore uses pieces of language in much the same way as other poets use images.

For the critic familiar with Moore's work, these notebooks provide a history of her creative process, which has less to do with finding out what she wants to say than it does with selecting and reordering what has already been said. Long passages in these notebooks will appear unfamiliar, but unexpectedly the student of Moore will find a phrase or a line that the poet has preserved for the verse. A single poem may include lines from an unpredictable range of materials read over a long expanse of time. Moore seems to have little regard, as she writes, for the context of her quotations. As Laurence Stapleton has pointed out, she sometimes collected materials on a specific "subject" in order to write about it.[26] In this sense the sources may "influence" her product, but even then she tends to equalize these materials and to redirect them in the poem. As often as not she radically distorts the original meaning of the words by juxtaposing them with materials from quite distinct contexts.

"An Octopus" is a collage of voices culled, as Moore's own notes tell us, from sources including Newman's *Historical Sketches*, Baxter's *Saint's Everlasting Rest*, Hyde's *Five Philosophies*, Trollope's *Autobiography*, the Department of National Parks Rules and Regulations, and a conversation overheard at a circus. Among the sources Moore cites for "An Octopus" are articles from *The Illustrated London News* and *The London Graphic*, both of which have to do with the octopus. But since the poem is really about Mt. Rainier and the glacier on it, and not about an octopus at all, Moore has already taken considerable liberties with her sources. If we look at these "sources" we see how much freedom she exercises in reordering the materials presented in these articles. I will quote a section from each copied part of the article, in order to give the reader a sense of how Moore draws from her source. Here is the beginning of Moore's notes from *The Illustrated London News* concerning an octopus:

The arms seemed to approach the prey from all directions [. . .] To the uninitiated the ill[ustration] would suggest that the cephalapod is looking to the left, but this is not so. The animal is facing right, 8 arms long tapering cones all joined at their bases to form a crown around the mouth [. . .] The cep[halapod] itself is very powerful; photograph 3 showing large stones wh[ich] the animal has pushed aside w[ith the] greatest ease [. . .] Arms injured not infrequently & in time regenerated. Usually rests w[ith] its dome on [the] ground and the arms extended in front at an acute angle under some shelving rock or in a dark corner [. . .] Often the animal digs itself in. This is done in a slow deliberate manner. If disturbed escapes by swimming away backwards, arms trailed horizontally [. . .] during these movements the color changes to an extraordinary degree. Normally large patches of reddish buff are seen on a cream background. When excited the animal's skin [turns] a deep terracotta. If frightened an intense ghostly pallor passes right over the animal except on the undersurface of the suckers & the web. The

> delicate green metallic tinge (etched on [the] wan green air)
> is due to iridocysts below the layer of the color cells [which]
> lie in the skin[.] Only swims when he wishes to escape—at
> other times he creeps suggesting meditated stealth.[27]

This long excerpt "provides" Moore with two lines: "Creeping slowly
as with meditated stealth, its arms seeming to approach from all directions" and "its ghostly pallor changing to the green metallic tinge of an
anemone-starred pool." In fact the last clause of this second line comes
not from the *London News* but from the *London Graphic*; Moore saw
the connection only by inference.

> The octopus is really a timid creature [and] makes his home
> in the rock pools in quite an innocent fashion. Off the Bre-
> ton coast he is undoubtedly very destructive [. . .] Care must
> be taken when exploring the wonderful anemone starred
> pools [. . .] to avoid . . . treading on an "arm" [. . .] The fish-
> ermen are very scornful of the tourists' alarm of these queer
> beasts [. . .] The big arms, double rowed [with] 140 suckers
> each are of amazing strength [and] unimaginable delicacy
> combined with extreme delicacy of touch [. . .] It can pick a
> periwinkle out of a crack, [and] yet crush a larger prey [with]
> the grip of a small python.[28]

Moore does cite this source for "picking periwinkles" but clearly made
other uses of it; she may even have drawn from this passage the idea of
putting tourists in her poem.

Honesty and humility, then, are clearly not Moore's only motives
for quotation. Indeed a large percentage of her borrowings remained
undocumented. A statement she copied in her reading notebook is
closer to her actual practice: "A good stealer is *ipso facto* a good inventor."[29] Like a contemporary sculptor who rummages in junk yards,
Moore welds together the shards of language to invent an individual reality. One of the functions of her quotations, then, is to show that the
poem is constructed of other verbal constructions, and to pull the poem
back into that plurality, even while she tries to unify the plurality. In
this sense the notes are an important part of the poems. We see this
especially in poems like "Marriage" or "An Octopus," which are made
up almost entirely of quotations from a disconcerting range of sources.
When Pound read Eliot's draft of *The Waste Land* he marked
"Marianne" in the margin. Mrs. Eliot has asserted this is not Moore,

but Pound could have been warning his friend against borrowing another poet's trademark. In any case Moore's quotations and notes are entirely different from Eliot's. Her borrowings do not extend the meaning of her poem into the worlds they allude to. While in a sense there is no surface immediacy in *The Waste Land*, in Moore's poetry the surface is everything. The remarks she quotes are not always reflective or profound; they are more often accidental displays of style which retain the flavor, but seldom the intention, of their source. Moore demonstrates both a continuity and a discontinuity with ordinary language. This peculiar relation to language is most graphically presented in the form of an index, not of titles or first lines but of subjects, at the end of *Observations*, which equalizes concrete and abstract words, proper and ordinary nouns. Such an index brings the multiplicity of the world into the volume of the poem, but it likewise denies the poem its exclusive function and its autonomy of form.

Quotation is also a mark of the poet's reticence; this is not only a matter of humility, but of the definition of poetry. For Moore, a poem is *not* a functional utterance; rather, it is an ordering of language. The poet's function is not to say something, so much as to creatively order and reimagine our sayings.

That constant sifting and rearranging went on not only from her notes to her poems, but from her notes on poems and her revisions of poems. While Stevens is right in seeing Moore's poems as individual realities, they are always tentative and open-ended, emerging from and returning to the larger pool of words. This is revealed most clearly in the poetry workbooks, which indicate not separate acts of composition but rather one endless act of composition from which lines would spin off into distinct poems.[30]

Moore's idea of "plain speaking," then, is connected to her idea of the genuine. Since words mediate and thus distort experience, plain speaking is an interesting impossibility. The self-proclaimed plain speakers of the world have mistaken rhetoric for reality. Moore's formal techniques are designed to resist the complacent and illusory conventions of speech. By setting internal and external levels of organization against each other in the poems, she involves her readers creatively in the process of interpreting experience.

7. *Ut Pictura Poesis*
Moore and the Visual Arts

$\mathbf{M}$OORE'S APPROACH to form was influenced not only by other contemporary poets but by artists of several generations and styles. Her awareness of the power of conventional form in determining thought, and her techniques for creating dynamic effects in the static frame of art, were often stimulated by visual sources. To understand fully Moore's approach to both representational and formal problems, we must acknowledge and investigate her long fascination with the visual arts.

Moore's dominant sense, most would agree, was sight. Her metaphors are based on visual resemblance, her stanzas are arranged by the look of the page rather than by metrical rhythm or rhyme. Not surprisingly, she identified the objectives and problems of her art with those of visual artists. As she wrote to Samuel French Morse in 1934, "With regard to color and image, the arts are so closely interrelated it seems to me, that descriptiveness in any one of them can achieve itself in terms of another. Exact resemblance is, is it not, a major objective in each."[1] I have been examining Moore's poetry within the context of literary convention, but the problems and solutions described in the previous chapters developed in a context that included the visual arts. In this relation, again, Moore's own comments are misleading. For "descriptiveness" and "exact resemblance" are not really what she admires or practices. What she admires is style and conception, though often rendered in minute particularity. Visual art offered her models of thought and feeling captured in immediate sensation. Perhaps more important, visual art offered her a store of images and techniques from which she could draw in creating her own patterns of resemblance. Moore's mind was highly metaphoric— it lept across natural connections to see the resemblances in unlike things. But it was also very concrete, and the visual arts provided examples of abstract connections, of line, color, shape composing discrete particulars through visual rhyme.

In the modernist period the reciprocity of the arts is such that it makes little sense to talk in hierarchical terms of painting as the model for poetry or vice versa. They had common goals and exchanged insights. As the conventions of each medium were called into question, each looked to inherent qualities of the other as a means of redefining strategies. Painters considered how poetic metaphor leaps the boundaries of nature by its conceptual freedom. Poets considered how painting engages the body by its sensuous impact. It would be a mistake to isolate these disciplines, since they flourished by crossfertilization. In New York in the first decade of this century at least, avant-garde writers drew some of their inspiration directly from painters. According to Bram Dijkstra "imagism" was already second nature to poets in contact with painters.[2] And while others who generated their poetic out of an amorphous "imagism" gradually drew away from the visual arts, Moore, like Williams, continued to find in them a major stimulus for her poems. Since no study of Moore has paid any detailed attention to this well-documented interest, the whole topic needs examination.

Moore's interest in drawing and painting began early. Her favorite classes at Carlisle High School were in art, and she thought of becoming a painter after graduation from college. The Rosenbach Foundation has about thirty of her drawings of flowers and landscapes. Drawing was a habit with her, second only to that of writing. Sketches accompany many of her notebook entries, and though rapidly drawn, they show considerable draftsmanship.

Moore's scrapbooks and notebooks (from which she drew the material for her poems) include, from the beginning, regular entries on the visual arts. Besides keeping drawings and bibelots and a large collection of postcards and magazine reproductions, she copied out long passages from articles announcing auctions, describing shows, and assessing new artistic movements. Moore's book collection is dominated by this subject, and while it is not a reliable source (she occasionally sold her books for extra money and many books were sent as gifts) it is indicative of the place visual art held in her imaginative and intellectual life.[3]

After graduating from Bryn Mawr, Moore returned to her home in Carlisle, Pennsylvania, far from the fomenting excitement in New

York. But she lived it vicariously, clipping articles from *Letters and Arts, Literary Digest, Current Opinion, Literary Spectator,* all journals that were covering the revolution in the arts. From the articles in her scrapbook for this period one can discover the major poles in the controversy over modernism, which came to a head at the Armory Show in February of 1913. Moore seems to have been obsessed with this event, saving over a dozen articles about it.[4] She also saved articles on modernism in the theater, ballet, and fashion; articles on offshoots of cubism such as futurism and fauvism; and theoretical discussions, in particular a review of *Cubism* by Gleizes and Metzinger, the chief spokesmen for the movement. Her curiosity took her beyond the casual article to more serious reading, and her notebook includes long passages copied from W. H. Wright's *Modern Painting* and *Creative Will,* both of which discuss European modernist painting in detail. Naturally, her own developing forms were stirred by the waves of such news.

Moore's interest was not an outsider's for long. In her 1909 notebook she jotted down an address that came to symbolize the New York avant-garde, and which would become important to her as well:

Paul Haviland

291 Fifth Ave

Alfred Stieglitz

This was, of course, the address of the 291 Gallery, the "acropolis" of American modernism.[5] In 1915 Moore finally saw some of the spectacle first hand. Her first visit to New York City included, as a high priority, a visit to 291, and a letter to her brother records what she saw there.[6] A picture of the sea she refers to was probably done by John Marin, whom she would get to know well. She also mentions a Steichen photograph of Gordon Craig, the set designer whose work and personality Moore had read about with interest and who would shortly emerge in poems ("To a Man Making His Way Through a Crowd," and "Picking and Choosing.") Moore's principal host on this trip, however, was not Alfred Stieglitz but Alfred Kreymborg, editor of *Others* and a major sponsor, with his coeditor Walter Arensberg, in bringing poets and painters together.

When Moore moved with her family to Chatham, New Jersey, she was only a short train ride from this mecca, and as she told Donald Hall, she became more and more bold in "venturing forth to bohemian parties"[7] at 291 and elsewhere. At any of these places, she met artists from the area—William and Marguerite Zorach (who did the covers for *Others*), Marsden Hartley, Charles Demuth, Paul Strand, Elie Nadelman, Bertram Hartman, Charles Sheeler, Gaston Lachaise, to name only a few. She also might have met some of her future colleagues at *The Dial*, Paul Rosenfeld and Henry McBride, the art critics, Scofield Thayer, the literary editor and a major collector of American and European modernism (whose collection Moore would certainly have seen), Sibley and Hildegaard Watson, art editors and later intimate friends of Moore's.

Moore was obviously dazzled by these companions, and her conversation notebooks in the early Twenties are dominated by their lively interaction. We get to know not only their informed opinions of each other's work, but a great deal about the gossip of the day; and of course the occasional observation finds its way into one of Moore's poems.[8]

Moore was also interested in the work of "precisionists," as she observes in "Bowls." She may well have had in mind the work of Charles Sheeler, Georgia O'Keeffe, and others from 291 who borrowed ideas and techniques from photographers like Alfred Stieglitz and Paul Strand and who called themselves precisionists. Like Moore, they aimed for visual accuracy in rendering the objective world and attempted to preserve an emotional quality in an impersonal medium.

As Moore grew closer to the circle of *The Dial*, of which she eventually became editor, her exchange with leading figures in the art scene became part of everyday life. Her interest in Paul Rosenfeld is clearly recorded in her commemorative essay on him, and in "*The Dial*, a Retrospect" she speaks with personal as well as professional warmth of Henry McBride and Gaston Lachaise. That the painting in *The Dial* was an integral part of the magazine is clear in the paragraph she devotes to it in which she mentions Rousseau, Stuart Davis, Arthur Dove, Georgia O'Keeffe, Wyndham Lewis, Brancusi, Picasso, Seurat, Cocteau, among others. Moore was responsible primarily for literary decisions during her years as editor of *The Dial*, but since Scofield Thayer and Sibley Watson were both living some distance from New York during that time, she undoubtedly had an influence on what pictures were printed. (She was directly responsible, for instance, for printing some American Indian art.) Her comment on Charles Sheeler shows both her awareness of the goings-on of the art production and an attention to the qualities of the works themselves: "I think of Charles Sheeler coping with the difficulty of photographing for reproduction Lachaise's polished brass head of Scofield Thayer, mounted on glass—glitteringly complicated from any angle—and have never seen anything effected with less ado or greater care; these scientifically businesslike proceedings reminding one of the wonderfully mastered Bucks County Barn and winding stair turn."[9]

With their native genius for putting pictures into words, poets have traditionally taken on the challenge of art criticism. Moore had written an article on sculptor Alfeo Faggi in *The Dial* in 1921, and often in her "Comment" she would discuss a book on the visual arts. She was regularly called on to write catalogue introductions, reviews of exhibitions, and similar articles presenting contemporary events to the public, and she seems to have enjoyed and worked hard at this activity. Quite often, it provided her with an occasion to consider the moral value of art, and the self-reflexiveness of such passages is always striking. Clearly she saw herself as involved in the same enterprise that occupied the visual artists. In her writing about the poster artist E. McKnight Kauffer, we see her empathy in clear echoes of her own poetry:

> Instinctiveness, imagination, and "the sense of artistic difficulty" with him, have interacted till we have an objectified logic of sensibility as inescapable as the colors refracted from a prism . . . Kauffer is a parable of uncompromise—a master of illusion . . . verifying Democritus' axiom, "Compression is the first grace of style." "What is to be feared more than death?" the man asked; the sage replied "Disillusion." Here, actually, we have a product in which unfalsified impulse safeguards illusion.

Throughout her career artists reciprocated, making sketches, busts, and photographs of her.[10]

But in her embrace of the new Moore never turned away from the old masters. "The past is the present," she is always reminding us. She was a regular reader of the arts column of the *Illustrated London News*, and she went to many exhibitions of earlier European and Oriental art. Museums bring the mind almost into contact with the dead, as we learn in her unpublished poem "Museums." They awaken, as the urn did for Keats, an insatiable curiosity. Gusto, in the visual arts, was for Moore as it was for Hazlitt, "the impression made on one sense [which] excites by affinity those of another."

Museums
are good things, never wholly barren, superficial, ignorant.
"Where was it
made and by whom was it worn?" The collection of armor, at
first sight no more than so much hardware, becomes

upon examination, cause for burning speculation.[11]

"The museum exists / for those who are able to enjoy what they see,"
and part of the pleasure to her greedy eye is simply the grab bag of fact.
"But there is there, something more mellow than information." Perhaps more important, "one goes to a museum to refresh one's mind
with / the appearance of what one has always valued." Museums are,
for Moore, a way of concentrating and renewing her relation to the
world. And indeed, the qualities of the objects she describes in this
poem are on display everywhere in her work. Finally, museums attract
by their variety, and by the variety of reactions one can have to them.

This variety, in the poetry, as in museums, can overwhelm us at
first. While William Carlos Williams and Gertrude Stein focused primarily on modern painting (Williams's interest in the old masters did
not develop until late in his career), Moore's interest in art took her as
far back as Egypt and as far afield as fashion design. From the beginning, her poems make references to artists as different as Giotto, Gargallo, Giorgione, Da Vinci, El Greco, Dürer; to Chinese painting and
Persian miniatures; not only to painting and sculpture but to decorative
arts, tapestry, pottery, glassware. Her documents demonstrate a considerable interest in cartoon art, theater design, armor, and costuming. She
read in the philosophy, psychology, and sociology of art as well, and
took notes on the biographies of artists.

The student of Moore needs to learn how to place a certain document of interest (a picture, an article, a note) in the system of Moore's
responses. As we can see from "Museums," she is sometimes drawn by
artistic sympathy or identification, sometimes by curiosity, sometimes
by distaste. She may attend to the representation, to the art object itself,
to the artist who made it, or to the critic observing it. (Moore's notebooks are full of detailed descriptions of particular artworks, many of
which she never saw. It often seems true that she is more attracted to
the particularity of critical language than to what it describes.)

Sometimes a work of art offers Moore a ready-made image of her subject; at other times she acts as art critic, interested in the kind of visual imagination or artistic virtue or vice represented by a particular work. The artwork may become an occasion for considering the stoniness of art in the stream of life. And indirectly it may provide a model for her own formal problems and solutions. Selection was, for Moore, a means of expression, and we can begin to outline the imagination moving across these diverse visual surfaces.

Almost every poem Moore wrote involved a picture or art object at some stage of composition. She drew her materials, and often her subjects, from art, from representation, not from life. Sometimes the painting or object served as a quick reference, a kind of visual shorthand (as in her allusions to Dürer and El Greco in "The Steeple Jack" and "The Hero") the focus of reflection ("Nine Nectarines," "No Swan So Fine"), or less directly, as a source of aesthetic principles and techniques (Chinese painting and porcelain, emblematic art, cubism). Within these three basic areas we find Moore constantly alert to visual suggestion, but always adapting visual materials to the special requirements of her literary constructions.

In a sense, Moore quotes painters, sculptors, ceramicists, just as she quotes other writers. Rather than convert a picture into a description, she will refer to particular works of art that capture a quality or image she wants to convey. Her "research" on prospective subjects always included collecting visual representations, and often she would make her own thumbnail sketch from a picture she had seen.[12] But as in her style of quotation, the references to art are often taken from contexts entirely unrelated to the occasion of the poem, so that in thinking of the pangolin, for instance, she will suddenly imagine "Gargallo's hollow iron head" or "the Westminster Abbey Thomas of Leighton Wrought-Iron Vine," or in thinking of imperial display she will refer to "Lord Nelson's Revolving Diamond Rosette." This is just one more example of the scope of Moore's imagination, her ability to create a poetic order out of widely divergent materials, often culled over a period of several years. Something more than visual precision is involved in the specificity of these references. Often they will advance not only the visual accuracy, but the theme of a poem, so that "the Chinese brush technique" of the basilisk's tail enhances our sense of his elusiveness, the "Parthenon" curves of the paper nautilus contrast Greek ideals of beauty with mercenary interests.

Characteristically, Moore reads moral meaning into aesthetic qualities. The chameleon-like iridescence of a French brocade (out of which she had a jacket made) will be a guard against dejection in "No Better Than A 'Withered Daffodil' "; the curves of the chambered nautilus express emotional restraint in "Paper Nautilus"; the curve of a Swan's neck "like the mathematic sign: greater than," suggests moral gracefulness in "See in the Midst of Fair Leaves." Her delight that all the surfaces of nature are functional provokes her insistence on experiencing meaning in visual terms. Moore was fascinated by color psychology and kept notes on the subject in her early years.[13] "The Buffalo" opens with an assignment of moral distinctions along the lines of visual distinctions:

> Black in blazonry means
> prudence; and niger, unpropitious. Might
> hematite—
> > black, compactly incurved horns on bison
> > have significance? The
> > soot-brown tail-tuft on
> > a kind of lion
>
> tail; what would that express? [CP, 27][14]

Often the pictorial source of a poem or line will remain secret. A photograph Moore preserved in her scrapbook of 1909–1913 was the source of "Snakes, Mongoose, Snake-Charmers and the Like"; a postcard reproduction of an anonymous nineteenth-century American work, "Meditation by the Sea," may have helped her in thinking about "A Grave." There are covert visual reserves as well as covert verbal reserves for most of these subtle poetic surfaces.

Moore's references to visual artists are often ways of capturing aesthetic attitudes, which for her always imply moral attitudes as well. We have an especially striking example of this method in the paired poems "The Steeple-Jack" and "The Hero," whose resident artists are, respectively, Dürer and El Greco. Dürer is the first word of "The Steeple-Jack" which is in turn the first poem in *Selected Poems* and subsequent collections.[15] The artist's work comes up often in her poetry (in "Apparition of Splendor" she mentions Dürer's rhinoceros, and in "Then the Ermine" his violets), and she included an article on him among her "Comments" in *The Dial.* Moore's interest in this artist is predictable, for the two have a great deal in common. Like Moore, Dürer was absorbed by the particular. His etchings and paintings are richly detailed in representing the physical world. His passion for observation, and his fascination with the strange in the real (so like Moore's), drove him, Moore observes in her article, "to the Dutch coast to look at a stranded whale that was washed to sea before he was able to arrive." This bit of information, in coincidence with another story of stranded whales on a local beach, gave her the opening of the poem. (Of course in the article Moore may have been as taken by the fact that the vision was denied to Dürer, as that it was pursued.)[16] Moore admires Dürer as an artist at once of originality and precision (criteria she also set for herself), but points out that in the best pictures he has obtained his sense of fact second hand, filtered through prior representations, a tendency of course akin to her own drawing of the particular from books, pictures, films. She writes of Dürer that "liking is increased perhaps when the concept is primarily an imagined one—in the instance of the rhinoceros, based apparently on a traveller's sketch or description." Like Moore's poems, this etching, while "minutely detailed and measured, seems altogether fantastic, an example of the conjunction of fantasy and calculation." Moore's ambivalence about this indulgence in the particular for its own sake, which shows in her constant revision and cutting, shows also in her cautious praise of Dürer. "There is a danger of extravagance in denoting as sacrosanct or devout, an art so robust as to include neither." But she reaffirms the virtues of his enthusiasms—his "sensitiveness to magnificence in apparel" (to which she too was sensitive, if ambivalent). But like Moore, Dürer is, finally, a realist of the imagination and not of nature. As W. H. Janson has put it, happily to my point, Dürer creates "imaginary gardens with real toads in them."[17] His art, for all its richness of surface particularity, is built on abstract principles of geometric proportion. Dürer was famous for his confidence in the relation of geometry to nature, and in the objective validity of perspective; he often designed figures from ideal calculations rather than from models, as in his etching of Adam and Eve in the Garden. His were finally optical unities rather than topographical records. Moore's poetry repeatedly questions such confidence, but it too is conceptually organized. Moore's mathematic sensibility, which shows in her prosody, her rhetorical balances, her leaps of association based on repetitions of design, is in sympathy with this tendency in Dürer if at other times in rebellion against it. The play between the particular and the general is typical of Dürer as well as Moore. Janson observes, "Dürer emphasizes the flatness of black and white pages with vertical compositions, but makes the details rich." He was known for combining the Northern and Italian modes, mixing ideally proportioned figures with passionate particularity. He also attempts, like Moore, to give a sense of the spiritual within the worldly, and of apocalyptic moments within everyday situations.

If we look carefully at "The Steeple-Jack" we can see some of the ways its resident artist is effecting the presentation. Aside from the direct references to Dürer we notice his implied vision in the choice and treatment of detail. The water is "etched / with waves as formal as the scales / of a fish." The seagulls fly "one by one, in two's in three's." The wealth of detail is carefully measured, symmetrically balanced. The highly pictorial quality of the scene is heightened by color as well as shape, but again the stylization is emphasized both in the comparison of the scene to a water color by Dürer and in the balance of the seagulls with other birds (peacocks, guineas) present only metaphorically.[18] The emphasis on pictorial harmonies suggests that we are already looking at an idealized, not an actual, objective scene.

The pastoral world of this New England town (a little like Robert Lowell's Castine in "Skunk Hour") seems to be a microcosm of sorts, but the negative elements of the larger world have been absorbed and transformed by its overall serenity. The storm is a "whirlwind fife-and-drum"; the terrain sponsors a variety of flora and fauna, but the most exotic and most threatening elements have been displaced by milder surrogates. "You have the tropics at first hand," but a diminutive tropics of trumpet-vine and snap-dragon, not banyans or frangipani. "The diffident little newt" substitutes for "exotic serpent life." (As with Dürer, Moore's robust enthusiasms for the particular led her to long, enchanting lists of flora and fauna which she canceled and then reinserted with her usual ambivalence toward such excess.)[19] It could not be dangerous to be living in a town like this, without the lures of destructive ambition; self-contained as it is, it seems the dream of the tourist, a heaven on earth where he can escape the harsher aspects of life. Or can he? Moore may be taking the lead from Dürer in planting apocalyptic symbols in everyday settings. Dürer would not have lived in a town like this to escape mortality, but to study and represent it. What could be more apocalyptic, more humbling than a vision of a stranded whale, though a conventional tourist might not see the meaning, and take it only as a natural wonder. The seagulls fly over the clock, again recalling our mortality. Danger is here, disturbing "stars in the sky and the / star on the steeple." It does not overwhelm the scene or violate its representational surface with its symbols, but rather creates a mild "confusion." The church spire has a quaint pitch which reminds us that it is "not true," both in the architect's and in the moralist's sense. The neat balance of the opening is offset by tremors. This town has the natural human tendency to pride and pretense, irony and self-deception, though its "four fluted / columns" are "made / modester by whitewash." Moore writes not in harsh judgment but as an observer, one who can both admire the setting and read the signs, who can see the flaws and compromises in this town which seems so prim. In this sense she identifies not only with Dürer but with "the student named Ambrose" (returned to the poem in 1961), who sees this world as someone who has gone beyond it, who appreciates its aesthetic "elegance" while he sees its moral limits.

The art of Dürer is concerned with minute particulars and mathematic principles. El Greco's art is concerned with bold outlines and mysterious sources. If the meanings of Dürer's paintings are gradual, directed to the movement of the studious eye and to the intelligence, El Greco's meanings are sudden, forceful, passionate. He has no interest, as Dürer has, in resemblance, but emphasizes paint itself, thus the subjective state of the artist and the unreality of the visual illusion. Both artists are after the real, but they have different notions of what constitutes the real. El Greco's version of the real ("the startling El Greco / brimming with inner light")[20] is close to that Moore discusses in her essay on Alfeo Faggi (whose elongated figures indeed resemble El Greco's). In asking "is the real the actual?" she discovers that the spiritual may be more real than appearances. Here and elsewhere Moore uses the image of the crystal with its dramatic asymmetrical lines, drawing toward a center that eludes the eye, its three-dimensional hardness, to represent this spiritual art which knows the invisible beneath the visible.[21]

The hero is explicitly contrasted to the imagination absorbed in appearances. He does not live in or pursue the material—"it is not what I eat that is / my natural meat." Because his sustenance is drawn from spirit, "he covets nothing that he has let go." The "decorous frock-coated Negro / by the grotto," / another kind of hero, transcends the foolish trappings the agents of tourism have dressed him in because he barely lives in this world of appearances, "standing like the shadow of the willow." Moore's hero has no interest in the exotic or bizarre in nature but has a "reverence for mystery," for the wonders of the spirit.

It is important that these poems be separated but paired, for they represent two positive tendencies in constant tension in Moore's vision. This tension and ambivalence caused her not only to make regular revisions in her poems, but to write poems that sometimes defy the lessons they purport, and at best to write poems that engage both impulses, that insist on the visible and the invisible. A great many of Moore's poems discuss the faults of overcalculated, baroque surfaces that risk obscuring spiritual depths by becoming stylized and static. The frequent excesses of her own style with its long, convoluted sentences, flittering syllables, and effusive lists, are often the implicit targets of such criticisms. She may have seen in Dürer a model of how one might properly engage the general and the particular in a composition that did not obscure "the spiritual forces that have made it." In El Greco she saw an artist whose work was indeed "lit with piercing glances into the life of things." But the strength of his inner light may have obscured the variety and individuality of the observable world. Moore needed to apprentice herself to both artists in order to develop her own pluralistic sense of reality.

For all her eclecticism, Moore returned continually to a fundamental, if troubled, and violated piety: excess is dangerous, simplicity is virtuous, in art as in life. "The Jerboa" (CP, 10–15), discussed briefly in Chapter 3, is perhaps the most famous poem on the virtues of simplicity and naturalness, and one of Moore's personal favorites. As she does so often, Moore immediately focuses her cultural criticism in terms of art criticism, here particularly the art of Rome and Egypt.

Too Much

A Roman had an
artist, a freedman,
   contrive a cone—pine cone
   or fir cone—with holes for a fountain. Placed on
      the Prison of St. Angelo, this cone
      of the Pompeys which is known

now as the Popes', passed
for art. A huge cast
   bronze, dwarfing the peacock
   statue in the garden of the Vatican,
      it looks like a work of art made to give
      to a Pompey, or native

of Thebes.

Although a "freedman," this artist is ordered to enslave nature (art, appropriately, ornaments a prison). The obsession of this culture for "imitation" (what Moore calls "Rome's taint" in "An Expedient—Leonardo da Vinci's—and a Query"), is part of the Roman desire (both Pompey's and the Pope's) to create the illusion of power (Moore later noted with interest that the Persians banned imitation as blasphemous). Nature is similarly the Pharaoh's "subject" in two senses. Again Moore is implicitly asking, "why dissect destiny with instruments / more highly specialized than components of destiny itself."

In these societies, ornament has overwhelmed function, tools have become toys, and worse, nature is put on the rack. Indeed, the authorities of nature and art have been inverted, as they were by the "decadents" of the 1890s. "Lords and ladies put goose-grease paint in round-bone boxes—the pivoting lid incised with a duck-wing or reverted duck head." Similarly, locust oil is put into stone locusts.[22]

In the completely aestheticized world of the Egyptians, the grotesque is assimilated into an overall symmetry and "dwarfs here and there lend an evident poetry to frog grays, duck-egg greens and eggplant blues." Life is a composition, "a picture with a fine distance," though a closer look details disaster. The failure of art to achieve the grace of nature is a constant theme. Where art tends to separate form and function, nature discovers the beautiful harmony of the two. The pangolin's armor is not "extra," it has the aesthetic virtue of a Gargallo or a Da Vinci, but is also perfectly adapted to his needs. Nature presents an ideal of economy for art.

But nature also satisfies our most lavish desires.[23] Many of Moore's positive descriptions of natural scenes or creatures have the same rhythm and momentum as her negative descriptions of decadence and luxury. (Moore's ambivalence about luxury may be evinced in her zest for copying out in her notebooks long passages describing wealth in minute detail.) The lush surroundings of Bluebeard's Tower, described in "People's Surroundings," where "the Chinese vermilion of the poincianas / set fire to the masonry and turquoise blues refute the clock," where lizards glitter "without thickness / like splashes of fire and silver" would seem to be Moore's idea of the sublime, given her celebration of iridescence and luminosity in nature. Indeed, we can feel Moore's obvious delight describing these scintillating colors and fine textures, but we must recall that while the plumet basilisk had all the shimmering qualities of Bluebeard's surroundings, he was no "Tower of London jewel."

His vitality depended on his being left in nature and only imaginatively possessed.

This, like so many similar moments in Moore's poetry, presents a dilemma for the artist, a dilemma she attempts to solve by presenting imaginative constructions that display the enchantments of association rather than the power of usurpation.

The world from which Moore draws her poems is already ordered, by painters as often as by writers. Just as she takes materials from books, she takes materials from pictures rather than from life. Her visual representations are already at one remove from nature—the world they construct is already interpreted. This is clear not only from her ready references to visual arts and artists, but from the many poems that take an objet d'art as their subject. Occasionally the artwork is simply a pretext for considering the representational subject, but most often Moore integrates the subject and the aesthetic qualities of the artwork. And often her reflection on an art object is a way of focusing her thoughts about the status of art in relation to life. "The Buffalo" divides the world into types of representations as they "express" "human notions." Like so many of Moore's poems, this one deals with the problem of reproduction, as it relates to problems of representation. The same poem that protests that no modern ox can equal the magnificence of "the Augsburg ox's portrait" also complains about the obscurity of an original caused by the process of reproduction. Originally the poem included the lines: "though prints like this cannot / show if they are black / birds, nor the color of the back."[24] The same association of biological reproduction with visual reproduction occurs in "Nine Nectarines" originally published with "The Buffalo" as "Imperious Ox, Imperial Dish." The search for an original in this poem finds infinite regress: the poem describes a picture of a "much mended" porcelain plate on which is depicted a cultivated fruit, which inspires thoughts about the "original" wild fruit. The asymmetry of the number nine, divided into twos "and a single one," repeats the asymmetry of origins.

Moore's interest in hybrids and derivatives extends not only to the subject of her poems but to their form. Most of the poems that seem to deal with only one work of art are nevertheless actually composites of several. While "Smooth Gnarled Crape Myrtle" focuses on a decorative patch-box, it draws upon Moore's experience of several specific works.[25] "Sea Unicorns and Land Unicorns" focuses on the single tapestry of the Virgin and the Unicorn, but draws not only upon Moore's knowledge of the other tapestries in the series but upon Elizabethan map drawing, Da Vinci's St. Jerome, and several paintings of the Virgin Mary. "Magician's Retreat" takes its title from an eighteenth-century drawing by Jean Jacques Lequeu but describes a painting by Magritte called "Domain of Lights." The two pictures are very similar but use inverse effects of light and dark.[26] "No Swan So Fine" draws not only from a Louis XV candelabrum but from pictures of the fountains of Versailles.[27] The most dramatic example of the composite poem is "Egyptian Pulled Glass Bottle in the Shape of a Fish," which, as Patricia Willis has pointed out, is the result of looking at three different pictures and reading three articles.[28] In the original poem, called "In Einar Jonsson's 'Cow,' " Moore described two works by the Icelandic artist as though she were looking at one:

> Here we have thirst,
> And patience from the first,
>   And art—as in a wave held up for us to see—
>   In its essential perpendicularity;
>
> Not chilly but
> Intense. The spectrum's cut
>   Out of the body of the world, laid on its back,
>   And made subordinate. We recognize no lack.

The two works covertly referred to, though by the same artist, are visually very different. One is a sculpture of a wave personified as a woman, called "The Wave of the Ages." The other, called "Ymir and Audhumla," included a caption indicating that "the giant Ymir suckles the cow Audhumla," the pair representing nebula and ether, the first things created according to Icelandic lore. Moore's association of the two Jonsson works (pictures of which appeared in different articles about the artist) seems to be based on a conceptual rather than a visual resemblance. Indirectly the poem is really perhaps about the artist. Indeed, both articles mark Jonsson out as an original and independent artist, qualities that would have been important to Moore (who often remarked them in Gordon Craig). Artistic originality is, as we have seen, connected in Moore's mind with the problem of historic origins, which she also usually associated with lost intensity, and in turn with prismatic color as an emblem of that original intensity.

When Moore came across a picture of "A Fish Shaped Glass Bottle from Tell El-Amarna" in an article about a recent archeological excavation, she found the perfect visual conjunction of images that had hitherto been linked only conceptually. As an ancient object, the bottle suggested origins and drew in the mythological quality of the Jonsson work. The wave was justified by the image of the fish, the spectrum by its multicolored surface, thirst by the fact that the artifact was a bottle.

The final version of the poem (CP, 83), its elements converging around the glass fish, is remarkable for its control of sound "like intermingled echoes / struck from their glasses successively at random" and its intensity of statement. The medium of the image (the bottle) and the image itself (the fish) are marvelously mingled, the qualities of each played off against the other to signify "thirst," "patience," and "art." The bottle and the fish are both container and thing contained. Different aspects intersect again when we consider the bottle as both image of thirst and image of patience, its function to offer drink, its permanent form a sign of endurance. The intersection is, in fact, "perpendicular," declaring the work of art both temporal and atemporal. The image is complicated by the fact that the bottle, which both holds water and radiates a spectrum, is itself, as glass, nearly invisible.

Moore's pleasure in this work of art is felt throughout the poem, and not surprisingly, the glass fish shares many of the qualities (perpendicularity, prismatic color) for which she is nostalgic in "In the Days of Prismatic Color." But we are reminded, finally, that this is art, not life, a "wave" again going over "truth," which for all its graces can finally only refract light—cannot, as the chameleon can, take the spectrum up for food. The poem is a beautifully compact expression of her ambivalence about art. It is no accident, I think, that this object was found in the same Egyptian ruin that contained the many luxurious toys of "The Jerboa."

For integrity that can outpace tedium, the Chinese were Moore's best models; her interest in their art began very early and continued through her entire career. David Hsin-Fu Wand has traced her preoccupation with Chinese thought and art;[29] I will consider here why this work appealed to her so much. In her typically indirect way, Moore comments in the introduction to *The Marianne Moore Reader* that Chinese art represents her ideal of integrity: "the Tao being a way of life, a 'oneness that is tireless'; whereas egotism, synonymous with ignorance in Buddhist thinking, is tedious." Moore explicitly contrasts European art with chinese art in her original version of "Nine Nectarines and Other Porcelain." While baroque art concentrates on covering space, expanding the domain of the artist, Chinese art reveals space. Indeed, the dragon is a symbol of space, as Moore notes in her *Reader:*

> The dragon as lord of space makes relevant Miss Mai-mai Sze's emphasis on "space as China's chief contribution to painting; the essential part of the wheel being the inner space between its spokes; the space in a room, its usefulness" in keeping with the Manual: "a crowded ill-arranged composition is one of the Twelve Faults of Painting; as a man "if he had eyes all over his body, would be a monstrosity."[30]

Of course she likes the Chinese "precision" and "passion for the particular," as she tells us in her poems, but, most important, she admires the Chinese master because he "understands the spirit of the wilderness," he retains a sense of the mystery and elusiveness of nature, depicting simple natural scenes while Europeans celebrate themselves in excessively cultured images of "hunts and domestic scenes." Perhaps it is because of this humility toward the mysteries of nature that the Chinese have so many symbols of longevity while European art is a museum of mortality.

As Wand had pointed out, Moore was partly attracted to Chinese art for its rich symbolism of the invisible and spiritual. The peach-eating kylin, the versatile dragon (Moore had a picture of one in her living room), are emblematic images in Chinese tradition. Moore was attracted to emblematic art from a variety of periods and cultures, and we can see clear reasons for this attraction in her poetry. Moore's was an emblematic imagination, in the long tradition of the *impressa* in which image is juxtaposed to abstract idea in order to give the latter immediacy and concreteness.[31] She conceived of moral situations pictorially before she developed them in logical or narrative sequence. It is not surprising, then, that she was attracted to emblematic art. Many of her poems can be understood as readings of these emblems. "An Egyptian Pulled Glass Bottle" begins "Here we have thirst," "Charity Overcoming Envy" begins "have you time for a story depicted in tapestry?" Most of the emblems that attract her stand for the spiritual value of restraint as a condition of revelation. The Virgin and the Unicorn, St. Hubert and the Stag, St. Jerome and the Lion all depict this value. When Moore uses emblematic materials in her poems she is usually occupied primarily with the subject, but the qualities of the work and the struggle for the artist are always brought in at least indirectly. Quite often, in fact, not only the image but the formal qualities of the work will illustrate the moral. In "Leonardo Da Vinci" Moore draws the artist as creator into the moral picture he has painted (in "St. Jerome and the Lion") by punning on Leo and Leonardo. For Moore the personal locus of this value of restraint is in the artist's own relation to his materials and to his vision. In a few instances the moral and artistic struggle of the painter is the explicit subject of the poem, his works the circumstances of that struggle. In "An Expedient—Leonardo Da Vinci's— and a Query" she describes the need for something surpassing analysis as a stay against dejection—a theme we have already seen in "Logic and the Magic Flute" and "The Mind Is an Enchanting Thing." The irony of the poem is that while Da Vinci created works that have the power of enchanting others, the artist was arrested in the failure of his mathematical principles.

Moore's poems, then, are galleries for art of the past. Surprisingly, while she often wrote about contemporaries in essays and reviews she almost never openly displayed their work in poems (in contrast to Williams and Stein). Instead, she kept the moderns in the workshop of her mind, as guides rather than subjects or references.

It was from modern painting that she drew formal and conceptual inspiration. As she wrote to Ezra Pound, "Over here, it strikes me that there is more evidence of power among painters and sculptors than among writers."[32] Many of Moore's literary inventions may have been the result of watching events in contemporary visual art. She is often quite direct in acknowledging such connections. In "Concerning the Marvelous," for instance, she notes: "The fictitiously architectural verisimilitudes of de Chirico, in his enamelled perspective period particularly, and Max Ernst's voracity for a definiteness that cannot defeat mystery, are effects of lasting value for poetry"—indeed, effects of which she made ready use.[33] This is not to suggest that Moore attempted to "paint" in words, or to accommodate a set of visual norms to a set of literary ones. But she was fascinated by the analogies between the two arts and to a certain extent developed her own work in the space between them.

With the decline of representational painting and descriptive poetry the old adage *ut pictura poesis* seemed no longer to apply. Painting and poetry were brought together in an entirely new way, both con-

cerned with combating the complacency of visual and verbal "ideo-
grams." In his essay "On Realism in Art" Roman Jakobson makes this
point in comparing tendencies in painting and poetry:

> It is necessary to learn the conventional language of painting
> in order to "see" a picture, just as it is impossible to under-
> stand what is spoken without knowing the language. This
> conventional, traditional aspect of painting to a great extent
> conditions the very act of our visual perception. As tradition
> accumulates, the painted image becomes an ideogram, a
> formula, to which the object portrayed is linked by contigu-
> ity. Recognition becomes instantaneous. We no longer see a
> picture. The ideogram needs to be deformed perception, if
> we are to detect in a given thing those traits which went un-
> noticed the day before . . . The motivation behind this "dis-
> order" was the desire for a closer approximation of reality.[34]

In this light painting is still considered to be like poetry, but neither is
bound any longer to a strict imitation of nature. Since "sight" is ham-
pered by convention, "insight" is necessary. Visual and verbal arts alike
in the modern period stress "conceptualization" over visual "imitation"
or emotional "impression." But since conceptualization involves a penetration of the forms dictated by convention, it necessarily contains a
deconstructive as well as a constructive moment. It requires the dis-
mantling, abstracting, confronting, and rearranging of the conventions
producing an illusion of the external world.

In the letter I quoted at the opening of this chapter, Moore remarked on her aim of "exact resemblance," which she claimed to share
with visual artists. But her definition of exact resemblance is closer to
that represented in the Armory Show than to that represented by nineteenth-century realism. One of Moore's earliest expressions of this rede-
finition of realism was her essay in *The Dial* in 1921, on the sculptor
Alfeo Faggi, "Is the Real the Actual?"[35] What she admires in Faggi is
his ability to break through the trivial form things take in secondary experience and to discover the absolute not as an idealized otherworld but
in the realm of the imagination.

Paul Rosenfeld's famous essay "On American Painting" appeared
in the same issue as "Is the Real the Actual?" and the two have a great
deal in common.[36] The struggle of his contemporaries, says Rosenfeld,
is to find the primary reality beneath the boldest versions of secondary
reality. Some artists can dismantle the secondary reality (given us by the

grid of perception). Others penetrate to a primary contact of the imagination with the world, presenting designs that are boldly independent of secondary illusions.

Moore's commemorative essay on Rosenfeld (which she liked enough to reprint in her *Reader*), shows the critic demonstrating in writing many of the same principles he admires in painting. Moore uses his remarks on painting to describe his writing (and what Moore admires in the work of others is usually a key to her own work): "Paul Rosenfeld was an artist. In his performances one finds 'a level of reality deeper than that upon which they were launched'; his experiences have not been 'made by fear to conform to preconceived theories.' "

It is precisely this quality of assertive, recreative composition, based on a displacement of old artistic codes with personal strokes of a nonexperiential type, that Moore admires in Rosenfeld's own writing. "The mind which has harbored this greater than great Noah's ark of acknowledgments was characterized by an early compliment to it in the Nation as 'courageous, clear, and biased.' Biased. Biased by imagination; a poet, as we see in Paul Rosenfeld's mechanics of verbal invention."[37]

With its dazzling surfaces and transparent hardness, the crystal was Moore's favorite image of primary reality. The crystal or prism also provided the cubists with a major metaphor of their new art. Albert Gleizes and Jean Metzinger, in an apology for cubism that Moore may have read in *Camera Work*, fuse the image directly: "Here are a thousand tints which escape from the prism, and hasten to range themselves in the lucid region forbidden to those who are blinded by the immediate."[38] In the days of prismatic color, of course, there was no difference between the visible and the invisible, and the struggle of art is to recapture some of that "inner light" in an outward form. The passage in "Novices" (CP, 60–61) in which Moore describes the power of Hebrew poetry could almost stand as a description of a cubist painting with its "precipitate of dazzling impressions," its "angle at variance with angle," and "fathomless suggestions of color."[39] The form of the poem repeats what it celebrates. The collage of phrases, the emphasis on infinitely crossing angles, contrasting colors, the rapid succession of images and words beyond a syntactic hold, are all elements of Cubist painting stressed by Gleizes and Metzinger and by W. H. Wright in the note Moore made from his *Modern Painting*: "Cubism depends on artists' abil. to express pure aesthetic emotion in relation to form, previously organization of line, volume, chiarosiuro, color . . . . . Cubism added [the]

illustrative device of disorganizing and rearranging objectivity so that
[the] separated parts would intersect . . . + partly obscure the image."[40]

What is satisfying about the variant angles of a crystal, unlike flat
surfaces and murky foregrounds, is that they seem to direct themselves
inward and outward at once. Since neither their extension nor their ultimate source is clearly delimited, they suggest the possibility of a total
inclusiveness and a unified center at once. Furthermore, the relations
among the parts seem indeterminate, as each angle directs the eye toward a different mode of relation creating a dialectic between the desire
to focus along a single-point perspective, and a sense of the myriad perspectives available for interpreting a single form. Thus the crystal provides a sense of action within a stabilized figure. As a model for the
poem, this figure suggests the urge to see a thing from all sides, giving
an impression of infinity to a finite subject. It suggests the duality of the
poem that expands the scope of its references while developing an internal formal coherence. It suggests the development of a conceptual
unity out of a representational plurality.

In "Peter," the subject matter, a cat, is easily recognizable, the
logical movement of the passages relatively accessible. But different
fashions of description—scientific, metaphoric—compete in the presentation:

> the detached first claw on the foreleg corresponding
> to the thumb, retracted to its tip; the small tuft of fronds
> or katydid-legs above each eye numbering all units
> in each group; the shadbones regularly set about the mouth
> to droop or rise in unison like porcupine-quills.   [CP, 45]

Each new mode of description redirects our attention, redefining what
precedes it. It is hard to retain through these lines a natural image of a
cat. The metaphors themselves represent different proportions and contexts, thus further complicating the visualization. Each part of the body
is a piece of another realm. The poem goes on to play the shifting figure
of the cat off against the shifting metaphors for it. That is, Moore presents a *moving*, multi-faceted creature, not by tracing that movement
along the lines of visual conventions, but by presenting multiple images
for it and thus conceptualizing motion.

In "Peter" our attention never fully breaks from a central image.
But the elements of the picture are cut out of disparate depictions of
life and the whole thing hangs together like nothing we have seen be-

fore. The play of the poem lies in the dialectic between the "natural" image of the cat and the internal, pictorial coherence of juxtaposed words. A tension is created between the sense of an external variety and an internal consistency, rewarding a desire for order while suggesting the inclusive density of life. It is this bidirectional pull that is the pleasure of many of Moore's "descriptive" poems. Of course poetry, with its temporal organization, has advantages over painting in presenting a thing from all sides. But Moore adopts from painters the double sense of looking at something. The impulse to find a conceptual unity within the visual multiplicity is one she shares with modernist painters. Her note from M. Krohgon on futurists could stand for her own work: "the Futurist . . . has got to see feel understand and interpret the front side and the back side of things, the inside as well as the outside and the bottom as well as or better than the top."[41]

To modernist painters, the object was a random occasion for analyzing the space it inhabited, and sometimes the object would dissolve within it. And as we struggle through Moore's briary syntax to reach the treasured subject, we often feel that she, too, is more interested in the briars. William Carlos Williams has had the fullest insight into this aspect of Moore's verse. "The only hint I ever got on how to read Marianne Moore is that she despises connectives."[42] Williams's discussion of Moore is shot through with analogies to the visual arts, and particularly with his favorite analogy between the geometric base of visual representation and the grammatical base of linguistic representation.

> A course in mathematics would not be wasted on a poet, or a reader of poetry, if he remember no more from it than the geometric principle of the intersection of loci: from all angles lines converging and crossing establish points. He might carry it further and say in his imagination that apprehension perforates at places, through to understanding—as white is at the intersection of blue and green and yellow and red. It is this white light that is the background of all good work . . . It grows impossible for the eye to rest long upon the object of the drawing . . . The unessential is put rapidly aside as the eye searches between for illumination . . . The intensification of desire toward this purity is the modern variant.[43]

Like many modernists, Williams aimed (and believed Moore aimed) to dredge up the nets of grammar and make them glisten. Williams is not alone in connecting geometry and grammar. Apollinaire writes in *Cubism* that "geometry is to the plastic arts what grammar is to the art of the writer," and Roman Jakobson has recognized the significance of this analogy to developments in both arts: "the relation of pronouns to non-pronomial words has been repeatedly compared with the relation between geometrical and physical bodies."[44] Moore's exploration of the geometry of grammar did not result in the violent rejection of linguistic code that characterizes the work of Gertrude Stein and some of Williams's writing. Moore remains within the conventions of statement, but challenges them to their limit in such a way as to draw attention to the medium through which a statement is being made. Grammar is thus no longer a transparent vehicle for expression; it takes on a reality of its own in her verse. This may be what caused Moore to make note of W. H. Wright's remark in *Creative Will*: "In (subjective art) [the] objects cease to exist as objects and create in us an emotion of form as in contra-distinction to a recognition of form."[45]

In Moore's poetry particulars are detached from nature and float free in the artificial realm of her designs. By the very concreteness of her images one expects description, but here is description in a space separate from nature, unfamiliar to the eye. It is at once "abstract" and "concrete," or, as Williams says, "a part, cognizant of the whole." "Marianne Moore escapes. The incomprehensibility of her poems is witness to at what cost (she cleaves herself away) as it is also to the distance which the most are from a comprehension of the purpose of composition."[46] In escaping illusion ("plagiarism of nature") to find instead "transcription" in "the realm of the imagination," one risks "letting life go completely," risks the "dislocation of sense." One can then return to "the forms common to experience so as not to frighten the onlooker away but to invite him." These forms, while particular, are, to Williams, no longer "representational." They are converted and are now "of the imagination." "Miss Moore undertakes in her work to separate the poetry from the subject entirely—like all moderns." The notion that art must be either a mirror or a lamp has vanished, replaced by an idea of art as a production, for which the physical world provides the materials. The product may resemble its sources, but it does not stand for them in a way that denies its own reality. But the poems are not just designs, pure form, they are, as Williams later argues, "diagrammatically informative," significant form. Williams focuses on the moment of engagement; the diagram points both ways, to the imagination of the poet and to the world to which the imagination is attuned.[47]

Williams's essays tend to be impressionistic and hortatory rather than critical, but he was right about Moore's attunement to the visual arts, particularly with respect to her impulse to "separate poetry from subject matter almost entirely," to break up several lines of thought and bring the fragments together to make new units, to "transpose" image and actions from the illusion created by conventional speech to a non-illusionistic design: "In painting, Ingres realized the essentiality of drawing and each perfect part seemed to float free from his work, by itself. There is much in this that applies beautifully to Miss Moore. It is perfect drawing that attains to a separate existence which might, if it please, be called mystical, but is in fact no more than the practicability of design."[48]

This tendency to exact particularity without illusion characterizes Moore's style. As we read her poems, we become absorbed in the articulation of an image for its own sake. The pangolin like the wrought-iron vine, the jerboa like a Chippendale chair, are comparisons that indeed seem to float free from the work, to suggest an independent, conceptual reality.[49]

Gleizes and Metzinger were similarly assertive in contrasting natural spaces and the space of painters. Their remarks, which Moore had read, apply well to some of her effects.

> The fact commonly invoked, that we find in a painting the familiar characteristics of the sight which motivated it, proves nothing at all . . . The worth of the river, foliage, and banks, despite a conscientious faithfulness to scale, is no longer measured by width, thickness, and height, nor the relations between these dimensions. Torn from natural space, they have entered a different kind of space, which does not assimilate the proportions observed. This remains an external matter. It has just as much importance as a catalogue number, or a title at the bottom of a picture-frame. To contest this is to deny the space of painters; it is to deny painting.

But elsewhere in their manifesto Gleizes and Metzinger adjust this indifference to external space: "Nevertheless, let us admit that the reminiscence of natural forms cannot be absolutely banished; as yet, at all events. An art cannot raise itself all at once to the level of pure effusion."[50] What these qualifications indicate is that though the relationship between the internal coherence of the picture and the external coherence of visual experience is different, it is still at work in the experience of painting. Indeed, the function of cubism is to declare that both exist, that there is a difference denied by illusionist art, and to articulate that difference. Even Juan Gris, one of the most stylized of Cubist painters, recognized that while the work of art has a life of its own, that life is relevant with respect to natural space; the painting is a fabric "all of a piece and uniform, with one set of threads as the representational aesthetic element, and cross threads as the technical, architectural or abstract element. These threads are independent and complementary and if one set is lacking the fabric does not exist." But this relationship need not follow a single, conventional hierarchy of art and nature. Gris was to take the tendency to abstraction so far as to invert the relation of art and nature: "Cezanne turns a bottle into a cylinder but I . . . make a bottle—a particular bottle—out of a cylinder."[51] Reality is not simply replaced by the canvas; it is reinvented there.

This play of priorities is always alive in Moore's verse. At the simplest level, objects in nature remind her of images she has already seen in art—the pangolin is "Leonardo da Vinci's replica." The associations pull away from the object and gather into independent aesthetic or thematic harmonies and yet the stimulus of association, the object in nature, remains in the mind as a point of origination and continuity.

In Moore's "Paper Nautilus" (quoted in Chapter 4) no illusion of an external object is intended, yet the poem moves with particularity from image to image drawn from a wide range of contexts, but all collected around a central figure. Moore establishes the poem first in a realm totally unrelated in the conventional scheme of things to the object around which she will organize her thoughts. Thus any illusionary function the image may have is obstructed at the outset. We are not in the presence of a real paper nautilus, but the language never abandons detail; any abstractions come from the links we make as readers from image to image. Though we realize these images are not the true subject of the poem, we have no direct access to that subject except across the stepping stones of particulars.[52]

Visual rhyme, rather than natural connection, helps Moore advance her design. Thus in "New York" she associates the world of furbearers with that of fur-wearers by imagining the ground dotted with deerskins—"white with white spots, 'as satin needlework in a single color may carry a varied pattern.' " Formal resemblance seems more important than thematic significance here.

Such leaps of perspective are Moore's method and her subject when she praises the paintings of Robert Andrew Parker, who illustrated an edition of *The Pangolin*:

> The design of the men and boat (Oarsmen) is integrated with the sea as seeds are set in a melon—the men braced by resistance to the mounding weight of deep water; the criss-cross of the oars, uninterferingly superimposed on the vastness of the sea without sky . . . Robert Parker is a fantasist of great precision . . . the balanced color pattern, dominated by white, of *East Yorkshire Yeomanry Disembarking from H.M.S. Cressy*—its caraway-seed multitudes pouring down the ship's sides in streams like sand in an hourglass, the sea choked with landing boats repeated to infinity . . . A platoon—sabers up—seen from the side, reduplicates identical-identical-identical boots that are as black as the men's tunics are flaming vermilion—with an effect resembling the leaves of a partly open book standing upright.[53]

In Moore's "Smooth Gnarled Crape Myrtle" the clusters of sound, shape, and color seem to generate the poem, and hold our attention. The title itself, with its contrasting qualities of smooth and gnarled, points to the emphasis on textures rather than things or ideas. This nonreferential visual order occurs not only in the visual rhymes of the poems but in their appearance on the page created by the syllabics. Sometimes Moore will use typography to create a startling concurrence of the reference and the physical presence of the poem—the "MEridian" of "Four Quartz Crystal Clocks," the "c r e e p i n g" cat of "Bird Witted"—but these devices are rare. More often, the experience of the composition is separated from the subject.

To bring life back into the haven of art, modernists went rummaging for junk—nails, newspapers, scraps of fabric. Though Moore uses words and only words, she "does not discriminate against schoolbooks and business documents." But imported into the canvas or poem, such trash becomes treasure. We find in Moore poems about paperweights and house cats, beside poems about roses and swans. The democracy of subject matter is extended by the style. Poems open casually: "I have a friend who . . . ," "you suit me well," "there is nothing to be said for you." The effect is not so much to break down the boundary of poetry as to draw the world into it.

Moore uses collage technique not only in this mixing of subjects and categories but through a literal scavenging of language from magazines, newspapers, atlases, overheard conversation. Collage gives the poet an opportunity to affect distance from the claims of the poem (she has only "found" the words of others, though, of course, context is all); in addition, the objects of collage become themselves the focus of attention, not for what they point to but as found subjects. Quotations inhabit a kind of middle space between their original meanings, and the function assigned them by the poet, reminding us that the poem is a construction of words. Moore has taken this habit so far in some poems as to append notes even after removing the quotations to which they refer.

Though poetry's medium is uniform (letters on a page), it can produce a more various surface than painting. Moore's poems, as we have seen, take advantage of the diverse relations among words; grammatical, imagistic, aural, visual, semantic, stylistic, contextual, to create powerful incongruities and bidirectional signals not just between the ways things are seen but between the fact of art and the fact of external flux. In its drawing together of diverse functions and modes of language into proximate and dynamic difference, Moore's work can be called "collage." The term collage itself signifies the explosive bond created on the canvas by multiple incongruous representations and materials:

> The word collage is derived from *coller* (to paste or glue) and means pasting and, by extension, that which is pasted. The name, like the pictures, had carried a shock, the word collage having the slang meaning of an illicit love affair, which must have delighted Braque and Picasso with its inference of shameful cohabitation between nobly born oil paint and the streetwalker newspaper. Beyond this, the past participle *collé* (pasted or glued) used as slang means faked or pretended.[54]

We might think of the title of the poem "Marriage," its techniques, and its view of married couples as "opposed to each other, not to unity" as especially pertinent to the idea of collage. Moore's words and images are "pasted" in the sense that they are fragments of other continuities, and their relation in the context of the poem pulls against these former groupings. Collage presents a process. Its forms are evolving, "incomplete" (in the positive assertive sense in which Paul Rosenfeld used the word of some of his contemporaries). Hans Arp claimed to create his collages out of old failures, and we can understand this tendency in a broader sense as applying to all collage, as the bringing together of old artistic codes.[55] *Dechirage* (torn paper) implies the destruction of former shapes. The edges are left rough to suggest the disassembling of the old and a newly forming synthesis. The complete form implies limit, exclusive definition. The rough form implies change, transition, which for Moore, as for the cubists, was the nature of things.

Moore's pastiche of images and quotations is not only a gesture of objectivity, an attempt to present an object from many points of view. It is also a gesture of democracy, as it challenges a tendency to order language according to its appropriateness for poetry. But it is finally a gesture of irony. The imaginary garden with real toads in it can never be secure. If we choose "not to discriminate" against any materials, we open the form to infinite revision, for the intrusion of one form necessarily involves the alteration of another. Artistic genius, Moore told us, is always in revolt. Finally, then, the fact of art, of its limits, must be announced if we are to acknowledge the warfare of imagination and medium, the permanent resistance of the world to our forms of expression. The last meaning of collage, that it is "faked," pasted or glued, is always latent in Moore's compositions. But while they do not objectify the world, they affirm the independent, participating reality of composition. The collage artist Robert Rauschenburg made the famous remark, "painting relates to both art and life . . . I try to act in the gap between." Moore is interested in that gap too, as an inspirational focus.

In talking about relations between painting and writing, Williams (and his critics) tended to overlook the differences in media for the sake of seeing likenesses. But Moore demonstrates repeatedly a keen awareness of the formal laws governing literature and distinguishing it from the visual arts, and though her work employs the techniques of painting, it also shows the differences between media, and an interest in the distinctive combinations those differences make possible. Literature is based upon a linguistic system of words and sounds and is consequently decoded linearly, while painting, composed of color and form, is decoded in a plastic block. Moore's poems are cognizant of this difference even while they attempt to work against it. Any effort to increase the spatiality of her poems, for instance, remains in a dialectic with the intrinsic linearity of words.

In poetry the play of composition and representation, which char-

acterizes so much modern art, is complicated by the unavoidable re-
ferentiality of words, which ranges beyond visual experience but is also
bound to extend beyond the surface of the composition. Indeed, in poetry there is an obvious radical discontinuity between words and the
physical world of a sort that cannot exist in painting. Language preserves none of the formal and sensuous properties of experience. An attention to the primary aspect of the medium of language, then, tends to
obstruct a sense of its reference. When we read a story we do not ordinarily think of ourselves as holding a book. We are conscious of reading
only when the story itself throws back images of our own activity or
otherwise interrupts the illusion. Generally we naturalize symbols according to the conventions of language in the condition in which we receive it at a given moment in history. As with painting, there are three
realities here, though somewhat differently aligned. There is the relation between the images and concepts drawn together in the reader's
imagination (the composition that words symbolize) and the external,
experiential world. There is the relation of the various images and concepts with each other in an imaginative space. And there is the relation
of this imaginative composition to the literal materials, letters on a
page, that project it. The surface of poetry has a uniform sensuous quality that runs counter to the possibilities of plural sensuousness in the
qualities it symbolizes and to the inclusive, dense totality of the world.
Language is organized into a transparent system of relations (grammar)
whose stability runs counter to the range of elements that can fill it.
Relations that do not occur naturally can be presented in a grammatical
system, and the play between grammatical accuracy and sensuous incongruity ("the house swims") is an aspect of metaphor. In painting, incongruity is produced by juxtaposition but the "grammar" of visual
symbols is determined by the gestalt of visual perception, whereas language requires a separate synthetic system.

With an almost Rube Goldberg–like spirit of invention, Moore
scavenged widely among the many materials around her, setting them
to surprising tasks in the unique machinery of her poems. But in the
teeming field of the visual arts she found one of her largest supplies of
ideas and images. She returned to the visual arts repeatedly during her
long career, not as to a shrine whose idols she would imitate, but as to a
fountain from which the imagination could always find renewal.

8. The Rhetoric of Reticence
Three Critical Essays

W HEN MOORE'S collected prose is published, she will be recognized as one of the most original and significant essayists of her time. The few pieces in *Predilections* and *The Marianne Moore Reader* are only a hint of her total achievement in critical prose. For all their excellences, however, which have been noted by Kenneth Burke and more recently by Laurence Stapleton, Moore's essays are bewildering.[1] As Burke has noted, they are a hybrid of pedantic literalism and impressionistic criticism. They elide distinctions between moral and aesthetic judgment and move erratically through quotations with only the briefest of indicators and transitions. Many of the quotations seem slack or bland by objective standards, her ecstatic response to minute technical matters a bit exaggerated. But if we look carefully at the quotations and their contexts, certain rhetorical and thematic structures emerge in the paratactic presentations.

It is a mistake, I think, to read these essays primarily as appreciations, as Stapleton does, following Moore's own modest way of presenting them. Some of the essays, I believe, offer fairly complicated commentaries, though only implicitly and through a chain of particulars. Just as in the poetry, Moore appropriates her examples and quotations, making them not simply illustrations but discreet assertions. As Burke has put it, "when she quotes in her special way of quoting, we see her carving a text out of a text, much like carving a personal life out of life in general."[2] Following her own standard, Moore practices restraint, but she speaks, even in her respectful silence, by means of arrangement and context and by allowing the content of her examples to show, while she addresses herself to technicalities.

I do not have the space here for a broad or thorough discussion of Moore's special talents and methods within the genre of critical prose. But I want to suggest something of her predilection for and strategy of indirection by a careful reading of three major essays: "Feeling and Precision," "Humility, Concentration and Gusto," and "Idiosyncrasy and Technique." In each essay Moore implicitly explores the relationship between impression and expression, or what Burke has called "the *liber scriptus* of art and the *liber virus* of nature." She connects intense feeling with formal deviation, but this dichotomy between feeling and writing becomes, for her, a model for the fundamental tension in all experience between the self and the world, tension out of which her paradoxes of failure emerge. In "Feeling and Precision" Moore locates a double bind: the artist needs to release the pressure of intense vision or desire through speech, and yet speech exhausts its subject and limits the power of the speaker. In "Humility, Concentration and Gusto," she begins to convert this double bind into a system in which the compositional flow of language is hindered to indicate a difference between "the genuine" and the forms of speech. She calls these marks of difference "impulsive intimacies," and their affective power, she suggests, is "gusto." In "Idiosyncrasy and Technique" Moore explores the irreconcilable tension between "imaginative awe" and "the burning desire to be explicit" by shifting from organic metaphors of continuity between feeling and form to mechanical metaphors of discontinuity.[3]

"Feeling and Precision," the first essay in *Predilections*, is the most blatantly uncooperative. Moore bounds over examples of word-order inversion, antithesis, interiorized climax, anticlimax, and concealed rhyme, casting the reader, as explanation, only an occasional, impressionistic phrase. This instance is "virile," another shows "strong feeling," one is "precise," another is "fresh." But the "natural reticence" that this condensed and ambiguous essay displays is, in fact, its subject. The essay presents two urges that seem to be at odds: plain speaking, at the expense of spirit, and "natural reticence," in which the spirit is pent up. She seeks a form that mediates these urges. The deepest experiential counterpart of this is the quest for self-preservation, discovered in paradoxes of freedom and restraint and in their stylistic equivalents, antithesis and sustained climax.

Moore presents her first remarks in this essay as tangential ones, but they are in fact central to her argument: "Feeling at its deepest—as we all have reason to know—tends to be inarticulate. If it does manage to be articulate, it is likely to seem overcondensed, so that the author is resisted as being enigmatic or disobliging or arrogant." In the next paragraph she apologizes for her rudeness to a pedantic literalist who would have her "analyze her sentence structure." The essay, we expect, will make up for her curtness earlier. But from what she elaborates immediately, and from what follows in the essay as a whole, it seems clear that she has chosen to begin this way not to provide a corrective but to make her own case a frame and an illustration of her point; though we wish to oblige (ourselves and a public) with explicitness, we also wish to hold out in silence for the optimal expression.

> My instinctive reply might have seemed dictatorial: you don't devise a rhythm, the rhythm is the person, and the sentence but a radiograph of personality. The following principles, however, are aids to composition by which I try, myself, to be guided: if a long sentence with dependent clauses seems obscure, one can break it into shorter units by imagining into what phrases it would fall as conversation; in the second place, expanded explanation tends to spoil the lion's leap—an awkwardness which is surely brought home to one in conversation; and in the third place, we must be as clear as our natural reticence allows us to be.

Moore here begins with a fairly specific, technical point and advances to one slightly more general and impressionistic, concluding with another enigma to replace the first. Though she began by obliging the "painstaking" magazine with "painstaking" explicitness, "reticence" is reaffirmed and displayed as "natural." Furthermore, the rules, such as they are, seem to go in two directions. The first two curtail excess, the third overcomes silence. The first two propose a "natural" standard, conversation, as a measure of excess, the third proposes resisting (as far as possible) a "natural" tendency. As aids to composition these seem to control contrary wishes, or to mediate some basic ambivalence about composition itself. As usual, what Moore presents as explanation is really illustration.

   In this essay Moore offers examples in which "natural reticence" disrupts the conventional flow of words, which might arrive at ready conclusions. In this way feeling flows into words but never runs out in them, keeping the line alive with expectancy. To represent the need for forcefulness in poetry, Moore quotes Wallace Stevens, "referring to poetry under the metaphor of the lion, 'It can kill a man.' Yet the lion's leap would be mitigated almost to harmlessness if the lion were clawless, so precision is both impact and exactitude." She goes on to suggest that the force of this lion's leap is achieved through the storing up of feeling until "the writer seems under compulsion to set down an unbearable accuracy." She also quotes Williams's comment that writing "denotes a certain unquenchable exaltation." The writer, it seems, must defend himself against two opposite dangers. He must set down an "unbearable accuracy," in which case writing is self-preservation because it provides some mediation between the writer and his most intense experiences. And he must be "galvanized against inertia," must avoid expiring in easy, available language that involves no personal insight and glides without friction into conclusion. The poet, like the hero of the poems, must be "hindered to succeed." There are, of course, innumerable examples of this in her own verse, not only in the form of paradox, but in her tendency to revise her assertions as she makes them ("when I buy pictures / or what is closer to the truth") and her deliberately cumbersome, layered comparisons ("the old thick, low-leaning nectarine that is the / color of the shrub-tree's brownish / flower"). The peculiar result of such "precision," peculiar since it is presented as restraint in process, is not fewer words, but more. In this essay Moore's example of "maximum impact" is Gerard Manley Hopkins's "description of the dark center in the eye of a peacock feather as 'the colour of the grape where the flag is turned back.' "[4] Why should exactitude require these obliquities, these metaphors of metaphors? The phrase doesn't describe (or define) an absolute endpoint or "dark center" but postpones that reference, describing instead a process of penetration and intense desire, "turning back," metaphor by metaphor, to some final exposure. The accumulation of words denotes a "refusal to be false." In this way Hopkins gives the impression of releasing the tension of "unbearable accuracy" and avoids finite definition, which would snuff out the energy of the line.

The Hopkins example is neutral enough in its own right, but surrounded by descriptions of the creative process as "unbearable" and lethal, the "dark center" of the peacock's feather picks up the intensity of other, more ominous dark centers. The same images and structures, in more explicitly moral subjects, reveal Moore's sense of writing as a mode of self-preservation. Metaphors of combat and armor abound in these essays, as in the poems. The next example Moore discusses is Louis Ginsberg's "Command of the Dead," and though she points out only the technical appeal of the poem's word order, it is clearly "galvanized against inertia" in thematic as well as technical ways. Appropriately, to illustrate that a struggle against one's own verbal inertia can aid victory in language, Moore chooses a poem about the battle against emotional complacency as an aid to victory in war. It is precisely the sense of an unframable "dark center" that gives vigor to both physical and symbolic action. The inversion of word order is not simply a matter of semantic clarity. It is a difference of intensity that appeals to Moore. She observes that Ginsberg has written "we feel them when we most are free" where the natural word order calls for ". . . are most . . ." Moore writes, "but that would mean . . . being free makes us feel them—gross inaccuracy since these 'mosts' are the essence of compassion." The natural "advance" of speech, which places the verb before the adjective and hurries the sentence to conclusion, does not acknowledge the fear of endpoints as a poem about "the dead" should. Through the inversion "we" are "hindered to succeed." The Ginsberg passage is a perfect example of Burke's insight that Moore's imagination works on the principle of "nevertheless" even to the point of coming around to the mainstream by her own circular current. Here she has gone against her own hard and fast objection to the trend for inverted word order in poetry. Verbal hesitation (the result of "natural reticence"), like hesitation in battle (which acknowledges our mortality), allows us to continue speaking while preserving a "refusal to be false," silence and false conclusion both being threats to self-preservation. Complacency or inertia in diction is like death in life; Moore's warning against complacency is charged with absolute fears. It is with such overtones that she later quotes Ezra Pound's remark that "the great writer is always a plodder; it's the ephemeral writer that has to get on with the job."

Moore doesn't give us much help with the Ginsberg poem, but there are some central ambiguities that probably drew her to it. In the primary sense of this poem the dead "command" us to acknowledge mortality. Imagining something beyond what is expressed may be a matter of compassion, of "feeling with," but since compassion involves, to some extent, imagining yourself in someone else's boots, it can also cause anxiety. The image of the dead is incomplete, "they" and "we" both fundamentally set apart and tied by association ("we" will become "they"). But while the subjects of the poem receive "the command," the poet can, in a sense, "take command" by introducing elements that "sinew" his "work," by allowing the dead to "live" in his "works."

Moore goes on to applaud the feeling evident in hindered expression in the Book of Daniel. Again the language is aligned with a situation of uncertainty and vulnerability.

> Explicitness being the enemy of brevity, an instance of difficult descriptive matter accurately presented is that passage in the Book of Daniel (X: 9, 10, 11) where the writer says: 'Then was I in a deep sleep on my face, and my face toward the ground. And, behold, an hand touched me, which set me upon my knees and upon the palms of my hands. And I stood trembling.' Think of what *we* might have done with the problem if we had been asked to describe how someone was wakened and, gradually turning over, got up off the ground.

The literal "descriptive matter" is not difficult at all. The criterion of brevity would seem to favor the paraphrase. The passage from Daniel seems to contradict the strict rule to "avoid expanded explanation" introduced just a page earlier. But the trembling language is the source of gusto. Here we see a speaker struggling against his own bewilderment (his speechlessness, perhaps) with an excess of language, as though no phrase could adequately describe his experience, or as though he were still uncertain just what the experience was. As in "the unforced passion of the Hebrew language," intensity of experience produces here an overflow of words. As in Ginsberg's lines, the speaker is aware of a presence and its effect on him but is not able to articulate that presence. Verbal impediments are the signs of an impression greater than his verbal power. While Daniel's natural reticence prevents the usual advance of words, his intensity requires release in expression. The humble posture of the figure in the description (on his knees) reinforces the humble posture of his language. However, in Moore's restatement, brief and to the point, the posture described is different. While in Daniel the figure is helped from a prostrate position to a position of kneeling, the figure in Moore's alternative statement turns over facing away from the ground and gets up without assistance. There is no undefined "presence" in the restatement, which demonstrates complacent confidence in the conventional flow of words. Perhaps Moore is making a parallel between the good writer and the figure in the Daniel passage, both maintaining a humble posture, vulnerable, uncertain of what has hit them, struggling for articulation. In any case, it is clear that the content, as well as the form of the passage, is important to her point here. The posture of humility (which we have already seen depicted in "St. Nicholas," "Sea Unicorns and Land Unicorns," and other poems) is directly connected to the style of verbal excess and awkwardness.

In each of the passages I have discussed the need to break silence with speech is met with the need to avoid a second silence of premature conclusion. Moore's next instance of "strong feeling" is "antithesis," the perfect verbal means of having it both ways. Moore's love of antithesis showed up early. *Poems* is shot through with moments like the one at the end of "Radical," in which content reflects form: "that which it is impossible to force, it is / impossible to hinder." Antithesis is not only the structure of individual couplets but of whole poems. It is, indeed, a basic element of her wit, as we have seen.

Moore gives no reason why antithesis should be "an aid to precision," but her examples suggest more than she is willing to say directly. Chief among these is a fragment from W. H. Auden's "The Double Man" ("The New Yorker Letter"): "For, torn between conflicting needs, / He's doomed to fail if he succeeds." Antithesis here impedes the advance of the sentence by throwing it back to its beginning, equalizing clauses in a striking, combative relation. The Auden lines are said of the devil, but also seem to be directed to the human condition, particularly, for Moore, the condition of writing. Indeed, the paradox contained in Auden's lines can be found throughout Moore's poetry, in very similar language. Torn between imaginative awe and the desire to put one's feelings into words, she is "doomed to fail if she succeeds." Through antithesis, in which assertions are made but held in check, she can convert this conflict to an enigmatic statement. Again, "natural reticence" is a principle working against "plain speaking."

The standard by which Moore measures the "precision" of poetry is "naturalness," but nature, in her terms, confounds rather than ingratiates our understanding. "Voltaire objected to those who said in enigmas what others had said naturally, and we agree; yet we must have the courage of our peculiarities. What would become of Ogden Nash, his benign vocabulary and fearless rhymes, if he wrote only in accordance with the principles set forth by our manuals of composition?" The "effects of helpless naturalness" that enliven Shakespeare, Chaucer, Spenser, and others are "well nested," however. They are deliberate deviations, feigned awkwardnesses. Natural reticence becomes an active principle of style, manifest in certain kinds of language under ordinary circumstances considered "inarticulate": excessive use or absence of connectives, inversion of word order, anticlimax, enigmatic phrasing, repetition, and wordiness, all of which can be found throughout her verse, though she "tries to be neat." Restraint is usually connected with decorum, but for Moore it is shown in indecorum.

Enigmas, of which the characteristic form is antithesis, unlike matter-of-fact statements, keep the text open to imply a source greater than it can contain. Moore's most famous enigma is the definition of poems as "imaginary gardens with real toads in them." And we should recall her temporary self-accusation "enigmas are not poetry." The rules of composition that Moore delights in violating are generally those with closural force. That antithesis can be a means of having it both ways, of saying something and yet nothing, is comically clear in the Ogden Nash poem she quotes ("I love the Baby Giant Panda"), again without commentary. It is an example of antithesis taken to an extreme, where one meaning cancels out another. We see the full force of Moore's love of antithesis when she adds this comment: "This, it seems to me, is not far removed from George Wither's motto: 'I grow and wither both together.' "

Sustained climax (a technique Moore uses often in poems, as at the end of "An Octopus") may be seen as an extended version of antithesis, in the way it undermines the force of singular endings. And what better example of sustained climax (though Moore never makes the connection of form and content explicit) than Tantalus, who was indeed "hindered to succeed." "In 'Orpheus and Eurydice,' Henryson tells how Tantalus stood in a flood that rose 'aboif his chin'; yet

> quhen he gaipit thair wald no drop cum In;
>
> .   .   .
>
> Thus gat he nocht his thrist [to slake] no[r] mend.
>
> Befoir his face ane naple hang also,
> fast at his mowth upoun a twynid [threid],
> quhen he gaipit, It rollit to and fro,
> and fled, as it refusit him to feid.
> Quhen orpheus thus saw him suffir neid,
> he tuk his harp and fast on it can clink;
> the wattir stud, and tantalus gat a drink.

Moore's only comment is "one notices the wholesomeness of the uncapitalized beginnings of lines, and the gusto of invention, with climax proceeding out of climax, which is the mark of feeling." Presumably she admires these qualities because they work against the formal closures of composition and suggest a subject matter and vision stronger than those closures. By deemphasized structure (such as she accomplishes through her syllables and eye rhymes) the poet sustains the energy of the language throughout the whole passage, rather than truncating it through firmly defined units. But Tantalus's situation tells us more. It is precisely "unquenchable" desire, like Williams's "unquenchable exaltation," that torments him. He feels a magnetism, an ardor, which requires the music of Orpheus, of the poet, to be released. The poet, as he is presented here, has the power to break the strain of intense desire by obstructing the progress of time. The poem is tantalizing; it delays its conclusions.

Moore recalls Longinus's disapproval of "weak rhythm" of the kind that " 'enables an audience to foresee the ending and keep time with their feet' "; to avoid this she rejected metrics altogether. Here again she is interested in techniques for hindering the easy advance of language toward conclusions. Here again, the energy of intense desire is incorporated into the language to give it force. Moore presents Henry Treece's "Prayer in Time of War" as an example of interiorized rhyme (a device she used regularly), and the poem itself makes explicit the relation of desire and writing. Perhaps too, part of the "temptation" to present one's feeling to another that Moore spoke of in the foreword, comes from an anxiety about the "running panther of desire," though in less violent terms than Treece invokes. The language of the poem recalls Moore's earlier suggestion that "when writing under maximum impact the writer seems under compulsion to set down an unbearable accuracy," and the suggestion that the poem is an enormous release of energy, a "lion's leap" that "can kill a man," though in this case the energy goes to "rock the mountain."

Each of the poems Moore quotes indicates the inhibitive force of what she calls "natural reticence." Precision in poetry seems to be a matter of infusing speech with signs of silence, through oddities of diction and syntax. That is, "natural reticence," which is antisocial, however eloquent, becomes "rhetorical reticence," variations within speech that indicate a speaker's unconsummated desire to see or possess an object fully. While natural reticence tends toward total privacy (either in silence or private speech), rhetorical reticence uses conventional speech forms, making its subject communicable while interrupting the conclusiveness of these forms, thus continuing a channel of verbal energy. The vanity of natural reticence, the "refusal to be false," is that we hold out for the ultimate word, for a *mot juste* that can fully circumscribe our experience. Rhetorical reticence admits failure and simply demands continuance.

The thrust of Moore's essay, certainly, is on the side of personal intensity, or feeling. We must have the "courage of our peculiarities." In the penultimate paragraph feeling is viewed in its maddening intensity, the artist "aware of nothing but his subject." "Fear of insufficiency is synonymous with insufficiency, and fear of incorrectness makes for rigidity. Indeed, any concern about how well one's work is going to be received seems to mildew effectiveness." Several examples of "rapt attention" and "intensively private soliloquizing continuity" follow. "Mr. McBride in the New York Sun, once said of Rembrandt and his etching, 'The Three Crosses': 'It was as though Rembrandt was talking to himself, without any expectation that the print would be understood by others.' " She recalls Bach's moment of vision, which produced "Behold I Stand Before Thy Throne." This kind of concentration seems to favor the side of "eloquent silence" and "natural reticence." Sublimity is connected with privacy.

But the last paragraph of the essay has a peculiar qualifying effect on the celebration of "rapt attention."

> Professor Maritain, when lecturing on scholasticism and immortality, spoke of those suffering in concentration camps, "unseen by any star, unheard by any ear," and the almost terrifying solicitude with which he spoke made one know that belief is stronger even than the struggle to survive. And what he said so unconsciously was poetry. So art is but an expression of our needs; is feeling, modified by the writer's moral and technical insights.

The "poetry" of the passage for Moore was surely the invocation of a terrifying condition: speech that has no audience, a "language of sensibility" without any portrait. Totally private speech isolates the speaker. Total concentration (eloquent silence) is akin to concentration camp isolation. What we "need," it turns out, is "expression," however imprecise. Perhaps one of the "temptations to write" is the chance of breaking up the intense magnetism of "eloquent silence." The "poetry" in Maritain's passage has the sublimity of tragedy, which presents a terrifying condition at one remove. The strength of his parallel is partly its contrast to the condition from which he presents it. Maritain, seen and heard by his audience, invokes a condition of absolute desire, the repetitions in his "poetry" adding to the intensity. The "technical insights" that "modify" feeling are those which can imply the pressure of inarticulate feeling, and thus avoid the horror of finality.

As in all her arguments, in verse or prose, Moore's tactic in "Humility, Concentration and Gusto" is to acknowledge principles and then violate them. Humility (a motive of natural reticence) begins as a standard of simplicity and objectivity, but its effect is the opposite. "Concentration" gives way to "impassioned explicitness." What was presented as a dialectic in "Feeling and Precision" here becomes a process: "Humility is an indispensable teacher, enabling concentration to heighten gusto." Only implicitly does she tell us how.

The essay opens in the more than metaphorical context of war:

> In times like these we are tempted to disregard anything that has not a direct bearing on freedom; or should I say, an obvious bearing, for what is more persuasive than poetry, though, as Robert Frost says, it works obliquely and delicately. Commander King-Hall, in his book *Total Victory*, is really saying that the pen is the sword when he says the object of war is to persuade the enemy to change his mind.

The notion of "persuasion," along with the idea that "the pen is the sword," would seem to be on the side of established rhetorical formulas. But what is persuasive, it turns out, is an uncertainty about rhetoric and a sense of oneself and one's experience as somehow beyond form. That is, an internalized war between one's desire to be sincere and one's desire to speak, a "warfare between imagination and medium," becomes, when one's language implies it, a powerful weapon in external wars. Humility, embarrassment, are attention getters: "could anything be more persuasive than the preface to [William] Caxton's *Aeneid*, where he says: 'Some desired me to use olde and homely termes . . . and some the most curyous termes that I could fynde. And thus between playn, rude and curyous, I stande abasshed'?" One is generally "abasshed" because of some failure of decorum (whether social or linguistic), some personal exposure. Caxton's response is provoked by an awareness of style and self as somehow at odds. The passage describes an unresolved relation between sincerity and expression. Good writing and embarrassment are, then, connected.

Moore's ideal style is flawless and impersonal; in humility she admits she often falls short of the mark:

Daniel Berkeley Updike has always seemed to me a phenomenon of eloquence because of the quiet objectiveness of his writing. And what he says of printing applies equally to poetry. It is true, is it not, that "style does not depend on decoration but on simplicity and proportion"? Nor can we dignify confusion by calling it baroque. Here, I may say, I am preaching to myself, since, when I am as complete as I like to be, I seem unable to get an effect plain enough.

This is a designed humility on Moore's part. What is persuasive is her preaching to herself. Certainly we should not expect her to be less complete than she would like to be, so what seem like excesses are justified as honesty. The ideal may be a pure resolution of "completeness" and "simplicity and proportion," but for her, at least, these aims remain at odds. Humility may have a standard of quiet objectiveness, but it becomes, in failing this ideal, a willingness to acknowledge that the forms we use are inadequate. We must *undignify* forms in an effort to indicate their inadequacy. That is, we must break up their formality. As usual, the poet says more than her "feigned inconsequence of manner" would suggest:

We don't want war, but it does conduce to humility; as someone said in the foreword to an exhibition catalogue of his work, "With what shall the artist arm himself save with his humility?" Humility, indeed, is armor, for it realizes that it is impossible to be original, in the sense of doing something that has never been thought of before. Originality is in any case a by-product of sincerity; that is to say, of feeling that is honest and accordingly rejects anything that might cloud the impression, such as unnecessary commas, modifying clauses, or delayed predicates.

This passage starts out, again, upholding "objective" simplicity and proportion over self-assertive decoration. We should, it would seem, humbly submit to the forms available, pass on a tradition, acknowledging that there is no possibility of an "original" form. But the second half of the passage takes a slightly different tack, asserting that "originality is the by-product of sincerity." Since the mere rejection of unnecessary commas, clauses, and delayed predicates would not amount to originality, Moore must mean something more by it. If we go back to sincerity as Caxton expressed it, it seems to be at odds with form rather than subject to it. Originality, that is, is a by-product of sincerity because sincerity creates personal violations of form, *un*dignifies it with "minor defects." Style, then, is deformation, and humility, to invert Moore's theorem, becomes an agent of originality, of "regal awkwardness." What is persuasive in art is the artist's rebellion against decorum, the embarrassment of authorship. Paradoxically, to ensure that form does not become hermetically sealed and detached from experience, to give signs of her embarrassment within form, Moore often uses commas, modifying clauses, and delayed predicates, for these break up the continuity of form, its artificial totality, and suggest, give an "impression" of, a greater totality. Of course commas, modifying clauses, and delayed predicates used in this way are to Moore "necessary," not decorative. As usual, the purpose of making rules is to break them.

Concentration, seeming to take the lead from humility as a principle that rejects excess, "avoids adverbial intensives such as 'definitely,' 'positively,' or 'absolutely',", presumably in favor of inherent emphasis. But quickly that principle of simplicity becomes a principle of ambiguity, eating away at the "clear impression." Perhaps what Moore wants to avoid is concluding "definitely," "positively," or "absolutely" at all. Though we "cannot dignify confusion by calling it baroque," we may give a "clear impression" of confusion; "unconfusion may submit its confusion to proof." "Concentration—indispensable to persuasion—may feel to itself crystal clear, yet be through its very compression the opposite, and William Empson's attitude to ambiguity does not extenuate defeat. Graham Greene once said, in reviewing a play of Gorki's: 'Confusion is really the plot. A meat-merchant and a miller are introduced, whom one never succeeds in identifying even in the end.' " Concentration intensifies an uncertainty about the identity of characters and perhaps a more basic uncertainty about the meaning of the play. It is in this sense that Moore applauds Stevens's remark that "a poet may be a wall of incorruptibleness against violating the essential aura of contributory vagueness." It is concentration of this kind that attracts Moore to the partially concealed figures of the chameleon and the jellyfish. And these elusive figures in nature are directly connected, in her mind, with the elusiveness of the author within his text. Concentration, a result of humility, becomes an agent of gusto when identities are raised. Moore implicitly connects Gorki's mysteries of identity with the broader question of authorship.

The assumption behind Moore's stress on "concentration" is that "complete" information is an illusion, which disguises the essential am-

biguity of the world and limits meaning. It is in this sense that "vagueness" is contributory: by avoiding completeness of expression the poet
allows for imaginative inclusiveness. It is important that the sense of inclusiveness is usually produced by an insoluble difference presented at
close proximity. Concentration, that is, is ambiguity, compressed differentiation. The lines Moore quotes Auden quoting show this particularly well: "In any case, a poem is a concentrate and has, as W. H.
Auden says, 'an immediate meaning and a possible meaning; as in the
line, a wedged hole ages in a bodkin's eye.' "

It seems peculiar that instances of "concentration" should be followed by an instance of "impassioned explicitness." The main investment of the essay so far has been toward the reduction of words, and
what follows is an instance of expansion. We saw this same pull from
compactness to expansion in the Book of Daniel passage in "Feeling
and Precision." The ambivalence shows in her simultaneous publication of the short and long "Poetry." And the pull in all her poems, between definition and epigram on the one hand, and description, list,
qualification on the other, again repeats this tension. For Moore concentration and explicitness are but two responses to the same problem—that experience cannot be squeezed into form. Her long poems
are like explorations of the ambiguities and paradoxes presented in her
short poems, but in neither form are these "confusions" resolved. "Impassioned explicitness" is, rather, a narrowing down of differences
through an accretion of words, a regular technique in her descriptive poetry. If the concentrated phrase "a wedged hole ages in a bodkin's eye"
can produce "forever in a microscopic space," the following passage can
produce microscopic space in an endless expansion of words. And
again, it is the content as well as the form which interests her here. "I
am prepossessed," she writes, "by the impassioned explicitness of the
Federal Reserve Board of New York's letter regarding dangerous count-
erfeits, described by the Secret Service:"

> $20 FEDERAL RESERVE NOTE . . . faint crayon marks have
> been used to simulate genuine fibre . . . In the Treasury
> Seal, magnification reveals that a green dot immediately
> under the center of the arm of the balance scales blends
> with the arm whereas it should be distinctly separate. Also,
> the left end of the right-hand scale pan extends beyond the
> point where the left chain touches the pan. In the genuine,
> the pan ends where it touches the chain. The serial numbers
> are thicker than the genuine, and the prefix letter "G" is

sufficiently defective to be mistaken for a "C" at first
glance, . . . the letters "ry" in "Secretary" are joined together. In "Treasury" there is a tiny black dot just above the
first downstroke in the letter "u." The back of the note, although of good workmanship, is printed in a green much
darker than that used for genuine currency.

      December 13, 1948   Alfred M. Olsen, Cashier

At the end of this quotation Moore adds, "I am tempted to dwell on
the infectiousness of such matters, but shall return to verse."

Coming right after "concentration," "impassioned explicitness"
is odd enough. But there are extra layers of fascination here. This example is not, as Moore's others are, "literary" (the shock is marvelous,
as this excerpt is followed by an Edward Lear ditty). Indeed, it is
Moore's democratic policy to include "business documents and school-
books." But clearly Moore does not see these words as the cashier does
(while we can assume intention in Spenser or Lear). To call this "impassioned" explicitness requires considerable projection. What Moore
has done with this passage, as with so many of the quotations in her
verse, is to make a "found poem" of her own. Unlike the language of
Spenser or Lear she quotes later, the language here is dispossessed. She
claims it (or it "prepossesses" and "infects" her), thus revising its function. The "genuine" or "sincere" poet does not depend for his or her
enthusiasm on subjects marked for their sublimity. And since the *explicit*, for Moore, lies in the direction of the particular, the work is done
for her and she need only foster it. The passage does not become easily
assimilated in its context of art. It remains a challenge.[5]

But it is not simply the shock of class that interests Moore in the
passage. The embarrassment to art goes deeper. Why is Moore so hesitant to go into these "infectious matters"? Infection spreads, and presumably she is afraid this variety could go on forever (a possibility most
of her poems indulge). But perhaps in preferring to "return to verse"
she is, implicitly, still "dwelling" on the passage. For in an essay dealing
with "the genuine" in art, who can resist a passage concerning counterfeit? Is it not the question of the genuine that art is always dwelling on?
As it turns out, we are here not only looking at an author (admiring her
power of possession) through her diffused identity in descriptive detail;
we are looking at a metaphor of the art of writing itself. But the question of the genuine can never, in art, be confronted head on. There is
silence and embarrassment at this most central of differences.

There are several compositions (copies) to consider here, and we find in the search for the genuine an infinite regress, as well as a perpetual fascination with the comparison. There is the cashier's composition, the counterfeiter's own "composing," and, since money is minted (*impressed* in a wonderfully complex sense), there is the composition of the "genuine" bill and all its "authorized" reproductions. On which does Moore focus in adopting the passage in her own composition? Or is she standing at a distance, fascinated by the interaction of identities here: the bold lettered, impersonal Secret Service in "unbiased" search for the truth nevertheless requires a private identity, Alfred M. Olsen, Cashier, December 13, 1948, to do its work. (Poetry as secret service with poets as agents is an inviting analogy.) The counterfeiter is identified for his "good workmanship" tested against the work without an author, the "genuine" bill, authorized by the impersonal Federal Reserve Board. Authorship always implies something short of their standards, or is Moore suggesting with tongue in cheek that authorship, and our interest in it, are inevitable? Questions of identity raised in this passage are not unlike the questions of identity raised in the imagination of a reader of Gorki's mystery. Indeed, one of the ways this excerpt functions in the essay is as a parody of the reader confronted with a work of concentration, a "satire on curiosity in which no more is discernible / than the intensity of mood."

To make matters even more complex (and more infectious certainly), the cashier deconstructs the words on the two bills (themselves symbolic and in a sense "artificial"). Moore's fancy flitted over all these identities, fascinated with the genuine counterfeiter whose distinctive marks are his undoing, the cashier whose careful eye dissects differences, and even the general institutions through which individuals pass. The interest is not in "the genuine" alone, in the sense of a resting place, but in the variants of it. Things in themselves are, to say the least, too mundane for Moore's curious eye. Her "relentless accuracy" in describing "an octopus of ice" or "the jerboa" and delighting in repeated defeat has the same quality of gusto.

Clearly this introductory example of "gusto" complicates our sense of the genuine, which we superficially associate with gusto. For once we acknowledge that gusto is generated by a basic difference between the real and the artificial rather than simply by the impression of the real, this discord becomes the type of all other forms of gusto, all created out of differences.

The Olsen passage has a privileged position in the essay by virtue of its length and peculiarity. Questions—of authorial identity and expression, and of the real versus the represented—that occurred obliquely before, are now central. Achieved objectiveness in art would eliminate a difference between imagination and media so that questions of the createdness of art would not obtain. Impostor artists pass off their creations as objective. Artists who possess the persuasive virtue of "humility" attest to the createdness of their objects by breaking up, with signs of authorship, formal continuities and illusions. This humility gains special respect through the passage above since no element (not even the genuine bill) is presented that does not, in one form or another, have an author.

Moore "dwells" on the counterfeit passage, then, by returning to literary examples in which gusto involves a subtle narrative intrusion into the fictions they present, "impulsive intimacies," to use Moore's phrase, which bring the fiction and its creation into close proximity: "You remember, in Edward Lear's 'The Owl and the Pussy Cat,' they said: 'Dear Pig, are you willing to sell for a shilling / Your ring?' Said the Piggy, 'I will.' The word 'Piggy' is altered from 'Pig' to 'Piggy' to fit the rhythm but is, even so, a virtue, as contributing gusto." What has gusto, though Moore does not make this explicit, is the introduction of an element that cannot be assimilated into the action, collapsing the distance though not the difference between narration and action. The source, not the subject, the mind working with words, becomes the focus of interest here, as in "An Octopus," "Walking Sticks," and so many other of her poems. Lear's rhythms are about language in the same way as are those of Ogden Nash. The playfulness with which he creates an illusion and then jumps into it with an intimate form of reference is what produces gusto here. Similarly Spenser's "impulsive intimacy" in the word "pumie" substituted for a repetition of "pumie stones," which Moore notes as an instance of gusto, brings "The Chase after Love" to life. These variations have no semantic value, but they produce a quantum of energy in the text by playing off a difference between the text and its author. Impulsive intimacies abound in Moore's poetry—in the form of sudden exclamation, ("Neatness of Finish!"), by shifts from description to admiration ("its leaps should be set / to the flageolet"), and most often by self-reflexiveness (the MEridian of "Four Quartz Crystal Clocks") or direct address (the "you" of "Camellia Sabina").

That gusto is related to signs of authorship and to the breaking of form is more explicitly clear in T. S. Eliot's tribute to Walter de la

Mare. Moore points to the words "By you," as a "yet more persuasive instance of gusto." The phrase "By you" inserts a special kind of "impulsive intimacy." The poem begins with a narration and abruptly interrupts it with questions (and eventually answers) as to the source of the illusion. The passage describes a process by which the speaker approaches an artwork with no sense of its source, becomes curious about its source, and eventually discovers it. What is remarkable is that the first lines can remain "an inexplicable mystery of sound" even after the author's identity has been revealed. The difference between the illusion and its creation is never fully collapsed. This is wittily complicated by the fact of a second author, Eliot, who has told the "story" of this unveiling.

Again Moore gives no hints of why she defends William Cowper's "The Snail" (a probable source of her "To a Snail") as "a thing of gusto although the poem has been dismissed as mere description."[6] But the poem is similar to the passage by Eliot in raising questions of authorship.

Give but his horns the slightest touch,
His self-collective power is such,
He shrinks into his house with much
    Displeasure.

Where'er he dwells, he dwells alone.
Except himself, has chattels none,
Well satisfied to be his own
    Whole treasure.

Thus hermit-like his life he leads,
Nor partner of his banquet needs,
And if he meets one, only feeds
    The faster.

Who seeks him must be worse than blind,
He and his house are so combined,
If finding it, he fails to find
    Its master.

The deflected allegory of man is clear enough. Undoubtedly Moore also found "gusto" in the precision of rhyme and meter in this poem. But precision, for her, should imply a personal interest pressing against the structure of language. In the case of Cowper that concern is always his isolation. The "mere description" takes on human pathos as soon as we focus on questions of inhibition and solitude, but especially when we identify them with the author. The rhyme repeats this sense, setting off a solitary last line against grouped rhymes. Similarly each sentence sets up an antithesis of plural and singular.

In the last stanza Cowper alters the focus from the snail to someone observing the snail, from inside to outside, and shifts the pathos more clearly onto the figure of the snail. But the real "gusto" of the poem, for Moore, undoubtedly comes with the recognition that the "master" *is* Cowper, the "who" the reader. Like Moore, Cowper brings his analogy to bear on the immediate circumstances of writing and reading. Such gestures are discreet, however, and do not dismiss the major analogy. Circumlocution, for Moore, as for Cowper, means bringing the image around to its source, the only place, after all, where the image and the idea are solidly united.

The closest we get to an actual definition of gusto is "that domination of phrase referred to by Christopher Smart as 'impression.' " What causes the domination, it seems here and by the examples Moore chooses, is an alteration of the reader's expectation, a complacency snapped alert by a difference in the form of deviation from conventional expression, or from the terms set up as decorum for the work. " 'Impression' he says, 'is the gift of Almighty God, by which genius is empowered to throw an emphasis upon a word in such wise that it cannot escape any reader of good sense.' Gusto, in Smart, authorized as oddities what in someone else might seem effrontery."[7] Gusto is one of those pivotal terms (like sincerity) that can designate either a response to something or a quality of something. Similarly, an "impression" is stamped and revealed. Smart frequently plays with this ambiguity in his own verse. The "oddities" that make an "impression" in Smart are signs of his idiosyncrasy and energy penetrating a formal, impersonal framework; they are, in a sense, "impulsive intimacies" that divert our attention from subject matter to source of creation. Like Moore, Smart plays with the surface of language, allowing formal connections to compete with semantic ones. In *Jubilate Agno* the surface of words is so obtrusive as to cancel other signals. Even in the lines Moore quotes from the more sober "Psalms" and "Song to David," we feel the force of the lines in alliteration, inversion, metonymy, repetition, rather than solely in any "vision" they may conjure up. Smart's language cannot be justified in terms of "plain speaking." Indeed, at moments it is hard to establish the meaning at all. And yet the words have a compositional authority:

> To everything that moves and lives,
> Foot, fin, or feather, meat He gives,
> He deals the beasts their food.
>
> .   .   .
>
> Strong is the lion—like a coal
> His eyeball—like a bastion's mole,
> His chest against the foes.
>
> .   .   .
>
> But stronger still, in earth and air
> And in the sea, the man of pray'r,
> And far beneath the tide;
> And in the seat to faith assign'd
> Where ask is have, where seek is find,
> Where knock is open wide.

At the beginning of this essay Moore suggested that one should "reject anything that might cloud the impression, such as unnecessary commas, modifying clauses, or delayed predicates." Here the "impression" is in fact made by such variations. In this part of the essay gusto is described as excusing "minor defects," but it is soon clear that it in fact thrives on "minor defects," that they are the source of the energy and are very consciously, artificially, made. The strong impression is made by the force of language and nothing else; it is no accident that the "strongest" figure in the poem should be "the man of pray'r" since the force of the language draws attention to its speaker.

Where textbook "plain speaking" may not justify an element, then, the pull of a composition may. As Moore's examples continue, it is clear that the experience must be one with the composition, with words interacting with words. It is the words, not the subjects, of "Bowls," "The Plumet Basilisk," "Peter" that will not escape the reader of good sense. Moore makes the general observation that "in any matter pertaining to writing, we should remember that major value outweighs minor defects, and have a considerable patience with modifications of form," but if we consider the examples she chooses it is the very modification of form, and the charge their difference creates, that *de-*

termines the major value. As she elsewhere quotes Edmund Burke on the sublime, "deformity is striking as beauty is striking, in its novelty."

> With regard to emphasis in Biblical speech, there is a curious unalterableness about the statement by the Apostle James: The flower "falleth and the grace of the fashion of it perisheth." Substitute, "the grace of its fashion perisheth," and overconscious correctness is weaker than the actual version, in which eloquence escapes grandiloquence by virtue of gusto.

What has happened to humility, which only four pages back upheld "simplicity and proportion"? Humility has become a means of indicating that the violations of form are unalterable, not decorative, but the distinction is ambiguous and it is clear that the force of the interest is with deviation, which can imply an energy pressing against conventional boundaries.

The impression of "uninhibited urgency" is extremely artificial, often not at all reflecting the patterns of "natural" emotional utterance, but nevertheless, within the poem, energetically "standing for them." The point is that the energy is always compositional for Moore, created not by an experience outside the verse imposed on language, but within terms the language itself sets up. Humility, concentration, and gusto interact as modes of speech to produce the energy of a work of art. "Gusto" involves the curious phenomenon of a language system that admits a principle of recalcitrance against the complacency of any mode of speech. Moore has moved from "humility," which admits that speech is fallible, to "gusto," which is achieved by deliberate linguistic deviation. At the root of these deviations is the notion of "the genuine," of a personal imagination pressing its way through an impersonal system. The difference between "art" and "life" can only be implied, artificially, by differences within a composition.

Toward the end of the essay Moore quotes some writing she considers "pithy" because of its word order:

> In a certain account by Padraic Colum of Irish storytelling, "Hindered characters," he remarked parenthetically, "seldom have mothers in Irish stories, but they all have grandmothers"—a statement borrowed by me for something I was about to write. The words have to come in just that order or they aren't pithy.

But did she include the line in "Spenser's Ireland" for its word order? Or does the order itself, "hindered" from the usual advance of the sentence by the interruption of the prepositional phrase, simply reinforce the notion it proposes? The relation of a fiction to its creative source (like that of these characters to their biological source) is always obscure; the difference betwen artist and artifact cannot be recovered. And yet a sense of a source remains. Hindrances and deviations in the "correct" advance of speech imply, though they can never fully identify, a source behind verbal constructs. While "correct" forms disguise their origins, as if they had no authors, "minor defects" open up an interest in origins. Moore's is a "native genius for disunion" like that of Irish grandmothers. Between the poet and the work a space remains; poems don't have mothers, but they do have grandmothers. Hindrances in language give a sense of personal energy at one remove. In this way Moore manages "impulsive intimacies" without ever speaking of herself.

In "Idiosyncrasy and Technique" Moore takes up the question of the genuine from the point of view of the writer rather than the text; again she is caught between "natural reticence" and "omnivorous perspicacity." She never overcomes this double bind, but she explores two possible ways of thinking about it. In the first half of the essay she relies on organic metaphors, which imply a continuity between vision and expression, making the work an outgrowth of its author, making art "natural." In the second half she shifts to mechanical metaphors, which imply a discontinuity between authors and works, making form a symbol rather than an extension of the genuine. We have already seen this tension at play in Moore's poems on poetry, discussed in Chapter 1.

In response to the question "why does one write?" Moore first quotes Auden: "Every poem is rooted in imaginative awe." She proceeds firmly to exclude "money and fame" as motives and to stress "a species of intellectual self-preservation." What she is preserving herself against is not clear; she seems to imply that expression is itself a matter of life or death. "One writes because one has a burning desire to objectify what is indispensible to one's happiness to express." The sentence is curiously circular. Why *does* one write? Though she argues against a public orientation in writing, she never can fully resolve the difference between "imaginative awe" and the "desire to express."

While the title of the essay gives priority to idiosyncrasy, the essay begins under a secondary notion, "Technique." And Moore's discussion of technique begins, curiously, with revision. "Writing was resilience. Resilience was an adventure. Is it part of the adventure to revise what one wrote?" Apparently yes, since she goes on for another page giving examples of revision. Revision and writing become synonomous for Moore, thus she includes her revisions as part of her poems. But resilience suggests a kind of continuity, whereas revision sounds more mechanical. Two main tendencies emerge. "The revisions of Henry James of his novels, are evidently in part the result of an insistent desire to do justice to first intention." And she quotes T. S. Eliot's definition of revision as "that power of self-criticism without which the poet will do no more than repeat himself." One of Moore's tendencies stresses idiosyncrasy of vision, "imaginative awe"; the other stresses idiosyncrasy of form, originality in expression. One assumes a base in private experience; the other assumes that the self is continually recreated in expression. To begin the discussion with "technique" rather than idiosyncrasy suggests that idiosyncrasy exists as a modification of technique, that idiosyncrasy is secondary to technique, an invasion of it. But to begin the discussion of technique with revision suggests something prior to technique which is directing it. The two possibilities are raised again through two different theories of revision. What is the relation of idiosyncrasy and technique? Which comes first? Is original art an outgrowth of unique vision, or the modification of form? Is art organic, continuous with and expressive of the artist's nature, or mechanical, discontinuous and allegorical? Developing a dialectic of organic and mechanical theories of poetry, she again resorts to paradoxes of nature and form, viewing art as a blossoming citadel. Moore makes similar conjunctions in the poetry. The pangolin is both a natural creature with the appearance of an artichoke and an "armored animal," "the night miniature artist engineer." Similarly, we are never sure whether the plumet basilisk is an independent spirit in nature or the effect of form, whether he is metonymic or metaphoric.

Moore's discussion of technique moves on from the subject of revision to discuss art which is difficult but nevertheless has a "private air of interest." "What is said should at least have the air of having meant something to the person who wrote it—as is the case with Gertrude Stein and James Joyce" (and, we would add, in the case of Marianne Moore). "One should be as clear as one's natural reticence allows one to be." In the close proximity of language "as an expedient for making one's self understood," and "natural reticence," obscurity becomes intimacy. The "air of interest" establishes a kind of continuity between "imaginative awe" and "a trade embodying principles."

To ensure that her notion of technique links private and expressive moments, Moore uses a series of organic metaphors. A poem is "rooted" in imaginative awe. She admires the "noble firmness" of some writers over the "structural infirmity" of others, which "truly has, under surrealism, become a kind of horticultural verbal blight threatening firmness at the core." "If precise, one weeds text of adjectives, adverbs, and unnecessary punctuation." One must avoid the "mildew" of skepticism. Moore admires for stylistic precision Dr. Edmund Sinnots's notes in his book *The Biology of the Spirit*, but again she implicitly connects his stlye with his subject. Sinnots "discusses the self-regulating properties of protoplasm—digressing, with a shade of outrage, to deplore untidiness in the use of terms: 'It is not the purpose but the function of roots to absorb water.' " Since Moore surrounds the passage with biological metaphors for writing, we can guess she noted more than technical precison. Moore implicitly borrows the "biology of the spirit" in developing her concept of writing. She aligns the distinction between purpose (which suggests a degree of self-consciousness) and function (which suggests natural gestures) with a plea for naturalness in style. Technique, as she understands it, "*teknikos*, from the Greek, akin to *tekto:* means to produce or bring forth." Art springs from the private imagination as naturally as a plant springs from the earth.

Moore's discussion of "technique" which has come to mean "how to cultivate your garden" ends with a rather long excerpt from "My Garden" by the Duke of Windsor. The passage is there, Moore says, as an example of "straight writing" (natural, not overconscious or mannered). To consider the full relation of subject and style in this excerpt, which provides, for Moore, "an impression of individuality, conviction, and verbal selectiveness," I shall quote it in full. Once again Moore makes a rather humdrum piece of writing come as alive as an imaginary garden with real toads.

"I think my deep enjoyment of gardening must be latent," the Duke begins. "At least it was not inherited . . . The gardens at Sandringham and Windsor . . . made a fine show in summertime [a word with flavor, for me] but people did not really live with them. A garden is a mood, as Rousseau said, and my mood was one of intimacy, not splendor." Of his present gardening at The Mill, not far from Paris, he says, ". . . French gardens can be remarkably beautiful things. They look like continuations of the Savonnerie or Aubusson carpets in the great chateaus rolled outside the windows onto the lawns, perfectly patterned and mathematically precise . . . I wanted an English type of garden, which means green grass and seemingly casual arrangement of flowers, and here I had the perfect framework." Commenting on one of the color photographs which supplement the account, he says, "The main entrance to the property has an old covered gateway with ancient oak doors and a cobbled drive which leads to the main building. There is a big sundial above the front door, put there when The Mill was restored about 1732. In the foreground is Trooper, one of our four pugs." Technically an oversight, the f-o-r-e ground and the f-o-u-r pugs in close proximity, this clash lends authenticity, has the charm of not too conscious writing. Unmistakably all along, the article embodies a zeal for the subject, a deep affection for flowers as seen in the complaint, "the mildest stone mason turns scourge when it comes to plant life." The piece smiles, whereas saturnity is a bad omen. "We do not praise God by dispraising men."

Even if we grant Moore's preference for "straight writing," this piece does not, from the excerpts she's given us, seem particularly remarkable stylistically. Her instance of "verbal selectiveness" (the word "summertime") and her instance of "authenticity" (earlier "intimacy": the clash between "fore" and "four") sound almost arbitrary. It is unlikely that the Duke took much care over these words. In any case they hardly justify her dwelling on this long passage when she skips over so many other more impressive bits of writing. Perhaps, then, as in the counterfeit passage, Moore has some investment in *what* the Duke is saying, as well as in how he is saying it.

In the context of an argument for "straight writing" and an organic view of the creative process, the writing of a Duke who has abjured the throne, about his enjoyment of gardens, is richly suggestive. He has preferred the common to the royal, the natural to the rhetorical. Moore introduces these excerpts by anticipating hesitation. "Prosperity and royalty are always under suspicion. 'Of course they had help,' people say. 'Someone must have written the piece for them.' " Her concern with the authenticity of this piece, its "helpless sincerity," recalls her concern elsewhere that writing be "genuine." Perhaps suspicion of authorship here carries the force of suspicion elsewhere in her essays about technique as fraud when it is not generated naturally from the author's "vision." As we've seen in "Feeling and Precison" and "Humility, Concentration and Gusto," Moore works to disguise or modify form. The poet, like the Duke, must abjure the throne of "poetry" as an absolute cultural value, and marry a commoner, penetrate perfect forms with imperfect, "natural" elements. The Duke begins with the originality of his sentiment, which is connected to gardens that are "lived with" rather than displayed. His enjoyment is "deep," personal, not inherited, and appropriately he prefers gardens that are "intimate." It is easy to see why the Duke should prefer a latent to an inherited taste (considering his decision), and even why he should prefer a "lived with" garden to one on display (considering his change of position). His preference in gardens clearly repeats Moore's preference in poetry, for that which seems "lived with" and not a showy "technical display." For both, humility and intimacy seem to be connected.

A garden that is "lived with" implies a form of communion between its life and the life of the gardener-enjoyer, and Windsor's imagined relation to a garden parallels Moore's imagined relation to her writing. Both prefer "intimacy" to "splendor" because the former seems more "natural." The next excerpt repeats the contrasts of the first: showy gardens and "intimate" ones. The distinctions are elaborated. Showy gardens are "mathematically precise" and "perfectly patterned," stressing culture over nature to the extent that the indoors threatens to dominate the outdoors. These are contrasted to gardens that play down the signs of cultivation, of royalty, with natural green grass and "the seemingly casual arrangement of flowers." We see such contrasts in many of Moore's poems—"Novices," "Those Various Scalpels," "The Jerboa," "Virginia Britannia," to name just a few. In eighteenth-century terms, the contrast is between the beautiful and the picturesque. But this picturesque garden that is "lived with" is no less artificial than the highly ornate gardens that one can only behold. What is supposedly "lived with" is a highly cultivated *image* of a mood. The Duke does not live with the garden but with a projection of himself. The artificiality of the setting is all the more clear when we consider that his "English" garden is nothing like the ones he knew in native England, and that the "perfect framework" for this garden is France, where "English gardens" are alien transplants. His "intimacy" with the flowers is an imaginative projection, perhaps of a failed intimacy at home. In the poems, too, it is the incongruity of forms or elements that portrays "naturalness."

Moore says she appreciates the second part of the passage for the clash of "fore" and "four," as lending "authenticity" by a breach of decorum. But this hardly warrants such celebration. Perhaps the details of the description enhance this effect. The "naturalness" (which she seems to associate with authenticity) of the place is implied in the rusticity of its materials: the estate is constructed, but out of "organic" materials. The authentic seems connected in her mind with the intimate, and the sense of intimacy is carried in the gradual drawing into the building from the drive. The sudden reference to the foreground after this description of an entrance sounds odd, not just because it clashes with "four pugs": it clashes visually as well. Pugs are probably the most grotesque of dogs—unusually small and compact, their tails tightly curled, their faces disproportionately broad and densely wrinkled, they are "supreme in their abnormality." Hardly "charming" in the way one would describe the garden of the estate. Why is fierce, highly bred "Trooper" introduced just where the scene seems most "intimate"? The "authenticity" of this element is something like the authenticity of the real toad in the imaginary garden. He does not make the garden more real; he belies the "imaginary" nature of the garden. The garden "reflects" the mood of the speaker symbolically, not naturally. The introduction of the pug is alarming; it shakes up the sense of continuity, of intimacy, that the estate is "designed" to render. The pug has this effect not simply because, as an animal, it is in a sense more animate than the rest of the scene, but because it is in fact a product of cultivation, a breed, and in fact more like man than anything else in the scene, closer to its master on the scale of nature. It is a sign of authenticity because it designates a conflict between art and nature. Intimacy occurs in art where the difference between imaginative awe and expression seems minimal. But Moore's quotation here shows that these are only "myths" of intimacy, like the myths surrounding the basilisk, which, drawing the reader into a desire for intimacy, make the shock of difference all the stronger. And it is just at this point that Moore turns from organic to mechanical metaphors, from continuity to discontinuity.

Moore indirectly relates writing to this scene by juxtaposing Windsor's comment "the mildest stone mason turns scourge when it comes to plant life" with a comment on her preference for language that "smiles" over "saturnity," which is a "bad omen." Saturnity and stonemasonry seem connected in that they destroy or negate images of growth and continuity. As stonemasonry is the sign of culture over nature, saturnity is a kind of hyperconsciousness (conscious fastidiousness) over the intuitive conditon of writing Moore calls "straight talk" (or unconscious fastidiousness). Moore continues the organic view of writing in the section headed "Idiosyncrasy." The writer should have "a sense of upthrusting vitality and self-discovery" and "reject the attitude of philosophic distrust." But it turns out that "straight talk" is based on violations of decorum, not the absence of it. It is a matter of modified technique, of stonemasonry, not the plant life of "helpless naturalness." The essay as a whole, then, sets up an ideal of organic expressiveness but gradually converts images of natural growth to images of construction; we must build a tower so perfect that it will seem to grow naturally from ourselves.

Curiously, it is in the section on idiosyncrasy, usually associated with the natural, not that on technique, usually associated with the cultural, that metaphors of armor, stonemasonry, and mechanical construction become dominant. First this occurs with the simple transfer of the idea of organic "upthrusting vitality" to a mechanical image of "upthrusting vitality," the citadel. But "the mildest stone mason turns scourge when it comes to plant life." The organic view of continuity between experience and expression is gone. We are now in the realm of symbols for the artist's imagination, not extensions of it. "I borrowed, at all events, Ambassador Conant's title *The Citadel of Learning*, taken for his book from Stalin: '[Facing us] stands the citadel of learning. This citadel we must capture at any price. This citadel must be taken by our youth, if they wish to be the builders of a new life, if they wish, in fact, to take the place of the old guard.' " Unlike the garden, the citadel and its analogues are not "natural" but constructed, as learning is acquired, not "brought forth." The poem the phrase was taken for, which Moore next quotes in full, is about how "denigration" of any spirit of construction "is treason"; but martial power is on both sides here. One *combats* saturnity. The last stanza reads:

> Blessed the man whose faith is different
>   from possessiveness—of a kind not framed by "things
>   which do appear"—
>   who will not visualize defeat, too intent to cower;
>   whose illumined eye has seen the shaft that gilds the sultan's
>   tower.

The artist here is someone enchanted with a cultural ideal, not a natural one, with images of power. The supreme emblem of individual strength is not "rooted" in imaginative awe, but the artist's "illumined eye has seen the shaft that gilds the sultan's tower." An artist's individuality is displayed by the building of cities, the displacing of old images with new ones.

Moore presents an anecdote connected with the writing of the poem which tends to revise its meaning by introducing the idea of revision. Though "denigration is treason," "another's expertise might save one considerable awkwardness." To further oppose the notion of natural self-extension, then, she draws in the notion of external assistance as an aspect of creative achievement. Here "assistance" is approved, not suspected as it is in the Duke's writing. Rolfe Humphries's advice against excessive alliteration (often the result of unselfconscious, "authentic" writing) casues her to reconsider the line "blessed is the man who does not sit in the seat of the scoffer." She proceeds to give more examples in which another's expertise has advantaged a writer. Though these are particular, a general rule applies, that "technique" is not "brought forth" but acquired, a "trade embodying principles attested by experience." What has happened to her praise of "authenticity," of writing that receives no help? Technique, as external rules of composition, seems to receive more appreciation here, as part of the citadel of learning. Naturalness is sometimes limitation.

The chief virtue or "secret" of good writing is now not "naturalness" but "steadfastness." The great artist is original not through the natural extension of himself into form, but through the construction of a unique form, a "portrait" of the language of sensibility, that can stand for an intensity of vision. Great art indicates the dynamic form of life by continually renewing the static forms made to represent it.

> Creative secrets, are they secrets? Impassioned interest in life, that burns its bridges behind it and will not contemplate defeat, is one . . .
> The master secret may be steadfastness, that of Nehemiah, Artaxerxes' cupbearer, as it was of the three youths in the fiery furnace, who would not bow down to the image which the King had set up. "Why is thy countenance sad, seeing that thou are not sick?" the King asked. Nehemiah requested that he be allowed to rebuild the wall of Jerusalem and the King granted his request; gave him leave of absence and a letter to the keeper of the forest that he might have timber for the gates of the palace—subject to sarcasm while building, such as Sanballet's, "If a fox go up, he shall break down their wall." Summoned four times to a colloquy, Ne-

hemiah sent word: "I am doing a great work and I cannot come down." Then when warned that he would be slain, he said, "Should such a man as I flee?" "So the wall was finished."

The scourge of the stonemason is now the power of the artist to construct the wall of Jerusalem or the citadel of learning. Organic metaphors give us images of a resolved relation between imaginative awe and expression, but we remain in a condition of "burning desire" to "objectify what is indispensible to [our] happiness to express." The aim of art is the objectification of feeling, of subjective reality. This is never fully accomplished: art retains an element of saturnity, of skepticism.

> Thomas Mann, fending off eulogy, rendered a service when he said, "Praise will never subdue skepticism." We fail in some degree—and know that we do, if we are competent; but can prevail; and the following attributes, applied by a London journal to Victor Gollancz, the author and publisher, I adopt as a prescription: we can in the end prevail, if our attachment to art is sufficiently deep; "unpriggish, subtle, perceptive and consuming."

Organic metaphors are not simply negated; they are replaced by metaphors of construction. We "fail" but can "prevail" in that we continue building. Indeed, failure is an agent of continuance. The "impassioned interest in life" becomes the drive to create new citadels. Here is Eliot's version of revision, the continual renewal of art, but with the force of James's version of revision, the continual reference to a source, before art, as its unrestorable ideal. "Why does one write"? Moore's organic metaphors would suggest that writing is a matter of baring the soul; her mechanical metaphors would suggest, as Pound said of Moore's poetry in comparing her to Laforgue (a master of saturnity), that writing is a matter of "logopoeia," of "poetry that is akin to nothing but language which is a dance of intelligence among words and ideas and the modification of ideas and characters." What Moore has in mind, I think, is a sense of the difference between one's eloquent silence and one's writing, which nevertheless provokes a desire to eliminate that difference. What prods the construction, the interaction of words, is the sense of an order outside the text, which is continually redirecting its course. One aims to build a tower expressive of oneself. On the other hand, it is that very failure of expression, the force of "sincerity" challenging the limits of any given verbal structure, that allows one to "prevail," to go on writing energetically, to continue an interest in life. Sincerity, in this sense, is an agent of gusto. And in this sense we can understand a poet as talkative as Moore making a claim to "natural reticence."

Epilogue

OORE HAD a uniquely receptive imagination as well as an idiosyncratic one. She schooled herself in excellence wherever she found it, producing in turn many excellent poems that take their place in a broad tradition of literature in English. Because Moore's achievement is the product of so many rich soils, and because it transcends its particular time and place, I have considered these poems independently in terms of the unique imagination they display. But while Moore is both a universal and an individual artist, she is also, and especially, an American artist. We learn little about Moore's poetry by imposing on it preconceived notions of the American. But having worked our way from the inside of these unusual creations to a broad view of them, we can appreciate their American hues.

In the late Forties Marianne Moore walked into a milliner's shop and asked to be fitted as Washington Crossing the Delaware. The tricorn hat and cape soon became the trademark of this deliberate American. Native themes, characters, places, idioms, often in contrast to those of Europe, find their way into many of Moore's poems—"The Steeple Jack," "The Hero," "New York," "England," "Virginia Britannia" among them. Moore cultivated an American mannerism in her style, as well; sincerity and gusto were, for her, the superlative elements of our national character.

But the native, the genuine, the vernacular in Moore, is well schooled in urbanity and restraint, though she remains a recalcitrant student. Originality and sophistication meet in her poetry, sometimes in collision, sometimes in cooperation, always in dynamic combinations: real toads and imaginary gardens, feeling and precision, plain speaking and artificial form.

It is not surprising, considering how often Moore couples anti-thetical elements of American culture—the native with the imported, the vernacular with the classical, the natural with the sophisticated—that Henry James should be her "characteristic American," quickly re-fined to "superlative American." Moore tends, in her essay "Henry James as a Characteristic American" (*Predilections*, 21–31) to beg the question of the American, defining it as what she admires in James. But if nothing else, the essay suggests how she liked to think of America, and consequently, which of its qualities she identified with her own. On the principle that what one says of another is descriptive of oneself, Moore always borrowed an author's praise of others to define his own virtues. We can take her typically indirect method one step further on her own behalf, converting what she says, sometimes through James, about him, to an appreciation of her own virtues as an artist.

Of course Moore sees "sincerity" as the key to James's American character: "Underlying any variant of Americanism in Henry James's work is the doctrine, embodied as advice to Christopher Newman, 'Don't try to be anyone else'; if you triumph, 'let it be all you.'" From the outside, American sincerity can look like idiosyncrasy, and cause James to think of us that "we were somehow queer." But Moore insists that the American in Europe is "not quite so unconscious a bumpkin as Henry James depicts him." Moore's own sincerity, indeed, "savors of the connoisseur." Her naturalness and her idiosyncrasy are not arch, but they are a product of manner.

Common sense, instinct, directness, are aspects of sincerity, for Moore, and traits of the superlative American. "There is something at-tractive about a mind that moves in a straight line," she remarks in "People's Surroundings":

> straight lines over such great distances as one finds in Utah or in
> Texas,
> where people do not have to be told
> that a good brake is as important as a good motor;
> where by means of extra sense-cells in the skin
> they can, like trout, smell what is coming—
> those cool sirs with the explicit sensory apparatus of common
> sense,
> who know the exact distance between two points as the crow flies;

There are straight lines in Moore, though always vine-entangled. Her American directness makes her exclaim, outright, "I, too, dislike it," makes her eschew "the classic multitude of feet," and lets "expediency determine the form."

But there are drawbacks to this native way of thrashing through a dense, anfractuous reality, what she calls in "New York" "the scholastic philosophy of the wilderness." There are in America "no proofreaders, no silkworms, no digressions." If Moore's love of the genuine makes her embrace the American way, her relentless love of accuracy and of the neatness of finish makes her more restrained than her contemporaries. She shares her ambivalence about America with Henry James. Like him, she seeks a hybrid ideal combining American boldness with classical precision. Her student in "The Student" is American in spirit, but his books are "not native." He learns his lessons from "expatriates."

Sincerity is a moral as well as an aesthetic category for Moore, and many of her poems attempt to define an American brand of heroism. The superlative American, the artist, unlike the average American she sometimes satirizes, possesses restraint as an aspect of his sincerity. As she says of James, "his respectful humility toward emotion is brave, and in diffidence, reserve, and strong feeling, he reminds us of Whittier." The reserve of her American hero, as she depicts him in "The Student," for example, is always a sign of feeling, not of its lack. The student, like Moore herself, is "too reclusive for / some things to seem to touch / him, not because he / has no feeling but because he has so much."

Moore derives, in both personal and literary ways, from Protestant morality, but a distinctly American morality, that incorporates Emerson's iconoclasm, his self-reliance, and his "determination with resistance."

> in France or Oxford, study is beset with
>
> dangers,—with bookworms, mildews,
> and complaisancies. But someone in New
> England has known enough to say
> the student is patience personified,
>   is a variety
> of hero, "patient
>   of neglect and of reproach"—who can "hold by
> himself."
>   . . . refusing to be less
> than individual.

Unlike the general American "public out of sympathy with neatness," Moore, Henry James, and the "student named Ambrose" show restraint, know "you can't beat hens to / make them lay"; that "wolf's wool is the best wool, but it cannot be sheared because / the wolf will not comply." Moore's superlative American, unlike the "fearless sightseeing hobo" of "The Hero," has a "reverence for mystery." "Idealism which was willing to make sacrifices for its self-preservation was always an element in the conjuring wand of Henry James," and equally in the wand of Marianne Moore. Idealism and pragmatism meet in the superlative American. Vision expires if it rises too far from the concrete. Precipitous expression is ephemeral.

In "The Student," Moore draws from Emerson's "American Scholar" more directly than she owns. The essay can tell us a great deal about her art, particularly her concreteness, which for the average literal-minded American is dead fact, but for the superlative American is poetry. The scholar, Emerson writes, adds "observation to observation," transforming a dull world: "it came to him—business; it went from him—poetry. It was—dead fact; now, it is quick thought." It is because of this transforming power, as well as this democratic spirit, that Moore "will not discriminate against business documents and schoolbooks."

Henry James, Moore affirms, had this power in abundance: "Things, for Henry James glow, flush, glimmer, vibrate, shine, hum, bristle, reverberate. Joy, bliss, ecstasies, intoxication, a sense of trembling in every limb, the heart-shaking first glimpse, a hanging on the prolonged silence of an editor." One cannot imagine a better description of Moore's own gusto in the appreciation of fact. For Moore, as for James, "the aura is more than the thing." "The bonfires of his imagination . . . are too alive to countenance his fear that he was giving us 'an inch of canvas and an acre of embroidery.' " Moore, like James, lingers in detail long after all practical function is complete, enraptured by the density and dazzle of the world's variety. In her letters and conversation, as in poetry, her imagination pursued the ecstatic momentum of detail rather than the measured progress of argument. Moore admired in James, and displayed in her own art, a "rapture of observation." But under it was always the stabilizing, directing "force of cogitation and aspiration, as to the explanation both of a thousand surface incoherencies and a thousand felt felicities." Thus engaged in the act of finding and ordering reality, the imagination justifies itself. In an immediate, thematic sense, much of Moore's poetry is digressive. But if, as Moore thought, the imagination has a power to tear the veil of dejection, like the frigate pelican "to foil the tired moment of danger," then "these things are important not because a / high-sounding interpretation can be put on them but be- / cause they are / useful." As she observed of Henry James, what may look to others like self-indulgent leisure is integral with freedom, and nothing takes more restraint than freedom. We may say of Moore, as she said of James, who said it of John La Farge, "one was . . . never to have seen a subtler mind or a more generously wasteful passion, in other words a sincerer one."

To Moore, James was American in his "instinct to amass." "The American is, as he thought, 'instinctively and actively ample . . . reaching westward, southward, anywhere, everywhere' "—"with a mind incapable of the shut door in any direction." Moore's own "omnivorous perspicacity" expands over the page with glacial force, taking in whatever the mind encounters so that her poems seem to have no closure but the world itself. Her long, breathless sentences, her wide associations, the democracy of her subject matter, her compendious quotation, all denote the adventurous American spirit of her poetry.

This instinct to amass can be as much a vice in the pejoratively "big" American, as Moore depicts him, as it is a virtue in a superlative American like James. Moore, like James, knew that "rapacity destroys what it is successful in acquiring." "The power to relinquish what one would keep, that is freedom"—and gusto, and even power, for Moore. Her images of rapacity are always ironic, the "man looking into the sea," "the mountain guide evolving from the trapper," of Mt. Rainier, the colonists of "Virginia Britannia," "not noted for humility." "It is not the plunder" Moore admires in her home state of New York but, invoking James again, "accessibility to experience." Possessiveness, which seeks to expand the domain of the self, but narrows the world by forcing it into the mold of the mind, she always distinguishes from "imaginary possession," which keeps the world large by setting it a little beyond our control. New York is a "savage's romance" but there are two kinds of savage in Moore, the acquisitive and the curious. When the "instinct to amass" becomes mercenary plunder, or in terms of poetry, becomes a crude, violent effort to impose an ego-serving order on the world, it is no better than the masked-ball attitudes of Europe, "the beau with the muff," "the gilt coach shaped like a perfume bottle," no better than "writers entrapped by tea time fame and by commuters' comforts."

By "imaginary possession" Moore is able at once to forage in the dense variety of the wilderness and to maintain her civilized bearing. She can "stand outside and laugh" and yet go in, even though she knows that "to go inside is to be lost." She is always simultaneously ironic and sympathetic. Like Henry James, she "feels the need 'to see the other side as well as [her] own; to feel what [her] adversary feels.' " It is Jeffersonian democracy, with its strong sense of aristocracy and authority, but also of tolerance and mercy, that she upholds against the cruder colonizing instincts of "Virginia Britannia."

Above all, America is, for Moore, a place of mixed soils, of an "inconsistent flowerbed" where "the hero, the student, / the steeple jack, each in his way, / is at home." Virginia Britannia, for all its colonizing arrogance, its raw, tactless, pugnacious, dashingly undiffident slogans ("Don't tread on me"), and for all its European pretensions "filled with anesthetic scent as inconsiderate as the gardenia's," is a "magnificent" totality. Moore always celebrates the whole of life, even as she picks and chooses among its parts.

Nowhere does Moore's love of American inclusiveness show better than in her language. In "Virginia Britannia" she draws attention thematically to the cacophonous variety of language (its blend of Indian, English, French, and Negro idioms) as a key to the crazy quilt of the landscape. But in a less thematic way she engages this variety in all of her poetry. Moore reflects in her art the American manner of appropriating native and foreign elements, inventing and redefining, bringing the high into the low and the low into the high, absorbing the technical, the musical, the hackneyed, and the novel.

Moore is a staunch defender of "plain American that cats and dogs can read." She had read H. L. Mencken in the Twenties, and responded defiantly to the protests of English purists that Americans had adulterated their tongue.

> The letter *a* in psalm and calm when
> pronounced with the sound of *a* in candle, is very noticeable, but
>
> why should continents of misapprehension
> have to be accounted for by the fact?

And yet Moore's ultimate defense of America is that it exceeds all boundaries. While England is noted for its suitability, Italy for its epicureanism, France for its frivolity, America is all of the above. "If not stumbled upon in America, / must one imagine that it is not there? / It has never been confined to one locality."

Moore's America is everywhere and nowhere because it is, like all her landscapes, like icy Mt. Rainier with its "relentless capacity for fact," like the impenetrable forests of New York, "the scholastic philosophy of the wilderness," a metaphor of the mind, and of the ultimate poem. The great American poem, for Moore, would be one in which a rich variety of experience would be imagined into a classic unity, a neatness of finish that would leave no stray particular. Thus poetry, like science, " 'is never finished.' " But if sincerity is the motive that will not tolerate approximation, gusto is the mood that will not tolerate despair.

Notes
Index

Notes

Introduction: Sincerity and Gusto

1. Marianne Moore, *Predilections* (New York: Viking, 1955), vii. All subsequent references appear in the text.
2. R. P. Blackmur, *The Double Agent: Essays in Craft and Elucidation* (1935), rpt. in *Marianne Moore: A Collection of Critical Essays*, ed. Charles Tomlinson (Englewood Cliffs: Prentice-Hall, 1969), 66.
3. Lionel Trilling, *Sincerity and Authenticity* (Cambridge: Harvard University Press, 1971); Henri Peyre, *Literature and Sincerity* (New Haven: Yale University Press, 1963).
4. T. E. Hulme, "Romanticism and Classicism," in *Speculations: Essays on Humanism and the Philosophy of Art* (London: Kegan Paul, Trench, Trubner, 1924); Ezra Pound, "Vorticism" (1916), rpt. in *The Modern Tradition*, ed. Richard Ellmann and Charles Feidelson (New York: Oxford University Press, 1965); Louis Zukofsky, "Sincerity and Objectification," *Poetry* 37 (Feb. 1931), 268.
5. Herbert Read, *The Cult of Sincerity* (New York: Horizon, 1968).
6. William Hazlitt, "On Gusto," (1819), rpt. in *English Romantic Writers*, ed. David Perkins (New York: Harcourt, Brace, World, 1967), 618–619.
7. "The Art of Poetry: Marianne Moore," an interview with Donald Hall (1961), rpt. in *Marianne Moore: A Collection of Critical Essays*.
8. Laurence Stapleton, *The Poet's Advance* (Princeton: Princeton University Press, 1978); Marie Borroff, *Language and the Poet* (Chicago: University of Chicago Press, 1979).
9. Craig S. Abbott, *Marianne Moore: A Descriptive Bibliography* (Pittsburgh: University of Pittsburgh Press, 1977).
10. "The Feminine Language of Marianne Moore," in *Women and Language in Literature and Society* (New York: Praeger, 1980).
11. *The Revolution of the Word*, ed. Jerome Rothenberg (New York: Seabury Press, 1974).

1. Defining the Genuine: Poems about Poetry

1. Alfred Kreymborg, *Troubador* (New York: Sagamore Press, 1957), 190–191. Grace Schulman, "Conversation with Marianne Moore," *Quarterly Review of Literature*, 16 (1969), 154.

2. For suggested sources of the lines "I, too, dislike it" and "the raw material of poetry" see *Marianne Moore Newsletter*, 1, no. 2 (Fall 1977), 10–11. Moore drew from conversation as well as writing in order to create these individual realities. Near the notation "Miss Nellie of N'Orleans—(Posters at W. H. School)" Moore writes in her notebook "there are things that are important beyond all this fiddle" (Rosenbach 1250/24, 34). She is probably quoting her mother when she enters "you are like the sinners who fight you—you can't enjoy what you do not understand" (ibid., 35) and "hands that can grasp, limbs that can run, hair that can rise if it must, eyes that can dilate" (ibid., 36).

3. The Rosenbach archive has some notes and drafts for the poem. Of the published variants, compare the first printing in *Others*, 5 (July 1919), 5; *Observations* (1924 ed.); *Observations* (1925 ed.); *Selected Poems*; *Complete Poems*. For a fuller summary of revisions of "Poetry" see Patricia Willis and Clive Driver, "Bibliographical Numbering and Marianne Moore," *PBSA* 70, no. 2, 1976.

4. Rosenbach 1250/2, 26.

5. Williams was probably influenced by this poem and often alluded to Moore's idea of "prismatic colorings." The centrality of the prism as an ideal image in modernist art will be discussed in subsequent chapters. It is related to, though not identical to, the image of the crystal, popular not only with Moore but with the vorticists Ezra Pound and Wyndham Lewis. The prism and crystal are often used synonomously, but they are slightly distinguishable as metaphors for art, in that the prism is considered a medium of light (the poem, consequently, a medium of external reality) while the crystal is a more autonomous structure, growing from its own inherent kernel of order.

6. Rosenbach 1251/24, 32.

7. The first printed version of the poem, in the Bryn Mawr College *Lantern*, 27 (1919), 35, depicted Truth as potentially parallel to Form. "Truth, many legged and formidable also, / is stationary by choice."

8. *The Marianne Moore Newsletter*, 3, no. 2 (Fall 1979), 3.

9. Perhaps this is why the end of the poem completely bewilders George Nitchie and why for Bernard Engel it is a protest against pretentious critical attitudes, while for Jean Garrigue it is a perfect description of art. See George Nitchie, *Marianne Moore* (New York: Columbia University Press, 1969), 22–26; Bernard Engel, *Marianne Moore* (New York: Twayne Publishers, 1964), 62–64; Jean Garrigue, *Marianne Moore* (Minneapolis: University of Minnesota Press, 1965), 20.

10. Donald Hall, *Marianne Moore: The Cage and the Animal* (New York: Pegasus, 1970), 92.

11. A curious conversation with Sibley Watson, which Moore recorded in

her notebook, gives some clues to these and subsequent lines from "Novices":

Dr. Watson:	Is that what you refer to in yr Novices?
[Moore:]	No I was thinking of Conrad Aiken to Norman Douglas.
Dr. Watson:	I think there shd be a footnote to that effect. It greatly adds to the interest.
[Moore:]	I'm afraid the rest of the intelligent world doesn't agree w me. They mt rise up and destroy me—I believe CA is very much admired.
Dr. W—	I don't know about Norman Douglas—it certainly fits Aiken. [Rosenbach 1250/25, 54]

But Moore got the main idea for "Novices" from her mother, who once remarked, "Novices like to talk about their work like Will Honeycomb who was jilted by a duchess."
12. In *Observations* Moore provided notes that she later removed, but which help in understanding the image:

> snipe legged hieroglyphic Egyptian low relief in The Metropolitan Museum
> "A silver fence was erected by Constantine to enclose the grave of Adam": Literary Digest, Jan. 5, 1918; a descriptive paragraph with photograph
> Michael taking Adam: wash drawing by Blake; "Adam and Eve taken by Michael out of Eden."

The indirect source of the "satire on curiosity" may have been a Biblical passage Moore made note of in her reading diary. Amos speaks of "the impossible caricature of exaggerated zeal" (Rosenbach 1250/1, 123).
13. Drafts in the Rosenbach archive suggest that Moore puzzled as much over this poem as she did over "Poetry." Some candidates for the final lines were: "It must be a distinct distillation of personal experience / that interests me impersonally"; "It must not need to plead its desirability"; "It compels analysis and does not disappear under admiration." All of these variants add to our understanding of Moore's evolving aesthetic.
14. Rosenbach 1250/1, 119.
15. Marianne Moore, "Comment," *Dial*, 81 (Dec. 1926), 535–536.

2. The Spontaneous Symbol: Emblems and Meditations

1. T. S. Eliot, Introduction to *Selected Poems* by Marianne Moore.
2. T. S. Eliot, "Observations" in *The Egoist*, 5, no. 5 (May 1918), 69–70.

3. Moore's work does not conform to a strict chronological development. She worked in several different styles simultaneously and often revived old poems. But we can see a general pattern of development from short, formal lyrics to syntactically complex epigrams, to long descriptive poems, and eventually back to simpler lyrics.

4. Bernard Engel, *Marianne Moore* (New York: Twayne Publishers, 1964), 77–78.

5. Many of these poems also contain very private references while they challenge public remarks. As often as not there is some detail in family correspondence or notes of private conversation to suggest a private layer of meaning.

6. Jean Garrigue, *Marianne Moore* (Minneapolis: University of Minnesota Press, 1965), 9.

7. Rosenbach 1250/1, 115. Moore copied the passage from Gilman's review, "Drama and Music," in *The New American Review* (April 1915).

8. Patricia Willis, in a slide lecture presented at the Rosenbach on April 12, 1980, revealed a hidden reference to Floyd Dell, who reviewed Moore's work in *The Masses*.

9. Keats to Reynolds, 22 Nov. 1817, in *English Romantic Poets*, ed. David Perkins (New York: Harcourt Brace, 1967), 1207.

10. The scrapbook, which Moore kept between 1909 and 1915, is preserved in the Rosenbach archive. The reading diary notes are in Rosenbach 1250/2, 141–142. See also Moore's notebook entry: "Leigh Hunt The Snail," Rosenbach 1250/2, 130.

11. A draft of this poem in the Rosenbach archive adds a clue to its meaning. It includes the lines "on obediently sifting out / the buried fact— / You ask about cause and effect." The instance and the figure of buried fact are the carrot, making the poem both literal and allegorical.

12. Moore first called the poem "To Disraeli on Conservatism." *Lantern*, 23 (Spring 1915), 60.

13. See Engel, *Marianne Moore*, 21. Engel also makes connections with the line from the King James Song of Solomon: "Black, but comely."

14. The poem has many images and themes in common with an earlier one, "Feed Me Also River God" (*The Egoist*, Aug. 1916). In each Moore displays her characteristic humility by repeatedly qualifying her assertions. The earlier poem ends: "if you may fulfil / None but prayers dressed / As gifts in return for your gifts—disregard / the request."

15. Kimon Friar and John Malcolm Brinnin, eds., *Modern Poetry, British and American* (New York: Appleton-Century-Croft, 1951), 523. Moore might also have read Valery's poem "A Graveyard by the Sea."

16. Rosenbach 1250/2, 56, from *Greek Anthology*, II, 631 (the edition published about 1913).

3. The Capacity for Fact: Descriptive Poems

1. See Harriet Monroe, "Symposium on Marianne Moore," *Poetry*, 19 (Jan. 1922), 208–216: "If one were to accept the challenge of the title, and of the geometrical verse-designs which frame these cryptic observations, one might be led straight to the ancient and rather futile inquiry, What is poetry? Poetry is evidently a matter of individual definition."
2. Rosenbach 1250/2, 68.
3. See the Moore/Eliot correspondence at the Rosenbach.
4. Rosenbach 1250/5, 6.
5. Rosenbach 1250/5, 63. See Hugh Kenner, *A Homemade World* (New York: Alfred Knopf, 1975), 96.
6. Rosenbach 1250/2, 194.
7. Marie Borroff, *Language and the Poet: Verbal Artistry in Frost, Stevens and Moore* (Chicago: University of Chicago Press, 1979), 113.
8. See Kenner, *A Homemade World*, 117.
9. See William Pratt, *The Imagist Poet* (New York: E. P. Dutton, 1963), 14; Kenner, *A Homemade World*, 98; Bernard Engel, *Marianne Moore* (New York: Twayne Publishers, 1964), 57.
10. In the earliest publication of "The Fish," in *The Egoist*, 5 (Aug. 1918), 95, Moore did not raise the first syllable of each stanza to a separate line, nor did she indent lines. The first word of each line was capitalized.
11. Engel, *Marianne Moore*, 84.
12. Louis Zukofsky, "Sincerity and Objectification," *Poetry* 37 (Feb. 1931), 269.
13. See Rosenbach 1250/1, 59. While there are no known drafts or worksheets for this poem, Moore's notes from *The Street of Jody Masefield* suggest a possible source: "The heron *stood* as if he *were* wise and the water were truth . . . Feminine minds are like pools of water in which images are sometimes reflected so clearly as to be mistaken for thoughts."
14. William Carlos Williams, "Marianne Moore" (1925), rpt. in *Marianne Moore: A Collection of Critical Essays*, ed. Charles Tomlinson (Englewood Cliffs: Prentice-Hall, 1969), 55.
15. William Carlos Williams, *Spring and All* (1921), rpt. in *Imaginations* (New York: New Directions, 1970), 100.
16. Moore and her brother Warren climbed the glacier on Mt. Rainier in 1922. The Rosenbach archive includes a photograph of the two of them with a small group of fellow hikers on the mountain side, dressed to mirror the L. L. Bean catalogue.
17. The pamphlet of *National Parks Rules and Regulations* includes an aerial photograph of Mt. Rainier that makes it look like an octopus, and the prose caption calls it an "octopus of ice." Most of what I call the "tourguide" language comes from this pamphlet. My discussion of "An Octopus" primarily follows the sequence of the poem, but I have made minor inversions of Moore's ordering to highlight specific features of the poem.

18. Edmund Burke, *A Philosophical Inquiry into the Origins of Our Ideas of the Sublime and the Beautiful* (1757), ed. J. T. Boulton (London: Routledge and Kegan Paul, 1958; rpt. New York: Columbia University Press, 1968), 57. The copious entries from Burke in Moore's reading diary suggest her thorough knowledge of his work. In "Picking and Choosing" she calls him (and perhaps also Kenneth Burke) "a psychologist of racoon-like curiosity."

19. Moore read Hegel before composing "An Octopus," and her notes suggest that he may have been an indirect source of her view of ancient Greece. See Rosenbach 1250/2, 28–30. Moore's language is quite often overdetermined in this way. But the direct source is the one she notes, Newman's *Historical Sketches.* Her notes from the text, in Rosenbach 1250/3, 24–26, include more key notions, images, and phrases than she acknowledges. "The Athenian chose propriety as became so exquisite a people, and professed to practise virtue on no inferior consideration, but simply because it was so praiseworthy, so noble and so fair. Not that they discarded law . . . but they boasted that 'grasshoppers' like them old of race and pure of blood, cld be influenced in their conduct by nothing short of a fine and delicate taste." In versions prior to *Collected Poems* Moore had referred to the "grasshoppers of Greece," perhaps also transforming the Biblical idea that "the grasshopper shall be a burden" (Ecclesiastes 12: 5). The first publication of "An Octopus" in *The Dial,* 77 (Dec. 1924), 475–481, includes several lines and variants that I have not mentioned. Most interesting in terms of the concerns raised in Chapter 4 are these lines about the Greek language: " 'rashness is rendered innocuous, and error exposed / by the collision of knowledge with knowledge.' "

20. Moore's interest in James began early and continued throughout her career. Her scrapbook of 1909 includes several articles on James, and in "Picking and Choosing" he is "everything that has been said of him." Moore's immediate source for the James references, however, was Percy Lubbock's *Craft of Fiction.* Her reading diary includes this entry on James's style: "I conclude that method on this paradox—the art of dramatizing the picture of somebody's experience." Rosenbach 1250/3, 82. Notes for the poem in her workbook develop the allusion to James more fully than the printed version: "and what is this: the novel you have written? / an essay exhaustive long poem, exhaustive / study of my life America—" (Rosenbach 1251/71, 63).

21. Rosenbach 1251/17, 27 and 53.

22. Kenneth Burke, *A Grammar of Motives* (New York: Braziller, 1945), 503–504.

23. The poem has been a favorite among critics, and Moore herself once named it her best accomplishment. But she couldn't resist tinkering after its publication in *Hound and Horn* 6 (1932) and in *Selected Poems.* She cut several lines of description even though (or perhaps because) her brother had written "very pretty" next to them on a copy she had sent him (see Rosenbach archive).

24. Rosenbach 1250/1, 99–100. Moore's choice of reading matter was indeed unique among poets. But her attention to Henri Fabre was not so peculiar. She read Pound's *How to Read*, in which he declares Fabre "essential to contemporary clear thinking."
25. Donald Hall, *Marianne Moore: The Cage and the Animal* (New York: Pegasus, 1970), 83.
26. Moore always had her ear open for bits of witty conversation. The remark on the French was made by her friend Sibley Watson, and Moore jotted it down in her notebook: "The waiter asked me if I wanted the cucumbers squeezed. The French are a brutal race. I ought to have said, Half squeezed, half not" (Rosenbach 1250/25, 135).
27. Moore kept detailed notes of her trip to Virginia, which can be read at the Rosenbach. A letter to Winifred Bryher (9/8/34) also describes many of the sights that would find their way into this and other of her Virginia poems ("Smooth Gnarled Crape Myrtle," "Bird-Witted").
28. Susan Sontag, *On Photography* (New York: Farrar, Straus, Giroux, 1977), 21.
29. Moore read a great deal before and after her trip, though she did not include her research as directly in her poem as she had tended to do earlier. Among the works from which she draws notes in her reading diary are *Life in the Old Dominion*, Rosenbach 1250/5, 40–43; and *Afloat on the James, Travaille into Virginia Britannia, History of Hapton and Elizabeth County, Virginia Highway Historical Markers*, 1250/6, 127–51.
30. In a draft (in the Rosenbach archive) the ending of "Virginia Britannia" was more like Moore's earlier poems, detail breaking the dam of closure. It also earned its ending and deepened its irony and complexity:

> the live-oak's rounded
> mass of undulating boughs, the white
> pine, the aged hackberry—handsomest vis-
> itor of all—the
> cedar's etched solidity,
> the cypress, lose identity
> and are one tree—as
> sunset flames increasingly
> against their leaf-chis-
> selled blackening ridge of green;
> and the redundantly wind-
> widened clouds, expanding to
> earth size above the
> town's bothered with wages
> childish sages,
> are to the child an intimation of
> what glory is.

The strongest version of the poem appeared in *Life and Letters Today*,

13, 2 (Dec. 1935), 66–70 in the same issue that published Wallace Stevens's essay on Moore called "A Poet That Matters."

> The live-oak's moss-draped
> undulating massiveness, the white
>   pine, the English hackberry—handsomest vis-
> itor of all, the
>   cedar's etched solidity,
>   the cypress, lose identity
> and are one tree, as
>   sunset flames increasingly
>   over the leaf-chis-
> selled blackening ridge of green
> Expanding to
> earth size, igniting redundantly
> wind-widened clouds, it can
>   not move bothered-with-wages
>   new savages,
> but gives the child an intimation
>   of what glory is.

The concreteness of the parallel (new savages/child) is superior to the
moralizing "dwarf arrogance that can misunderstand importance,"
while it retains the expansion/contraction parallel.

31. I will quote from the version in *What Are Years*. The poem went
through many revisions, which Moore discussed in one of her deliveries
of the lecture "Humility, Concentration and Gusto": "When instinct
falters, humbling and varied disciplines must be undergone … My
stanzas about watermarks and paperweights for instance. I revised 3
times at the suggestion of the magazine that had accepted them; then
still felt a lack of finality and revised them again for my present book;
and now that the book is printed, I see the need for another alteration."
The book Moore is referring to is *What Are Years*; she sent a copy of her
corrections to e. e. cummings shortly after it was published (see
Houghton Library, Harvard University: Moore/Cummings letters). The
poem was first published in *Poetry* 49 (Nov. 1936), 59–64, where it is
substantially different from the later version, and in someways more enchanting, if perhaps too ingenious for Moore's later quest for simplicity.
The lines that appeared in place of "Post mark … divisiveness" are particularly worth preserving.

> The post's jerky

> cancellings ink the stamp, relet-
> tering stiltedly, as a puppet-
>   acrobat walks
> about with high steps on his net,

an alphabet
of words and animals where the
wire-embedded watermark's more integral
expressiveness had first set
its alabaster effigy.

32. Lionel Trilling, *Sincerity and Authenticity* (Cambridge: Harvard University Press, 1971), 13.

4. From Adversities to Conversities: Images of Sweetened Combat

1. Wallace Stevens, "The Noble Rider and the Sound of Words," in *The Necessary Angel: Essays on Reality and the Imagination* (New York: Random House, 1951), 20.
2. Marianne Moore, "There Is a War That Never Ends" (1943), rev. of *Parts of a World* (1942) and *Notes toward a Supreme Fiction* (1942), *Predilections*, 41.
3. Marianne Moore, "Comment," *The Dial* 86 (April 1929), 359–360.
4. Moore writes in her notebook (Rosenbach 1251/2, 42): "The difficulty is one of language. The facts of modern warfare are outside normal human experience and strictly speaking only the facts of normal human experience are reproductive in words. (*Conquest of North Africa*, Alex C. Glifford)."
5. Moore, "Comment," 359.
6. See the draft in the Rosenbach archive.
7. Rosenbach 1250/6, 31–34. Eisenstein's article had appeared in *Close Up*, September 1931.
8. See Kenneth Burke, "Motives and Motifs in Marianne Moore" (1945), rpt. in *Marianne Moore: A Collection of Critical Essays*, ed. Charles Tomlinson (Englewood Cliffs: Prentice-Hall, 1969) 87–100; Marianne Moore, "A Grammarian of Motives," rev. of *Book of Moments*, by Kenneth Burke, (1956), rpt. in *The Marianne Moore Reader*, 233–236.
9. Kenneth Burke, *Permanence and Change: An Anatomy of Purpose* (1935), rev. ed. (Los Altos: Hermes Publications, 1954).
10. Marianne Moore, *Poetry and Criticism* (Cambridge: Adams House, 1965).
11. Burke, *Permanence and Change*, 262–263.
12. Some of these ideas were suggested by Karsten Harries, "Metaphor and Transcendence" *Critical Inquiry*, 5 (Fall 1978), 73–90.
13. See Laurence Stapleton, *The Poet's Advance* (Princeton: Princeton University Press, 1978), 130–131, and Rosenbach 1251/25.
14. Moore, "Comment," 359.
15. Ibid., 360.
16. See Roy Harvey Pearce, "Marianne Moore," in *Continuity in American*

Poetry (Princeton: Princeton University Press, 1961), rpt. in *Marianne Moore: A Collection of Critical Essays,* 150.

17. This notion of restrained power is a constant theme in Moore. As she writes at the end of "Then the Ermine" (CP, 161):

> Foiled explosiveness is yet
> a kind of prophet,
>
> a perfecter, and so a concealer—
>   with the power of implosion;
> like violets by Dürer;
> even darker.

This is very much like Kenneth Burke's notion of impulses released internally but never expended in external actions. The importance of Hegel as a source for these ideas is documented in Moore's reading diary. Among the many excerpts from Hegel (for which Moore unfortunately does not give references), this is particularly pertinent: "Constraint of brute emotions and rude instincts . . . is part of the instrumentality by wh only, the consciousness of Freedom and desire for its attainment in its true—that is its rational & Ideal form—can be obtained" (Rosenbach, 1250/2, 31).

18. Moore may have had Sophocles' *Antigone* in the back of her mind when she wrote "The Pangolin." The poem recalls much of the language of the chorus's "Ode on Man," its structure, its details, its ambiguities and ambivalence, though Moore's tone is less severe. It is hard to know which translation Moore might have read, but R. C. Jebb's version of the play was probably the most popular at the time, and contains many of the same words and phrases found in Moore's poem. See Sophocles, *Antigone,* trans. R. C. Jebb (Cambridge: Cambridge University Press, 1892).

19. Marianne Moore, "Comment," *Dial,* 81 (Dec. 1926), 535–536.

5. Fluctuating Charms: Images of Luminosity, Iridescence, and Metamorphosis

1. Lecture at Bryn Mawr, 10 Feb. 1953, notes taken by Samuel French Morse. The Santayana note is in Rosenbach 1250/3, 28.
2. Marianne Moore, "Conjuries That Endure" (1937), rev. of Wallace Stevens, *Harmonium* (1923), *Ideas of Order* (1936), and *Owl's Clover* (1936), rpt. in *Predilections,* 34. In 1950 Moore published a poem explicitly about Stevens, "Pretiolae," *Wake,* 9 (1950), 4.
3. Wallace Stevens, "A Poet That Matters," rev. of Marianne Moore, *Selected Poems,* rpt. in *Opus Posthumous* (New York: Knopf, 1972), 247–254.

4. *The Letters of Wallace Stevens* (New York: Knopf, 1966), 278–279.
5. Kenneth Burke, "Motives and Motifs in the Poetry of Marianne Moore" (1945), rpt. in *Marianne Moore: A Collection of Critical Essays*, ed. Charles Tomlinson (Englewood Cliffs, Prentice-Hall, 1969), 98.
6. This statement appears in a version of "Humility, Concentration and Gusto" in the Rosenbach archive.
7. Ibid.
8. Moore's pervasive fascination with these qualities is well documented in the Rosenbach collection. She kept many ornamental objects of opalescent or iridescent sheen—bits of brocade, stones, shells, and so on. Her reading notes evince a lasting interest in animal coloration and camouflage. Moore often uses the image of the prism or crystal to represent the fusion of the one and the many. Her fascination with the optical phenomenon of refracted light is clear from her detailed reading notes on Isaac Newton, especially from Brewster's *Life of Newton*. See 1250/2, 166. The notebooks also make clear that such qualities of diversified light attracted Moore not only by their scientific but by their metaphoric implications. From H. Festing Jones's *Diversions in Sicily* she copied this description: "His voice—listening to it was like looking long and long into a piece of Sicilian amber in whose infinite depth, as you turn it about in the sunlight, you see all the colors of the rainbow" (1250/2, 26).
9. Lecture at Bryn Mawr, 7 Feb. 1953, notes taken by Samuel French Morse.
10. Moore knew not only the poetry but the theory of the sublime. Her notes include many passages from Longinus and Edmund Burke.
11. Susan Sontag, *Against Interpretation* (New York: Farrar, Straus, Giroux, 1966), 13.
12. Marianne Moore, *Poetry and Criticism* (Cambridge: Adams House, 1965).
13. Moore kept voluminous notes on animals such as the ones that appear in this poem. As usual, the actual quotations are only the tip of the iceberg in dealing with the sources of her images and ideas. See especially Rosenbach 1250/6.
14. Laurence Stapleton, *The Poet's Advance* (Princeton: Princeton University Press, 1978), 81.
15. These lines were included in a draft of the poem sent to *Hound and Horn*, but were not included in the magazine's publication of the poem in 1933. The poem was again revised for *Selected Poems*, and once again for *Collected Poems*.
16. An early draft of the poem in the Rosenbach archive (1251/17, 126) included these opening lines: "Dedications are rubbish—, this is for the king duke prince the Costa Rican' I guess it is / One knows what is meant for him is his & what is not; / This rich era it is his the for him."
17. In commenting at a Harvard reading in 1964 on a similar use of the letter in "A Carriage from Sweden," Moore mentioned that *S* was her fa-

vorite letter of the alphabet. *The Poet's Voice: Poets Reading Aloud and Commenting on Their Work*, ed. Stratis Haviaras (Cambridge: Harvard University Press, 1978).

18. Isabel Cooper, "Wild Animal Painting in the Jungle," *Atlantic Monthly*, July 1924: Rosenbach 1250/5, 29–30.

19. A line was omitted, probably by accident, from *Collected Poems* and *Complete Poems*. It read: "the curve of whose diving no diver refutes. Upon spider-hands with."

20. Letter to family, 14 Feb. 1909. "Ennui" appeared in *The Lantern*, 18 (1909), 37. The "wish to be interchangeably man and fish" is an example of Moore's tendency to try out a line in many different contexts. She also experimented with these lines in "Sea Unicorns and Land Unicorns."

21. In *Selected Poems* this poem included the variant "to veil invisibleness ears must feel."

22. Jorge Luis Borges, *The Book of Imaginary Beings*, trans. and rev. Norman Thomas di Giovanni (New York: Dutton, 1959), 115.

23. See Rosenbach 1251/17, 127.

24. Donald Hall, *Marianne Moore: The Cage and The Animal* (New York: Pegasus, 1970), 86.

25. To my taste "The Plumet Basilisk" is far superior to a very short poem that Stapleton admires, "O to Be a Dragon." More interesting than that poem is Moore's long comment about it in the introduction to *The Marianne Moore Reader*, which suggests a great deal not only about "O to Be a Dragon" but about all of Moore's poems of mystery and magic, and further about the relationship between the long and short form in imaginative creations: "As antonym, integrity was suggested to me by a blossoming plum branch—a drawing by Hsieh Ho—reproduced above a New York Times Book Review notice of *The Mustard Seed Garden Manual of Painting* formulated about 500 A.D.—trans. and edited by Miss Mai Mai Sze, pub. by Bollingen Foundation in 1956 and as a Modern Library paper in 1959. The plum branch led me to *The Tao of Painting* of which 'The Mustard Seed Garden' is a part. The (not *a*) Tao being a way of life, a 'oneness' that is tireless; whereas egotism, synonomous with ignorance in Buddhist thinking, is tedious. And the Tao led me to the dragon in the classification of primary symbols, symbol of the power of heaven'—changing at will to the size of a silkworm; or swelling to the totality of heaven and earth at will invisible, made personal by a friend at a party—an authority on gems, finance, painting and music— who, exclaiming obligingly, as I concluded a digression on cranes, peaches, bats, and butterflies as symbols of long life and happiness, 'O to be a dragon!' (The exclamation, lost sight of for a time, was appropriated as a title later.)" (MMR, xiv).

26. A passage from Shelley's *Defense of Poetry* that Moore copied in her notebook (Rosenbach 1250/4, 37) is especially suggestive of this Romantic poet's influence on her: "373 All things exist as they are perceived: at least in relation to the percipient . . . But poetry defeats the

curse which binds us to be subjected to the accident of surrounding impressions. And whether it spreads its own figured curtain, or withdraws life's dark veil from before the scene of things, it equally creates for us a being within our being. It makes us the inhabitants of a world to which the familiar world is a chaos—it purges from inward sight the film of familiarity—wh obscures from us the wonder of our being. It compels us to feel that which we perceive, + to imagine that which we know. 376 (apropos of changes in opinion) At such periods there is an accumulation of this power of communicating + receiving intense impassioned conceptions respecting man + nature."

27. Keats to Richard Woodhouse, 27 Oct. 1818, in *English Romantic Poets*, ed. David Perkins (New York: Harcourt Brace, 1967), 1220.
28. This unpublished essay can be found in the Rosenbach archive.
29. The poem is in the Rosenbach archive (1251/27, 18 March 1909).
30. The notebook is in the Rosenbach archive. "A Jelly-Fish" was later published in *The Lantern*, 18 (1909), 110, along with "Ennui."
31. Rosenbach 1250/2, 127.
32. Moore's attraction to these images of multiplicity beneath surface unity is evident throughout her early notebooks. See especially 1250/1, 116: "It is like a snake sloughing its skin and appearing at each metamorphosis with a covering of rarer texture."
33. Again, there are many sources for this poem that Moore did not quote directly and therefore did not note. See especially Rosenbach 1250/6, 51–52.
34. For Moore's reading notes related to this poem, see Rosenbach 1250/6, 96–99.
35. For the sources of this poem, see *The Marianne Moore Newsletter*, 1 (Spring 1977), 10–13.
36. Moore made this note on the poem when it was published in Kimon Friar and John Malcolm Brinnin, eds., *Modern Poetry, American and British* (New York: Appleton-Century-Crofts, 1951), 523: "One of the winters between 1930 and 1940, Gieseking gave at the Brooklyn Academy, a program of Handel, Bach, and Scarlatti, the moral of this poem being that there is something more important than outward rightness. One doesn't get through with the fact that Herod beheaded John the Baptist, 'for his oath's sake'; as one doesn't, I feel, get through with the injustice of the deaths died in the war, and in the first world war."
37. Moore knew the paintings of Odilon Redon and may well have borrowed his image of the soul's eye, "feeling its way" across an abstract landscape.

6. Argument by Design: The Form of the Poems

1. Marianne Moore to Samuel French Morse, 7 March 1934.
2. Lecture at Bryn Mawr, 3 Feb. 1953, notes taken by Samuel French Morse.

3. Wallace Stevens, "About One of Marianne Moore's Poems," (1948), rpt. in *The Necessary Angel: Essays on Reality and the Imagination* (New York: Random House, 1951), 98.

4. Marianne Moore, "A Machinery of Satisfaction," *Poetry*, 38 (Sept. 1931), 338.

5. Moore's use of poetic artifice to counter the automatic reading of experience (directed by conventional syntax) is comparable to her use of detail to counter the automatic framing of visual objects.

6. Marianne Moore, rev. of e. e. cummings, "1 × 1" (1944), rpt. in *Predilections*, 141.

7. William Carlos Williams, "Marianne Moore" (1925), rpt. in Selected Essays (New York: New Directions, 1954), 128.

8. Geoffrey Hartman, notes for *Marianne Moore Reads from Her Works*, Yale Series of Recorded Poets.

9. William Carlos Williams to Marianne Moore, 23 March 1921 (Rosenbach manuscripts and letters).

10. Ezra Pound, "A List of Books," (1918), rpt. as "Marianne Moore and Mina Loy" in *Marianne Moore: A Collection of Critical Essays*, 46.

11. See *Marianne Moore Newsletter*, 2, no. 2 (Fall 1978), 7–11.

12. Thomas Carlyle, *Past and Present* (1897; rpt. New York: AMS Press, 1969). All subsequent references will be noted in the text under the abbreviation P & P.

13. George Moore, *Vale* (1914), rpt. in *Hail and Farewell!* (New York: Appleton, 1925), 221.

14. Marianne Moore, "Blake," *Others* 1 (Dec. 1915), 105.

15. Rosenbach 1250/23, 17.

16. See Jean Garrigue, *Marianne Moore* (Minneapolis: University of Minnesota Press, 1965), 13. I think Moore often strains syntax more than Garrigue admits, but the critic is astute in pointing out the aesthetic of incongruities, the movement by transposition rather than transition.

17. For sources of this line see Rosenbach 1250/24, 65.

18. Marie Boroff makes a similar comment on Moore's poem "Style": "At the end of the poem, descriptive terminology is abandoned in favor of a series of proper names, each of which 'means' only the individual it refers to." *Language and the Poet* (Chicago: University of Chicago Press, 1979), 127.

19. For details on the sources of this poem, see *The Marianne Moore Newsletter*, 2, no. 2 (Fall 1978), 18.

20. Geoffrey Hartman, notes for *Marianne Moore Reads from Her Works*.

21. Moore's note at the back of Kimon Friar and John Malcolm Brinnin, eds., *Modern Poetry, American and British*, (New York: Appleton-Century-Crofts, 1951), 524, details the importance of nonsemantic elements in determining her poems: "I tend to write in a patterned arrangement, with rhymes; stanza as it follows stanza being identical in number of syllables and rhyme-plan, with the first stanza. (Regarding the stanza as a unit, rather than the line, I sometimes divide a word at the end of a line, relying on a general straight-forwardness of treatment to counteract the

mannered effect.) I have a liking for the long syllable followed by three (or more) short syllables, 'lying on the air there is a bird,' and for the inconspicuous or light rhyme,—'let' in flageolet, for instance, being rhymed with 'set' in the lines, 'Its leaps should be set / to the flageolet.' I try to secure an effect of flowing continuity and am more and more impressed by the many correspondences between verse and instrumental music. I am against the stock phrase and an easier use of words in verse than would be tolerated in prose. I feel that the form is the outward equivalent of a determining inner conviction, and that the rhythm is the person."

22. Lecture at Bryn Mawr, 3 Feb. 1953, notes taken by Samuel French Morse.
23. "The Art of Poetry: Marianne Moore," an interview with Donald Hall (1961), rpt. in *Marianne Moore: A Collection of Critical Essays*, 33–34.
24. *The Poet's Voice: Poets Reading Aloud and Commenting on Their Work*, ed. Stratis Haviaras (Cambridge: Harvard University Press, 1978). She also mentioned at this reading that she was "fond of *non sequiturs.*"
25. Rosenbach draft of "Humility, Concentration and Gusto."
26. For a detailed record of this method in several poems, see Laurence Stapleton, *The Poet's Advance* (Princeton: Princeton University Press, 1979). For an interesting stylistic analysis of this method, see Borroff, *Language and the Poet*, 80–108.
27. Rosenbach 1250/4, 45–46.
28. Rosenbach, 1250/4, 47–48.
29. Rosenbach 1250/1, 118, from Samuel Butler's *Notebook*.
30. Rosenbach 1251/17. "Marriage," "An Octopus," "Sea Unicorns and Land Unicorns," and "Peter," for instance, appear intermittently over these pages. Moore obviously worked on all of them at once. Similarly, she worked on "The Frigate Pelican," "The Buffalo," "What Are Years," and "Walking Sticks and Paperweights and Water Marks" simultaneously. It is hard to tell at what point these became distinct compositions. It is clear that some primarily descriptive poems ("An Octopus," "The Frigate Pelican," "The Buffalo") contained larger sections of moral reflection which she deferred to other poems. We also see from these workbooks what an economical poet Moore was. She seldom threw out lines. Many phrases that arose in the composition of an early poem would be deferred to another at some later date. For instance, the basilisk was originally in the company of "An Octopus." The worksheet reads:

> the light green basilisk (sic)
> verdant green—disciple of Plato
> indulging in all kinds of noble vagueness.

The basilisk would go later to "The Plumet Basilisk" and "noble vagueness" to "Novices." Moore also deferred some rather austere lines about death in "An Octopus," which probably formed the basis for "What Are Years."

7. Ut Pictura Poesis: Moore and the Visual Arts

1. Marianne Moore to Samuel French Morse, 7 March 1934.
2. See Bram Dijkstra, *Hieroglyphics of a New Speech: Cubism, Stieglitz and the Early Poetry of William Carlos Williams* (Princeton: Princeton University Press, 1969), 67: "The concepts of Imagism, which, for that matter had itself been largely inspired by what was happening in the visual arts, became more or less self-evident for the poets of the Metropolitan area. The tenets of Imagism, as listed in *Poetry* in two separate articles by F. S. Flint and Ezra Pound, were all contained in the theories associated with the movements of painting that took their cue from Cezanne . . . Even in *Camera Work* the goals were being stressed as early as 1909."
3. The relevant items in Moore's book collection (in the Rosenbach archive) are too numerous to mention. The largest collections of art books are on Oriental and Modern art. As Moore's circle of friends in the art world expanded, so did her library. Monroe Wheeler, curator of the Museum of Modern Art, for instance, frequently sent her books, as did the critics Paul Rosenfeld and Henry McBride.
4. Among the articles in Moore's scrapbook are: "Post-Impressionism Arrived" *Letters and Arts* (1 March 1913); "The Greatest Exhibition of Insurgent Art Ever Held" *Current Opinion* (March 1913); "The Mob as Art Critic" *Letters and Arts* (29 March 1913); "Bedlam in Art" *Current Opinion* (April 1913); "Mr. Roosevelt and the Cubists" *Current Opinion* (5 April 1913). The scrapbook also shows Moore's early interest in Gordon Craig, with several articles on his new experiments in stagecraft.
5. The note is in the reading diary 1909–1915 (Rosenbach 1250/1), 11. See also Marianne Moore, "Stieglitz," in *Stieglitz Memorial Portfolio 1864–1946*, ed. Dorothy Norman (New York: Twice a Year Press, 1946). Moore writes of 291: "It was an American Acropolis so to speak, with a stove in it, a kind of eagle's perch of selectiveness, and like the ardor of fire in its completeness."
6. Marianne Moore to John Warner Moore in 1915.
7. Quoted in Donald Hall, *Marianne Moore: The Cage and the Animal* (New York: Pegasus, 1970), 23.
8. See Rosenbach 1250/24 and 1250/25. The bulk of these conversations are among or about visual artists. For example, Moore records a conversation with Bertram Hartman about Gaston Lachaise's plan to make a bust of her: "Surprised he wanted to do it as I wasn't typical of what he was esp[ecially] wild in—He said I know why he thinks that—because you are thin—but in sculpture it does not matter what you weigh we

will show them—what interests me is the spirit." And she records this amusing exchange with Kurt Wimmer: "Miss O'Keefe and Stieglitz— always make me think of an owl and a crow—watch her sometimes and see if her feet don't turn in and his out? I think she is very handsome. I'll never forget the impression her appearance made on me the first time I saw her—she was dressed in black w[ith] a black hat, and a bl[ack] cape of rather thin material. She didn't look just like a widow but ... Mr. Wimmer: a married one perhaps?"

9. Marianne Moore, "The Dial, A Retrospect" (1942), rpt. in *Predilections,* 103–114. The essay also recollects Gordon Craig. Much of the *Dial* collection was owned by Scofield Thayer, a personal friend of Moore's (he was rumored to have proposed to her). She would certainly have been familiar with his major collection of modernist art, which can now be viewed at the Worcester Art Museum in Worcester, Massachusetts.

10. Introduction for a catalogue of an exhibition of work by E. McKnight Kauffer held 18 October to 12 November 1949. See Rosenbach 1250/25 for Moore's lively discussion of her proposed sitting for Gaston Lachaise. The Lachaise bust, along with three rooms of photographs, paintings, sketches, and small sculptures, was recently displayed at the Rosenbach Museum in Philadelphia. Brooklyn's Prospect Park displays a contemporary sculpture by Victor Sularis called "Years Are What?" after Moore's "What Are Years?"

11. The poem was recently published in *The Marianne Moore Newsletter,* 1 (Spring 1977), 8–9. See also Moore's notes in Rosenbach 1250/24, 36. In her recollection to Donald Hall of her trip to Paris in 1911, Moore observed, "we went to every museum in Paris, I think except two." "The Art of Poetry: Marianne Moore," an interview with Donald Hall," in *Marianne Moore: A Collection of Critical Essays,* 25. Also see Moore's copious notes on art education, Rosenbach 1250/2, 120–122.

12. Moore's skillful sketches appear throughout her reading diary. They are most plentiful in the period 1930–1943 (Rosenbach 1250/6), when Moore was most regularly reading about the visual arts. But as early as the first notebook (1250/1) Moore was sketching favorite cartoons, among them "The Stand Patter" by Oberlander (1250/1, 82) which formed the basis of "To Be Liked by You Would Be a Calamity." The Rosenbach also holds a substantial collection of bibelots, pictures, and postcards saved by Moore, many of which are directly connected to poems she was working on. There are several reproductions of drawings and paintings by Dürer, Da Vinci, and Blake, also several reproductions of the Unicorn tapestries, of Holbein's "Melanchthon," various representations of St. Jerome, many photographs of Persian and Chinese artifacts, and primitive art. Moore habitually wrote away for catalogues and information on works that interested her. While writing "The Buffalo" she collected images of cows, buffalo, bulls, and ibexes. One amusing example of her unconscious fastidiousness appears in her marginalia to a catalogue of Brooklyn Museum Exhibits (1931). The caption for an "Ex-

ample of Rhages Pottery, 13th c" read "the Animal is a highly conventionalized ox." Moore corrects this to "bull."

13. See Rosenbach 1250/1, 87.

14. Moore's ambivalence about conventional color symbolism is most apparent in "Injudicious Gardening."

15. Moore first published these poems as part of a three-part poem entitled "Part of a Poem, Part of a Novel, Part of a Play" and included a section called "The Student."

16. Marianne Moore, "Comment," *Dial*, 85 (July 1928), 89–90. For other sources see *The Marianne Moore Newsletter*, 1, no. 2, (Fall 1977), 7. As she so often did, Moore had more than one image in mind in writing the poem.

17. W. H. Janson, *History of Renaissance Art* (New York: Abrams, 1962), 413.

18. See Rosenbach 1250/17, 96: "the blue water paled by—and there / the color of the peacock neck." These lines were probably originally connected with "The Plumet Basilisk."

19. One passage quoted on p. 178 is present in the 1932 ms and in the first printing in *Poetry*. It was dropped for *Selected Poems*, and even more lines were dropped for *Collected Poems*, but they were restored in 1961, and printed in *Complete Poems*. Moore may have derived not only details but prose rhythms from an article on Haiti she had been reading. See Rosenbach 1250/2, 163.

20. For the source of Moore's lines on El Greco see Paul Rosenfeld, "Greco's Portrait of Himself" *Dial*, 79 (Dec. 1925), 485–490, esp. 487.

21. Moore refers to El Greco again in "St. Valentine," comparing the eyes of his "Vera" to that woman's ring, prismatic in shape and effect.

22. Drawings of these objects appear in Moore's reading diaries: Rosenbach 1250/6, 48 (duck lid) and 6 (locust oil bug). The diary also includes many sketches of articles found in the Tell El Amarna site in Egypt, one of the sources for Moore's idea of luxury in "The Jerboa," and also the site on which her "Egyptian Pulled Glass Bottle in the Shape of a Fish" was found.

23. A major outlet of Moore's scribacious nature was copying out long passages from articles and books detailing the richness and variety of a given region's flora and fauna.

24. This draft can be found in the Rosenbach archive.

25. See Rosenbach 1250/6, 50 for sources of "Smooth Gnarled Crape Myrtle." From the *Illustrated London News* (Dec. 12, 1931) Moore notes the sale of a first edition of T. Lodge's pastoral romance "Rosalynde" to The Rosenbach Company. On the next page (51) Moore sketches a photograph from the *Illustrated London News* of a patch-box sold at auction imprinted with "clasped hands" and the words "By peace plenty. By wisdom Peace" around the edges. A random newspaper juxtaposition became for Moore a source of significant, poetic juxtaposition.

26. See *The Marianne Moore Newsletter*, 1, no. 2 (Fall 1977), 2–5.

27. Ibid., 2, no. 2 (Spring 1978), 2–5.
28. Ibid., 8–12.
29. "The Dragon and the Kylin: Chinese Symbols and Myths in Marianne Moore's Poetry," *Literature East and West,* 15 (1971), 470–484.
30. *The Marianne Moore Reader,* xiv. Moore's lifelong interest in Chinese art is well documented in the Rosenbach archive; see, for example, Rosenbach 1250/2, 106; 1250/3, 42; 1250/4, 5. Besides her many books and pamphlets on Chinese painting, porcelain, and carving, Moore's documents include regular clippings or notes from Arthur Hayden of the *Illustrated London News,* who specialized in Chinese art.
31. Moore's early interest in cartoon art undoubtedly influenced her biting, epigrammatic portraits. There is certainly an analogy to be made between the sharp anecdotal quality of cartoons and her way of encapsulating human behavior in quick snatches of speech or gesture. The union of illustration and caption in cartoons is like her own tendency to unite description and epigram.
32. Marianne Moore, "A Letter to Ezra Pound, 1919" rpt. in *Marianne Moore: A Collection of Critical Essays,* 18.
33. This unpublished review of a Museum of Modern Art Exhibition, dated 1 March 1937, is in the Rosenbach archive.
34. Roman Jakobson,"On Realism in Art," in L. Meteika et al., *Readings in Russian Poetics* (Cambridge: MIT Press, 1971), 39.
35. *The Dial,* 71, no. 6 (Dec. 1921), 712–714.
36. Paul Rosenfeld, "On American Painting," *Dial,* 71, no. 6 (Dec. 1921), 649–670.
37. Marianne Moore, "Paul Rosenfeld" (1946), rpt. in *The Marianne Moore Reader,* 208.
38. Albert Gleizes and Jean Metzinger, "Cubism" (1912), rpt. in *Modern Artists on Art,* ed. Robert L. Herbert (Englewood Cliffs: Prentice-Hall, 1964), 11.
39. The source of this passage (see Rosenbach 1250/2, 128) provides another interesting study in Moore's way of reinventing her quotations. Taking a passage from G. A. Smith's *The Expositor's Bible,* discussing the Book of Isaiah, Moore, like the cubists, takes it apart and reassembles it in her poem, to achieve a fresh vividness in her poem. Moore's notes read, "The phonetics of the passage are wonderful. the general impression, is that of a stormy ocean booming into the shore and then crashing itself out into one long hiss of spray + foam upon the barriers. The details are noteworthy. In ver. 12 we have 13 heavy M.-sounds besides 2 heavy B's to 5 N's 5 H's + 4 sibilants. But in ver. 13 the sibilants predominate + before the sharp rebuke of the Lord the great, booming sound of ver. 12 scatters out into a long yish-sha-von. the occasional use of a prolonged vowel amid so many hurrying consonants produces exactly the effect now of the lift of a storm swell out at sea & now of the pause of a great wave before it crashes on the shore."
40. See Rosenbach 1250/2, 29 and surrounding passages.
41. Rosenbach 1250/1, 74.

42. William Carlos Williams, rev. of Moore's work (1925), rpt. in *Marianne Moore: A Collection of Critical Essays*, 52–54.

43. Ibid., 52–53.

44. Guillaume Apollinaire, *The Cubist Painters*, tr. Lionel Abel (New York:1944), 12. Roman Jakobson, "Poetry of Grammar and Grammar of Poetry" *Lingua*, 21 (1968), 605.

45. Rosenbach 1250/2, 36.

46. William Carlos Williams, *Spring and All* (1921), rpt. in *Imaginations* (New York: New Directions, 1970), 101.

47. Ibid., 145.

48. Williams, "Marianne Moore (1925)", 55.

49. Something of this is suggested in another passage Moore copied from *Modern Painting*: "The true beauty of a work of art is subjective . . . a defect of one's having sensed the accumulated + sequential aspects of coordinated expression . . . . neither dolour nor depression results but always a feeling of exaltation and joy . . . . Comprehension aroused . . . not merely moved by . . . story wh sets in motion the associative process" (Rosenbach 1250/2, 29).

50. Albert Gleizes and Jean Metzinger, "Cubism," 11–12.

51. Quoted in Robert Rosenblum, *Cubism and Twentieth Century Art* (New York: Abrams, 1966), 112, 115.

52. Admittedly, poetry which is not descriptive may still be representational in articulating a theme. This is one of many basic differences between the media, for abstract painters "conceptualize" space in a more strictly formal, thus less directly thematic way than writers do. Nevertheless, we cannot really justify all Moore's images in terms of thematic, any more than representational, functions.

53. Marianne Moore, "Robert Andrew Parker" (1958), rpt. in *The Marianne Moore Reader*, 206.

54. Harriet Janis and Rudi Blesh, *Collage: Personalities, Concepts, Techniques* (Philadelphia: Chilton, 1969), 21.

55. Ibid., 35.

8. The Rhetoric of Reticence: Three Critical Essays

1. Kenneth Burke, "Likings of an Observationist" (1956), rpt. in *Marianne Moore: A Collection of Critical Essays*, ed. Charles Tomlinson (Englewood Cliffs: Prentice-Hall, 1969), 125–133. Laurence Stapleton, *The Poet's Advance* (Princeton: Princeton University Press, 1979), 52–67.

2. Burke "Likings," 125.

3. Marianne Moore, "Feeling and Precision" (1944) rpt. in *Predilections*, 3–11; "Humility, Concentration and Gusto" (1948), rpt. in *Predilections*, 12–20; "Idiosyncrasy and Technique" (1956), rpt. in *The Marianne Moore Reader*, 169–182. Burke, "Likings," 125.

4. The Rosenbach archive has several drafts of "Feeling and Precision." In

one draft Moore explains Hopkins's word "flag" as meaning "skin." The draft includes other revealing details. In the process of writing she clearly thought of feeling and precision as oppositions, writing in the second paragraph, in capital letters: "the CONFLICT between FEELING and PRECISION." The essay in its early stages also reveals Moore's association of luminous and iridescent qualities with feeling struggling to become form. She writes of "those EARLY RUSSIAN CHANTS in which emphasis weakens and strengthens, so that THE THEME IS MUTED BUT DISTINCT—like brocade seen through gauze." Imagination and enchantment play much larger roles in this early draft.

5. Moore presented this lecture several times, revising it repeatedly. Drafts in the Rosenbach show her uncertainty about including this long passage on counterfeit money, but also her temptation to keep it. Next to the passage, in one draft, she wrote "This doesn't seem to me extreme enough. omit? though I like this."

6. Identifying, as usual, with the peculiar, Moore wrote in an early version that she hoped it was not "over-perverse to regard Cowper" as an example of gusto.

7. In a draft Moore remarks that "in Christopher Smart himself there is an EFFLATUS that APATHY CAN'T RESIST." Once again she identifies gusto as the opposite of ennui.

Index